32-99 BK Bud July 99

NORTH CAROLINA
STATE BOARD OF COMMUNITY COLLEGES
LIBRARIES
SOUTHEASTERN COMMUNITY

P9-CDY-074

Hal Higdon's

SMART
RUNNING

SOUTHEASTERN COMMUNITY
COLLEGE LIBRARY
WHITEVILLE, NC 28472

NORTH CAROLINA
STATE BOARD OF COMMUNITY COLLEGES
LIBRARIES
SOUTHEASTERN COMMUNITY COLLEGE

GV
1061.5
.H539
1998

Hal Higdon's

SMART RUNNING

**Expert Advice on Training,
Motivation, Injury Prevention, Nutrition,
and Good Health for Runners of
Any Age and Ability**

By Hal Higdon, senior writer,
RUNNER'S *WORLD.* magazine and author of
Hal Higdon's How to Train
and *Marathon*

SOUTHEASTERN COMMUNITY
COLLEGE LIBRARY
WHITEVILLE, NC 28472

Rodale Press, Inc.
Emmaus, Pennsylvania

Notice

This book is written to help you make a decision regarding your fitness and exercise program. It is not intended as a substitute for professional fitness and medical advice. As with all exercise programs, you should seek your doctor's approval before you begin.

Copyright © 1998 by Hal Higdon Communications

All rights reserved. No part of this publication may be reproduced or transmitted in any form or by any means, electronic or mechanical, including photocopying, recording, or any other information storage and retrieval system, without the written permission of the publisher.

Runner's World is a registered trademark of Rodale Press, Inc.

Printed in the United States of America on acid-free ∞, recycled paper ♻

Cover and Interior Designer: Christopher R. Neyen
Cover Photographer: Tim De Frisco

Library of Congress Cataloging-in-Publication Data

Higdon, Hal.
     Hal Higdon's smart running : expert advice on training, motivation, injury prevention, nutrition, and good health for runners of any age and ability / by Hal Higdon.
         p.   cm.
     Questions and answers from the "Ask the expert" column on America Online.
     Includes index.
     ISBN 0-87596-535-0 paperback
     1. Running—Training—Miscellanea.   I. Title.   II. Title: Smart running.
GV1061.5.H539   1998
796.42—dc21   97-51801

Distributed in the book trade by St. Martin's Press

2   4   6   8   10   9   7   5   3   1   paperback

──────── Our Purpose ────────
*"We inspire and enable people to improve
their lives and the world around them."*

This book is dedicated to Amby Burfoot, winner of the 1968 Boston Marathon, executive editor of *Runner's World* magazine, and a close friend for many years. I first met Amby during the summer of 1965, when he was a student at Wesleyan University in Middletown, Connecticut. I had come to New England with my wife, Rose, and our three small children to participate in a series of road races. Races didn't offer prize money back then, but many of the New England events presented attractive merchandise awards worth considerable sums of money.

That was one reason why Amby and I both appeared at a 4-mile road race in Warren, Rhode Island, one weekend in August. Unfortunately, I was then driving a small car, loaded with luggage, so I couldn't carry much home to Long Beach, Indiana. Amby, however, lived just down the road in New London, Connecticut. Wise to the ways of New England road races, he had arrived with a station wagon. I won the race with Amby second, but he won the awards ceremony. Even though I had first choice of the items on the prize table, I had to settle for a wristwatch, while he stole the prize my wife and I coveted: a combination barbecue grill and rotisserie.

More than three decades later, my watch has long since stopped ticking, and Amby's rusted grill has been committed to a landfill, but we still remain friends, even though I no longer finish in front of him in road races. This book would not have been written if Amby Burfoot hadn't asked me to write the "Ask the Expert" column for *Runner's World Daily* on America Online.

Contents

Hal Higdon's Web site, which features his writing and offers additional training information, is at http://www.halhigdon.com

RUNNER'S WORLD.

For the latest running news and training tips, visit our Web site at http://www.runnersworld.com

Preface

My previous running books for Rodale Press (in addition to telling the history of the Boston Marathon) have provided information on racing at short and long distances and how to train. *Hal Higdon's Smart Running* covers all that territory and more. More precisely, it reprints the best answers to questions sent by runners to my popular "Ask the Expert" column on America Online (AOL).

The world has experienced a communications revolution with the end of the twentieth century. The World Wide Web suddenly made it possible for people to use their computers not only to access information but also to talk to each other online.

It certainly made a major change in my life, particularly in my relationship with *Runner's World* magazine, where I serve as senior writer. I now submit articles electronically rather than on paper. Executive editor Amby Burfoot and I exchange e-mail messages daily, sometimes hourly. My fax machine, which seemed such an electronic marvel only five years ago, sits barely used. Mail that still arrives in the box before my home in Long Beach, Indiana, seems duller lately. So much of my workday is spent in front of a computer that the precious hour I head out the door to run becomes even more important to me.

Meanwhile, the merger between running as business and running as recreation has gone smoothly. In January 1996, *Runner's World* magazine went online at www.runnersworld.com, providing instant news and information about our sport. Not only could runners get training tips and the results from track meets and road races held the day before but also links to other sites and sources. Our Web site proved instantly successful, and soon, we were getting as many as six million hits a month, with the numbers climbing fast.

By that summer, as runners everywhere focused on the Olympic Games in Atlanta, we signed a contract with America Online to provide a more interactive version of our Web site to that service's 10 million subscribers. We offered chat rooms where runners could talk online to celebrities in our sport and bulletin boards so they could send notes to each other. Seemingly, all of this "free" information should have made runners less willing to pay money to buy the print version of the magazine, but the opposite has proved true. During our first 18 months online, the magazine's circulation climbed from 420,000 to 458,000. More important, many more people began to learn about our sport through the Web, particularly young people. All of us discovered that we no longer had to depend on the sporadic coverage given to running by newspapers and TV. A new running boom had begun.

Independent of the magazine, I had established my own Web site: www.halhigdon.com. My *Marathon Training Guide*, which is an 18-week program for novice, intermediate, and advanced runners, proved particularly popular, and soon, I was getting as many as 50,000 hits a week myself from runners all over the world looking for help with their training.

Amby Burfoot next asked me to write a column for the AOL version of their Web site. I became an aerobic Ann Landers, dispensing advice on everything from knee injuries to how to improve your diet and lose weight to improve performance. Not only runners but basketball, football, and volleyball players with questions about running found their way to my column, which was titled "Ask the Expert." Keeping up with all their inquiries proved a chore since soon I was fielding more than two dozen questions a day. But it also was exciting and taught me a lot about what mattered most to runners. In the first two years of answering questions, I learned (*had* to learn so I could provide expert advice) more about running than I had learned in the previous two decades. Not surprisingly, "Ask the Expert" soon became the most popular feature on the site.

But not every runner has access to the Web, nor does every computer user always want to spend the time of going online. Sometimes when you need to know a fact, it's easier to reach for a book on the shelf. Despite the spell-checker and thesaurus on my computer, I haven't yet thrown away my dictionary or other reference books. Nor have I thrown away my Rolodex. It took more than one "expert" to provide the training advice for this book. While I was able to answer most questions, drawing on my four decades of experience as a runner, on other occasions I needed to call on the many coaches, scientists, physicians, and other experienced runners who so often have provided me with information for my previous books. It would have been impossible to write this book without their help. They are many, and I've tried to credit them within the text of my answers.

Thanks also to Glenn Hughes and Parker Morse, the two computer experts on the *Runner's World* magazine staff who have helped me cope with the vagaries of the Internet. John Reeser of Rodale Books worked with me in both selecting and editing the questions and answers offered in this book. Rodale Health and Fitness Books executive editor, Neil Wertheimer, came up with the book's title, which I endorsed immediately, because who wouldn't want their writing to be known as "smart"? Pat Corpora, president of Rodale Books, offered me his usual support and encouragement. Linda Mooney did an expert job at copyediting the text, and Chris Neyen designed the sharp cover and interior. Thanks also to Angela Miller, my agent.

Thus, I offer you *Hal Higdon's Smart Running*. What you find in the pages that follow may not necessarily answer all your running questions, but it will make you a smarter runner.

Beginners
Problems and Solutions for New Runners

- Adding Distance
- Switch from Walking
- Breathing
- Weight Lifting and Running
- Return to Fitness
- First Injury

- Fatigue
- Slow versus Fast Running
- Run More Often or Longer?
- Progress Check

All runners have one thing in common: a beginning. We all began somewhere. I went out for track as a sophomore in high school and discovered an unsuspected talent. I started to compete. Thus, before becoming a "runner," I was a "racer." Many young runners start this way.

But the majority of runners enter the sport from another route and at another and later age. Some participated in different competitive sports when they were young; others did not. Most simply looked out the window on a sunny spring day and thought, "Maybe I'll go for a run." These runners often are motivated by a desire to lose weight or look better or feel better or achieve physical fitness rather than from a desire to beat other runners or to win medals in track or road races. Sometimes they, too, become racers, competing for trophies and prizes in age-group competitions—but that is not what gets them going. They become runners before becoming racers.

Unlike young runners, they often don't have a coach telling them what to do and what not to do. Invariably, they have questions about breathing and side aches and shinsplints. These beginners don't always get the right answers from other runners they encounter on the road or from instructors at health clubs.

Whether your ultimate goal is to become a runner or a racer, here is how to begin.

Adding Distance

Q: I am a beginning runner who started running 1 mile on a treadmill. Now I'm up to 2 miles. I'm very proud of myself, but the problem is that I can't always get to 2 miles. On some days, I struggle to cover 1.5 or 1.75 miles. I eat right and run every other day. I also run with a heart monitor and stay within my target rate. What am I doing wrong? When I am able to get to the 2-mile mark, the last quarter-mile is really tough.

A: You're not doing anything wrong; you're just suffering normal beginner problems. It takes a while to condition the body to accept the training load that you place on it when you begin to run. Some exercise scientists suggest 40 days as the time when the capillaries suddenly develop within your body, allowing for a more efficient blood-transport system and allowing running to become so much easier. Of course, when that happens, you'll probably push your workouts to 3 miles and still struggle at the end. It's the natural inclination of people who exercise to push themselves to the limit.

I can't promise that you'll ever reach the point where the last quarter-mile won't be tough, but I know that you'll show dramatic improvement if you keep at it. We all have down days. Your slowdown at the end may be more a factor of what you're doing around your workout rather than the workout itself. Too little sleep the night before? Tension on the job? Too big a lunch? All these could be factors that cause one workout to be harder than another.

On these days, don't force yourself to go 2 miles. Stop at 1.5. Or train at a pulse rate 10 to 20 beats lower than normal. In fact, that's the secret to increasing distance. Slow down to run farther.

Also, you don't always have to run the entire distance or run that distance at the same pace. The speed of most treadmills can be adjusted by simply pushing a button. Try running for 5 minutes, walking for 2, running for 5, walking for 2. See if that allows you to go farther. The other suggestion is that you may eventually consider leaving the security of your treadmill and going for a run outdoors. Pick a nice day and go to a scenic area frequented by other runners. Don't be self-conscious about being seen running in public. Every runner out there once was a beginner, and even the general public has come to accept runners as part of the landscape.

Switch from Walking

Q: I was a walker for about six years but became bored with it, so I started running. What sort of program should I use to get accustomed to running so I can run longer distances?

A: Don't entirely abandon your old sport; I consider walking a valuable cross-training regimen for runners. You can still use walking as a training variation on "easy" days.

If you've been walking for six years, you certainly have a fitness base. You now need to start moving at a slightly faster pace. I suggest beginning with a routine that combines walking and jogging. Chuck Cornett, a coach for adult runners in Jacksonville, Florida, has an excellent program in which he sends those new to exercise out the door every day for 35 days to go 15 minutes in one direction, then turn around and come right back.

The first 5 minutes and the last 5 minutes feature obligatory walking. The 20 minutes between are for walking and/or slow running. Start by running, go a short distance until you begin to experience fatigue, then walk to recover. Run/walk/run/walk. Eventually, after 35 days, Cornett has his people running the full 20 minutes. Then he moves them into a more structured program featuring running on all days.

If you've already begun running, you may be ahead in your program and less inclined to back down to a walk. Some variation of alternating jogging and walking, however, will allow you to make the switch from walking to jogging easier and will lessen the chance of injury. The principle of alternating hard and easy running segments is used by world-class athletes in their training, usually on a track. They call it interval training, although it may be a while—if ever—

before you decide to incorporate such training into your schedule.

So start easy. Don't hesitate to take rest days or walking days. Eventually, you'll develop a regular routine best suited to your goals and talents.

Breathing

Q: What's the right way to breathe when running? Through the nose or mouth, or both? Shallow or deep? Two breaths in, one breath out? Everyone I talk to gives me a different answer. There must be a way to breathe efficiently.

A: This is a question that a lot of beginners ask. When someone asks about it, I like to quote legendary New Zealand coach Arthur Lydiard, who said: "Breathe though your mouth, breathe through your nose, suck it in through your ears if you can."

In short, don't worry about your breathing.

But more can be said on the subject. In an article in the December 1996 issue of *Runner's World* magazine, Jack Daniels, Ph.D., track and cross-country coach at the State University of New York at Cortland, offered additional insight on breathing technique. Dr. Daniels notes that most runners breathe on a 2-2 pattern: Breathe in for 2 steps, breathe out for 2 steps. They begin to inhale when either the left foot or the right foot strikes the ground. If they take 180 steps a minute (a common cadence), they inhale and exhale 45 times each per minute.

Other breathing patterns, Dr. Daniels notes, are 2-1 (breathe in for 2 steps, breathe out for 1), and 3-3. "You never want to use a 1-1 breathing pattern because it costs too much energy," advises Dr. Daniels. Also, shallow breathing can cause stomach cramps, sometimes known as stitches. (One way to cure a stitch is to slow your breathing.)

Your breathing pattern during a given run indicates how hard you're running. Marathoners may breathe in a 3-3 pattern—at least in the early miles. In a 10-K, the pattern is most often 2-2, or even 2-1 in the last couple of miles.

Dr. Daniels suggests that you gear your breathing to whatever rhythm feels comfortable. Warm up with a 3-3 breathing pattern. Once you begin to move at a faster pace (or in a race), shift to 2-2. For a faster-paced run, or toward the end of that race, you may be forced to shift to 2-1.

That's from a scientist's point of view, but I also think that Lydiard was right. Breathe any way you can that feels comfortable.

Weight Lifting and Running

Q: I am a weight lifter who is about 20 pounds overweight. I want to start running to increase my endurance and decrease my weight. I'm not sure how often and with what intensity I should start. Also, what modifications should I make in my weight-lifting routine?

A: While running with members of my marathon training class along the Prairie Path west of Chicago, I got into a conversation with a former weight lifter who's now a runner. He had been running for three years and was preparing for his first marathon. He found that lifting increased his weight because it increased his muscle mass. So you may not necessarily want to lose weight if it means losing muscle. A lot depends on your personal goals and whether you are really overweight. But since one of your goals is to increase endurance, you may want to modify your weight-lifting routine by cutting back on the heaviest lifts.

Blending running and lifting is a good idea. I suggest that your main focus as a beginning runner be on increasing endurance rather than on losing weight. Without knowing your body-fat percentage, you may not have that much fat to lose. Later, after you've been running for a few months, you can consider modifications in your program to lose weight.

But you wanted to know how to begin. I suggest beginning very easily: a few miles a day at a slow and comfortable pace, two or three days a week—and not on days when you're doing heavy lifting. Don't be afraid to walk in the middle of your runs, and don't worry about time and distance. After you've been running for several months and begin to feel comfortable about running, then it'll be time to consider taking the next step (which could include weight loss).

Return to Fitness

Q: I'm trying to get my body back. I was an athlete in college, but six years later, I've fallen sadly out of shape. I'm only 10 pounds overweight but I don't look or feel fit. I recently started running to improve my fitness and currently am running four or five days a week, about 2.5 miles in 20 minutes, more for time than distance, with a heart rate of about 160 following my run. What are some training tips to help me get started, to get over the workout hump, and then to keep enjoying the training?

A: It sounds as though you have made a good start. I suggest that you maintain your current routine of running for about 20 minutes until six to eight weeks after your starting date. Don't worry about distance or how fast you run that distance. Pick different courses so you don't always know how far you run (and therefore how fast). Give your body time to settle into its new routine. In the interest of what I'm going to suggest below, call this current phase of your training Phase 1.

By the end of this first six-to-eight-week period, your body should have passed through its aches-and-pains phase. Your muscles should have adapted to your new running routine. Only then should you consider some new variations on your training runs for a Phase 2 training period that can last another six to eight weeks. Two or three days a week, increase the length of your runs. Try some runs at 25 minutes, then eventually 30. Drop back to 20 every other workout so you don't progress too fast. Program periods of rest.

After you have been running for three to four months, you're ready for Phase 3. Pick one day a week when you have some extra time, probably on the weekend. A lot of runners save Sundays for their long runs, although you could pick any convenient day. Start lengthening your runs on this one day. Over a number of weeks, go from 35 to 40 to 45 minutes until you can run a full hour. Drop back in time every second or third week to make sure that you don't progress too fast. The easiest way to increase distance is to run slower than the 8:00-mile pace you are now doing. An hour at 10:00-mile pace will take you 6 miles, or about 10-K, a popular race distance.

I don't necessarily suggest that you turn from jogger to runner to racer immediately, but this three-phase program will give you a good start to becoming an athlete again.

First Injury

Q: I've never been a runner, but I began four weeks ago. I started out great: about 2 miles, six days a week. Everything felt fine until about 1½ weeks ago, when I suddenly had a lot of pain in my knees. I haven't been able to run since, and I miss it terribly. I'm using a cross-country ski machine and continuing with light weights in preparation for a 5-K race in another 1½ weeks. Currently, there is no knee pain. (I've tried running 10 to 12 paces just to see how it feels.) I want to get back into running, but I don't want to reinjure myself. Any thoughts?

A: I'd rethink your decision to run that 5-K so soon after injuring yourself. You could probably go the distance, but why risk further injury, even permanent damage? Assuming you paid your entry fee, show up at the race, grab your T-shirt, and walk the distance. Plan to run another 5-K when you recover.

I suspect that your problem was the typical beginner's mistake of doing too much too soon. (More experienced runners reading these words will immediately think: "Been there. Done that!") Usually, when someone begins a new activity, he can quickly identify his weak spot. In your case, it was your knees. I suspect that you simply strained the muscles, rather than pulled them, but it would take a doctor's examination to determine that for sure.

Your mistake is probably—and note that I said probably—not the 2 miles, but the fact that you ran every day. Once you have recovered from your injury (that is, no pain) and you resume running again, try running every other day. Blend some walking with the running or pick a cross-training activity (swimming or biking, for example) if you want to do something on the "rest" days. Gradually, you should be able to build your body up to a level where you can run without pain.

Fatigue

Q: I am trying to run every other day, schedule permitting. I usually run about 20 minutes each time. Instead of feeling stronger during my jogs, I seem to tire at the end and really need to push myself. It doesn't seem like my training is getting me in shape. What am I doing wrong?

A: You're not necessarily doing anything wrong, but you may need to exercise more patience. Twenty minutes every other day is probably at the bottom level of where your body will begin to benefit. That's not to say that you need to do more, but don't expect miracles to occur overnight.

It's also natural for a beginning runner to experience fatigue at the end of a workout. In fact, a lot of us who have been running for years also get tired toward the end of the run, if we push too hard or go too far. A more seasoned veteran might not experience fatigue until near the end of a 2-hour run, but it would be the same fatigue.

Stick with your schedule. Don't expect instant results. In a few weeks, or a few months, you may notice that your workouts seem easier, or at least that you are able to do them at a faster pace or run farther. In the meantime, be patient.

Slow versus Fast Running

Q: I have been trying to improve my health and fitness by running as often as I can. I don't know, though, which is better: running at a slow pace for a long time or running at a fast pace for a short time. Which one will help me more in terms of getting my heart and lungs into shape?

A: For heart and lungs and general fitness, running at a gentle pace will get you in good shape. Running faster and shorter will get you in better shape for racing. I recommend mixing the two in an organized training program, but there's no reason why anyone has to run any faster than he wants to if the main goal is fitness.

In determining which style is "better," one consideration is calorie burn. Frequently, people interested in losing weight ask whether fast or slow running burns the most calories. The speed at which you run doesn't matter. Rather, the distance you cover determines how many calories you burn.

Here's how the arithmetic works: An average person who weighs 150 pounds burns 100 calories per mile. (Weigh more or less and you'll burn slightly more or less, depending on your weight.) If you run 3 miles, whether fast or slow, you'll burn 300 calories. In fact, if you walk the same number of miles, you'll still burn that many calories. Calorie burn relates to foot pounds: how many pounds you push across so many feet of ground. Other sports such as swimming or cycling have different calorie-burn rates, but walking and running are approximately the same.

Fast running has somewhat of an advantage over slow running or walking because you can burn more calories in a shorter time. If you walk at a speed of 3 mph (20:00-mile pace), you'll burn 300 calories. But if you run at a speed of 6 mph (10:00-mile pace), you can burn 600 calories in the same hour's time. Run 10 mph (6:00-mile pace) and you can burn 1,000 calories. But if you run at that same fast 6:00-mile pace and only go 3 miles, your calorie burn is 300. But is one pace better than another? It depends on your personal goals.

There are other reasons why you may want to run fast or slow. Many runners get in a rut of covering the same distance at the same pace day after day. Eventually, they plateau and never improve. That is why advanced runners include slow, long runs in their weekly training schedules—and sometimes fast, long runs. As you progress as a runner, you will be able to determine which training paces and which training distances work best for you on different days.

Run More Often or Longer?

Q: I'm overweight (6 feet 4 inches, 265 pounds) but healthy, according to my doctor. I just finished my fourth run in four days. The first two days, I ran three-quarters of a mile, but my lungs hurt. Days 3 and 4, I went a mile. Am I better off trying to run a little every night or taking days off and trying to run longer?

A: You can continue adding to your mileage, but I'd stay at a conservative level for a while. Be content with that mile run for several weeks before pushing ahead. You also might be more comfortable if you took a day off now and then rather than trying to run every day. Your body needs time to recover between workouts. Also, you will burn as many calories walking a mile as running a mile. (For more information, see "Slow versus Fast Running.")

You may want to try a routine in which you run a mile one day and walk the next. You even could try blending walking and running on some of your workouts. There's no rule that says that you have to run continuously. Let pain be your guide. When those lungs start to ache, shift to a walk. When breathing comes more easily, start jogging again.

In time—and as running becomes easier—you probably will want to test yourself by going farther. After several weeks at the mile level, push forward one workout a week by adding a quarter-mile to your distance, then after another week or two, add an additional quarter-mile. Your total distance for that one workout will now be 1.5 miles. Alternate long runs, short runs, walking, and walk/runs. Play with the schedule. Listen to your body. You'll gradually begin to lose weight, and you should feel better, too.

Progress Check

Q: I am 26 and have been completely sedentary for eight years, since the day I bought my first car. Before that, I walked and biked several miles every day to school. I started running to get in shape three months ago and at first had difficulty finishing a quarter-mile lap. Now I can endure a 3-mile run, but my times are unbelievably slow—and I finish gasping for air with a heart rate of about 200. I am trying hard to get in shape, but am I pushing myself too hard? Just a brisk walk elevates my heart rate to 120. I have improved in distance and speed considerably in three months but don't want to put myself in danger.

A: It sounds like you're doing just fine. I wouldn't worry too much about times right now. You've had eight years away from any exercise, so you shouldn't expect to be contending for an Olympic title after only three months. One suggestion: Don't overlook the benefits of walking versus running. You may want to vary your routine by taking some long (but easy) walks where your pulse stays well below that 120 level you mention. And dig your old bike out of the garage. No need to put pressure on yourself to succeed since you've already achieved success by staying with it.

Equipment
Products to Aid Performance

- **When to Wear Tights**
- **Layering Clothes**
- **Total-Body Workouts**
- **Treadmills**

- **Inside versus Outside**
- **Heart Rate Monitors**
- **Baby Joggers**

Running is the simplest sport imaginable. Quoting a hit song by Billy Joel of a few decades ago, "Don't waste your money on a new set of speakers; you get more mileage from a cheap pair of sneakers." You actually need more than that, and shoes that are really "cheap" may be more costly in the long run if they cause an injury that sends you to an orthopedic surgeon.

When it comes to equipment, I don't like to recommend most products by name. And it's not entirely because I don't want to offend manufacturers of competing products. Manufacturers frequently change models, and stores ordinarily offer these same models and products at different prices. You'll find some products mentioned by name in this and other chapters, but that's because it's often more descriptive—and accurate—to offer a specific brand name than a generic title, particularly when one company dominates the market. NordicTrack, for example, almost single-handedly created a demand for cross-country ski machines. Just because I've mentioned a product by name does not imply an endorsement.

Actually, I try to avoid product mentions for a more practical reason: It's difficult for me, as an individual writer, to review dozens of brands and hundreds of models. When *Runner's World* reviews shoes or treadmills, they often recruit everyone on the staff (and frequently other runners not on staff) to help with testing. It just isn't feasible for me to do something like that.

When to Wear Tights

Q: I love to wear Spandex tights because they give me more freedom when running, and I like the feel of them. But is it good to wear them in the cold or in the heat?

A: There is absolutely no problem in wearing Spandex tights whenever you feel like it. In fall, form-fitting tights will permit you the freedom of running that you get bare-legged, plus they'll keep you warm. One research study even suggested that you could run more economically wearing tights than with bare (hairy) legs. In winter, when the cold winds blow off Lake Michigan, I often layer a pair of long johns beneath the tights both for running and cross-country skiing. Or, I'll use tights as an inner layer beneath a floppier garment.

Tights can feel a bit hot in summer, but I wore a pair one July while doing the *Des Moines Register*'s Annual Great Bicycle Ride Across Iowa. I donned the tights the second day into the ride, when it became apparent that my thighs, particularly, were becoming badly sunburned. The tights kept the rays of the sun off my thighs, plus I could stay cooler in the high-nineties weather by dousing the tights with water at rest stops every few miles. A number of bikers looked at them and commented that the tights must be hot—but they weren't, because the sweat wicks away and evaporates.

Layering Clothes

Q: Recently, I had a debate with a friend. I hope that you'll tell me that I was right in stating the following: Wearing several layers of clothing to sweat during a run forces the body to work harder in order to maintain a normal core body temperature. Now, if this is true, the body expends more energy, thus burning more calories. This should help with long-term weight loss. Am I right? She doesn't think so.

A: Sorry, but I have to agree with your friend. The main thing that wearing more clothes does is make you sweat more and lose fluids from your system. This causes a temporary weight loss, but you'll regain it as soon as you start drinking. Energy expenditure? Maybe a few calories, but certainly not enough to justify the discomfort of overdressing.

When I was in high school on the south side of Chicago, one of our former football players used to work out wearing a rubber suit to make him sweat more. He was trying to make the pros, which he did, but I don't believe that NFL coaches encourage such practices anymore. For one thing, it raises the threat of heatstroke while doing very little for your overall conditioning.

The only justification for wearing more than necessary is when you are training in a cool climate to prepare for a race in a warm climate. For instance, if you're running in Minnesota during late fall and preparing for the Honolulu Marathon, you might don an extra layer. That works, although you'll probably heat-condition yourself more by arriving in Hawaii a week before the race, plus it's more enjoyable.

Total-Body Workouts

Q: I am considering buying an exercise machine to add variety to my workouts. I want something that will provide a total-body workout, and I am thinking about a cross-country ski machine. Do you have any suggestions?

A: The most important words of advice that I can offer are to try out the machine(s) first before laying out a lot of money for something that might become just an expensive piece of sculpture in your basement. And I don't mean only to test the machine briefly in a store—although that certainly is a good idea, too. Try out the machine in a health club, preferably more than once. Do you know someone who owns the same machine? See if you can go over there and use it once or twice.

Cross-country ski machines certainly have proved popular in recent years. One of the first companies to produce such a machine was NordicTrack. I saw its advertisements grow in size from classified notices in the back of *Runner's World* to full-page ads in general publications—and those ads don't come cheaply. NordicTrack spawned countless imitators, but the company had designed a machine that met a specific need. Aside from being the proverbial "better mousetrap," it gives a good total-body workout. A cross-country ski machine can be tricky to use. Once you become comfortable with the rhythm, though, it's convenient, and some models can be stowed under the bed to conserve space.

One machine that I own is the HealthRider, which allows you to push and pull with your arms and feet, thus providing a good total-body workout. It's like a rowing machine with pedals. I first encountered the machine during a visit to Oklahoma City, where I lectured at a meeting of the local running club. My wife, Rose, and I stayed with a couple who had such a machine in their exercise room. I tried it, liked it, and purchased a model myself.

I also have an exercise bike that must be 20 years old now, but it's still quite usable. That's a point to consider: Look for a machine that will not break down within six months. You may want to spend a bit more to ensure that you are purchasing quality as well as whatever else the manufacturer promises.

Precor has developed what is called an elliptical trainer. This piece of equipment is a cross between a stairclimber, treadmill, and cross-country skier. It even allows you to run backward. Despite sounding difficult to use, it is actually quite easy to operate.

"Even an unfit person can get a good workout the first time he tries an elliptical trainer," says Budd Coates, health promotions manager at Rodale Press in Emmaus, Pennsylvania. Runners who have trained on elliptical trainers identify them as the ultimate cross-training machine for running. They are not cheap, however, and cost close to $3,000.

Treadmills

Q: My wife and I want to purchase a treadmill for our home gyms and we've seen models that go as high as $4,000. What should we look for when shopping for a treadmill?

A: In the December 1996 issue of *Runner's World* is a review of treadmills by the magazine's editors. They found no models under $1,500 that they would recommend for runners who are serious about the sport. Less expensive models, however, may work for casual runners. They did find, though, that all the models they tested could go fast enough and were smooth enough, so these issues were discounted when making a purchase. The editors decided on three factors if you're buying a treadmill.

1. The control panel shouldn't jiggle. You need a display that you can read.

2. The treadmill should have a handlebar across the front. When you change settings, you need the stability that the bar offers.

3. The treadmill should have a surface that's not too soft. Determining what is comfortable for you will require running on different models, but it's worth your time.

Inside versus Outside

Q: I have had a difficult time with runner's knee the past two years as the result of an earlier injury. I have built my mileage back up to 25 to 30 miles a week on the treadmill. My problem is that when I switch back to running on the roads, I have a hard time managing even 15 to 18 miles a week. Any suggestions for increasing my mileage on hard surfaces?

A: One advantage to treadmill running is that the machines can be more forgiving to the knees than hard concrete roads. And some models offer cushioned belts as an extra-cost option. But treadmills also carry you along. The moving belt, according to regular treadmill users, does provide an impetus to your running that the roads do not offer. So when switching from one surface to the other, act like a beginner. Don't assume that you can run as far, or as fast, indoors and out. The weather can affect how fast you can run, and there are other variations outdoors: everything from hills to potholes. There's also the possibility that your indoor treadmill may not have been calibrated properly, so distance inside may not equal distance outside.

Thus, when heading outdoors, back off on the miles, and on the speed. Gradually build from your current 15 miles weekly outdoors to your indoor distance of 25 to 30 miles. You can also continue to do some of your running on a treadmill indoors even as you shift outdoors. Still another strategy for the weak-kneed would be to seek softer surfaces outdoors, such as trails and/or golf course fairways. That might help you build your mileage back up to where you want it to be. And you would be less likely to know how far or fast you're running, and thus can avoid apples-and-oranges comparisons between indoor and outdoor running.

Heart Rate Monitors

Q: I need help in taking my heart rate. Can you please tell me how to take my own pulse? Or should I buy a heart monitor?

A: Purchasing a heart rate monitor is the easiest way. They work very well and give you a more accurate reading than you can get taking your own pulse. Plus, you don't have to stop running to get a reading. Heart monitors range in cost from $75 to $200.

You can take your pulse in two convenient places: 1) the inside of your wrist on the top vein nearest your thumb, or 2) the upper throat, right under the back part of your jaw. In taking your wrist pulse, use the first two fingers of the other hand and feel around until you can feel the pulse. Under your jaw, do the same. Practice doing this until you can easily count your heart rate.

The number of times your heart beats in a minute is your heart rate. The average pulse for most healthy people is 72 beats per minute, but people differ greatly. Those in very good shape typically tend to have lower heartbeats, but a talented young girl I coached had a pulse way above average. So don't be disturbed if your pulse is not "normal."

While exercising, you can take your pulse by stopping quickly and counting beats for 6 seconds (and multiply by 10) or 10 seconds (and multiply by 6). Do this quickly, since as soon as you stop running your heartbeat will start to drop. The better shape you are in, the quicker it will drop. That's one reason why I use a heart rate monitor when I want to measure my heart rate. The typical heart rate monitor features a chest strap that contains a transmitter capable of picking up the sound of the heart beating, which it transmits to a receiver worn on the wrist. Most monitors are comfortable, convenient, and quite accurate.

Baby Joggers

Q: A new baby is on the way, and I'm thinking of purchasing a baby jogger for my wife so she can get back in shape following her pregnancy without worrying about babysitters. And to be honest, I'm looking forward to both of us going for runs showing off our new family. What can you tell me about purchasing such a machine?

A: Your wife will appreciate it, and so will you. Baby joggers have replaced the more conventional baby carriages, at least for parents who enjoy running while pushing their children. The parents get a tougher workout, and the kids seem to enjoy going along for the ride. The most common models are lightweight devices on three-wheel frames. They cost somewhere around $200, more or less depending on the quality of the machine.

While appearing at a 5-K race in Davenport, Iowa, I visited Running Wild, where store owner Doug Foster demonstrated one such baby jogger for me. It was lightweight and featured a nylon seat that could be removed and thrown into the wash if it got dirty. Pop a few pins, and you could fold the jogger and throw it into the trunk of your car. Foster called it the Cadillac of baby joggers. It sold for somewhat more than the price quoted above. I was impressed.

Foster said that runners should make certain that the model they buy has wheels large enough so that they don't have problems pushing the jogger up and over curbs. Look also for brakes that come on when you let loose of the handle so that you don't see your child rolling down the hill faster than you can run to catch him. If you want a baby carrier or jogger that you can attach to a bicycle, be sure you get one that attaches low so it is less likely to tip. Be cautious, however, about placing very young infants in baby joggers. Babies under six months don't have neck muscles that are strong enough to allow them to sit safely. Use common sense when both buying and using this equipment.

Motivation

Tap Into the Power of Your Mind

- Stuck on a Plateau
- No More Stamina
- Time Management
- Goal Setting
- When to Run
- Wasted Talent

- Fast Finish
- Bailing Out
- Finding Partners
- Runner's High
- Why I Run

What keeps people from becoming runners? Any health professional will tell you that it is a lack of motivation. Building muscle, improving endurance, achieving the skill to run a 5-K or finish a marathon—such achievements come relatively easy. But how do you teach motivation? How do you convince someone that the quality of his life might improve if he ran, or walked, or biked, or even worked in the garden a half-hour or more every other day? Scientists identify that as the minimum amount of exercise needed to achieve a base level of physical fitness, but most sedentary individuals don't make even that much effort.

Questions about motivation are among the most difficult ones I receive. Most come from people who sincerely want to become physically fit because they sense it would be good for them. But they don't know how to motivate themselves to either start or keep going, and they're looking for a helping hand. They want me to lead them to the promised land. That's a heavy burden, and I wish that I possessed the gift to motivate others to change their lives.

Let me at least tell you about Susan. She didn't have a question, but Susan did write to my column to say that she had been running for several years. "Running has been my savior and has given me a purpose for living," she wrote. "My husband was killed in a commercial airline collision six years ago. Since then, I have suffered a long battle with depression. I finally decided to switch from taking antidepressants to running. Running has been an awakening to what happiness is. I recommend running, or any invigorating exercise, to those suffering from depression."

It worked for Susan, and I like to think that running can work for a lot of people—if only they would give it a chance; if only they would motivate themselves to get started.

Stuck on a Plateau

Q: I currently run 20 to 25 miles a week at about 8:30 per mile, but after doing this for a year, I have gotten very bored with the routine. I alternate between long-run days and short-run days and also cross-train on various exercise machines. My problem is that I don't seem to be getting any faster in my 10-K or 5-K times. Can you offer any advice?

A: Getting stuck on a plateau is not that unusual for runners. Since you've only been running for a year, though, I think that there may be some improvement left in you. Here are some recommendations to make running more interesting.

Seek scenic runs. Once a week, run somewhere special. Maybe there's a scenic park, a road rarely traveled, or a golf course that you can hit at dawn. Make this run an event with breakfast planned afterward. Recruit other running friends to go with you.

Join a club. Is there a running club in your area? Join it! Most clubs offer regular workouts. To identify a club, look for people at your next 5-K race who are wearing identical shirts. The Road Runners Club of America (RRCA) has a Web site (www.rrca.org) that lists its member clubs. Or contact the RRCA at 1150 S. Washington Street, Suite 250, Alexandria, VA 22314-4493.

Learn to run. You already know how to run—but have you ever worked with a coach? Young runners ordinarily learn their craft under the tutelage of a coach at school, whereas adult runners often start without any instruction. Increasingly, coaches have begun to work with adults in organized programs. The same RRCA, mentioned above, also publishes a booklet that I wrote titled *How to Find a Coach*. In that booklet, I identify a number of places to find coaches, prerace clinics, classes, camps, health clubs, schools, corporate centers, park departments, running stores, and running clubs.

Attend a camp. Some coaches organize running camps, usually held during the summer to get high school runners ready for cross-country. Lately, adult runners have begun to infiltrate these camps, which have been restructured for their different needs—such as having fun. *Runner's World* publishes a list of running camps each spring on its Web site (www.runnersworld.com). *Track & Field News*, 2570 El Camino Real, Suite 606, Mountain View, CA offers a similar list, usually in its June issue.

Run a marathon. This is a major move for many new runners, but maybe it is time to contemplate that 26-mile distance, or some interim distance such as the half-marathon. Get involved in a specific training program leading to that race. It will give focus to your training efforts.

Visit an expo. Whether you run a marathon or not, you may want to attend that race's expo, featuring not only all sorts of products and equipment but also lectures by running gurus. Seeing the excitement of runners getting ready to race may inspire you to a new direction in your own running.

Travel to a new place. If you're going to run that marathon (or other race), do it in some interesting location, whether it's Honolulu, Bermuda, or even in the next state. Combine running with a vacation. It will give you something to look forward to.

Hopefully, some of these strategies will get you moving so that running can be fun again. While every runner at some point in his career gets stuck on a plateau, that doesn't mean he has to stay there.

No More Stamina

Q: I have lost my desire to run. I used to love it and couldn't wait for 5:00 when my friend and I would go on a run. Now it just seems like too much effort. I don't have any of the stamina I had when I first began running. What can I do to spark my interest again?

A: Here's a list of possible reasons for your lack of stamina and interest. If one or more of these are applicable, simply make the appropriate correction to your training.

- You raced frequently during the past year and didn't bother to take time off at the end of the racing season to allow yourself to bounce back both physically and mentally.
- You have some undiagnosed medical problem (such as mononucleosis) related to that overtraining and overracing.
- You work all day on your feet, so begin your afternoon run feeling heavy-legged and tired.
- It has been hot in the late afternoon and you haven't adjusted your training patterns. (Or, in a different season of the year, it has been too cold.)
- You don't vary your running routine at all.
- You want to succeed so much that you are pressing too hard in your training.
- Other stresses in your life are distracting you, such as an increased workload at your job or financial worries.
- Your nutrition is poor, or you don't get enough sleep.

Time Management

Q: A dozen years ago when I was in college, I ran 3:57 for the 1500 meters. Now, as a father of three, I can't find time to train, and I've gained 25 pounds. I miss running competitively. How can I get back into the sport?

A: A lot of people your age have the same problem, which really relates to time management. You're busy with your job. You're busy with your growing family. You and your wife would like some time to yourselves, but babysitters are so expensive. When can you find time to train, much less compete?

The experts who advise people on how to balance their budgets usually recommend that they sit down and figure out how much money is coming in and going out. You and your wife should do the same in budgeting your time. How many hours of the day do you need for all of your activities? Where are the gaps of time that might allow you to get back into running? Can you find 30 minutes during lunch hour, even two days a week, when you might sneak in a quick workout or perhaps a short walk? Or can you set the alarm 45 minutes early, or stop by at the gym after work? What other activities would you be willing to eliminate so that you can run again? Try to schedule training time on the weekends when presumably you might have more time.

Work this schedule out with your spouse, since she's not going to be happy if you're stealing time from her. Find time for her to have some relaxing activities. If you get 30 minutes to run, give her 60 minutes while you mind the kids. When my children were young, I sometimes took them with me to the track. They played in the playground while I did interval training. Recently, my oldest son, Kevin, went on a trip to Alaska in a recreational vehicle with his wife and three children. While they were getting ready to depart the campground, he would start running down the road, and they would pick him up 30 to 60 minutes later and keep driving.

Hopefully, your wife will be supportive. Planning is the answer.

Goal Setting

Q: I ran on the college track team and pushed myself very hard: 10 miles a day, rarely taking a day off. Burned out, I thought that I would never have the desire to run again, but four months ago, I began again after a three-year hiatus. I now feel the same way I felt before—obsessed. I love running and the way I feel physically, but this time I don't want to burn out. Is there anything you can suggest to prevent, or deter, burnout?

A: Make sure that you have very precisely defined goals—then try not to exceed them. Usually, I determine my goals before the beginning of each year. Some years, I point for a marathon. Others, I may focus my attention on short track distances, looking toward the World Veterans' Athletics Championships. Still, other years, I run few or no races, happy to train for fitness only until the competitive bug returns.

You can do the same. Begin now to define your next goal in running. Do you want to achieve a certain weekly mileage, lose so many pounds, run a specific race time? Once having done that, reevaluate yourself at regular intervals: Am I on track for meeting that goal? Should I do more? Back off? Add speedwork? Cut long runs?

In your case, the initial goal may be to enjoy running but avoid becoming obsessed with it as in the past. At the end of the year, evaluate how you did in achieving your first goal, then set a new one. And go from there.

One word of warning unrelated to your specific question. You seem to have gotten through the first four months without injury. But if you push to anywhere near that old 10-miles-a-day routine, you may suddenly discover that you can't do the same type of workouts you did in your younger days. Take it easy and slowly build up your mileage if that is your goal.

When to Run

Q: I'm about to start a workout routine—mostly running and walking—and can exercise at any time of the day. When is the best time of the day to run? For instance, would running right before bedtime raise my metabolism so I would burn more calories while sleeping, and thus lose more weight?

A: The best time to run differs from person to person. Circadian rhythms have some effect. If you're a morning person (meaning your energy level is highest at that time), you may be better off training at that time. If you're competing in races that start in the early hours, you need to focus some of your training at the time you race. Since undigested food will probably slow you down, you probably don't want to run right after a large meal. But if too long a time has passed since your last meal, your energy level may be low. The bottom line is that you need to figure out when your energy level is the highest, and that would be your best time to train.

If you raised your metabolism by running right before going to bed, that might cause you to burn somewhat more fat while sleeping, but it also could adversely affect the quality of that sleep. Most important is when is it easiest for you? Compliance is more important than metabolism. If you pick the time of day when you enjoy exercising the most (maybe because it allows you to run with a friend), you are more likely to maintain your routine.

Wasted Talent

Q: I am an assistant track coach at a New Jersey high school. I love this job, but have one major point of frustration. Getting some of the kids to focus on training is like pulling teeth at times. There are a handful of runners who make running a priority, but others with real talent just play with the sport.

We had several sophomores who would clown around during practices to the point that they were told to go home. Meanwhile, a first-season runner trained his tail off and placed eighth in the state. This caused several runners to quit because their egos were bruised after getting beaten by the new boy. Now, while they are "taking a season off to get ready for cross-country," runners from other towns are having breakthroughs.

One junior, who used to be the model of dedication, decided to go out for baseball and actively campaigned against joining the track team. How can I get the younger athletes to focus and be more serious, and how can I impart my love of the sport to them?

A: Relax, and let the drifters drift. Every high school coach I've known could spin countless stories of young athletes with seemingly limitless ability who have wasted their talents and never achieved success, either in track or in life. Indifference claims some. Peer pressure claims others. Activities that interest them more than running claim still more.

But that overlooks the obvious point that it takes more than fast legs to become a champion. The greatest talent is dedication and a willingness to focus on a single objective. Maybe those who skipped track season aren't as talented as you (or they) may think. A lot of them are simply afraid of failure. By skipping track, they now have a built-in alibi if they get beaten in the fall. Give me a hard-working plodder any day over a finicky thoroughbred.

I recall one incident when I was coaching in high school. Two letter-winners on my boys' team had done little running during the summer. They showed up the first week of "official" practice in August badly out of shape. At the end of the week, the team was doing interval 400s on the track. I had the boys and girls running together, but split in three different groups, starting 5 to 10 seconds apart. Finish last in your group and you move back; finish first and you move up.

In the final 400, the two letter-winners mentioned above were running at the back of one group, when a freshman girl swept by them as though they were standing still. That was the last time I saw them that season. Both quit the team, and I wasn't too unhappy to see them go, even though our boys' squad was weakened by their absence. The freshman girl went on to finish second at the state meet her senior year; and the school won two state titles with her as the lead runner. She now has a scholarship at a Division-I school.

So continue to work with the dedicated students, and don't worry about the might-have-beens, who probably never had the right stuff to become top runners anyway.

Fast Finish

Q: I coach boys' and girls' cross-country at a small high school. I'm looking for new and different workouts that might help motivate my athletes. The district meet is five weeks away. Any suggestions for workouts would be appreciated.

A: Here's one that I used when I coached the teams at Elston High School in Michigan City, Indiana. I always had the boys and girls train together, meaning there was a wide range of ability from the fastest boy to the slowest girl. Keeping all of them motivated so they would enjoy the sport was my greatest challenge as a coach, more than merely winning meets.

One workout I favored on Wednesdays (after a Tuesday meet and before a Thursday workout of hard 1000-meter repeats) was to head to the Indiana Dunes State Park, everybody's favorite training spot. I'd send everybody out together for a 40-minute "easy" run, heading in a single direction along a trail in the woods. At the end of 20 minutes, we'd be spread out over a lot of territory and separated by trees, but everyone was supposed to stop, turn around, and come back at a faster pace.

Theoretically, this allowed the slow to finish at the same time as the fast, but more important, it took the edge off training too hard that day. There was no advantage to running fast at the start, because that meant you had more distance to catch up when you turned around. Of course, the faster runners somehow usually caught and passed the slower ones anyway, but everybody got to see and encourage each other toward the end of the run.

Adult athletes looking for motivation can use a similar easy/hard approach even when running solo. Not every day, but do some workouts where you start very slow and finish very fast. It's invigorating to train that way and will send you home eager for the next day's run.

Bailing Out

Q: I've been a runner since the eighth grade, continuing through high school and into college. In high school, I was on a nationally ranked cross-country team. We won the distance-medley in the Penn Relays. I never questioned why or how I ran. I just did.

I joined a nationally ranked college team but had a difficult time adjusting my freshman year. To make a long story short, I quit college and the team right before the NCAA Championships. I tried to keep running, but something was—and still is—missing. Since then, I have made several attempts to try running again, but it never lasts. I love the sport and all that it has to offer. I just don't know what to do or where to start. Can you give me any direction?

A: It sounds like you're suffering a classic case of burnout. All of those years in high school, you were living on the edge of success and fame, but after a while, living on the edge begins to wear. Not to criticize your coach—because if I were in his position, I'd go for the glory, too—but living on the edge does put young athletes under a lot of strain.

My recommendation is that you take a year's sabbatical from intense running, or even thinking about intense running. I didn't say stop running, and don't yet abandon the idea of running in college, but you need some downtime away from running as a job.

About your running: Forget about training. How about running just for the sensual enjoyment you get from the discipline? Run for yourself, not for others or the fame it brings you. If you do want to enter a road race to collect a T-shirt, start in the back row with all the walkers. (I'm serious; they're very pleasant people.) That will take away the pressure of having to run for a fast time, or victory, and you can enjoy the sights and sounds of running. Push the last mile or two if you absolutely must with no worry that you're going to have to stick around for the awards ceremony.

If a return to college and competition sounds like it might appeal to you after your year's sabbatical, find some school where you can walk on without pressure and where the coach isn't going to expect you to live up to your high school reputation to justify a scholarship. I've known runners who have bailed out of running for a year or two and come back to make Olympic teams and win major races (Bill Rodgers comes to mind). Whether or not there's a gold medal in your future, I hope that running can again become an enjoyable (if not dominating) part of your life.

Finding Partners

Q: I'm training for my second marathon, and so far I have been on track with my training schedule. Recently, though, I have started to lose my motivation. Can you suggest anything to get it back?

A: The first marathon usually is magic, but sometimes the second, third, or fourth fail to match up—particularly when crunch time comes in the last months and you need to force yourself to do increasingly longer workouts.

One way to keep going is to seek training partners, some person or persons with whom you can meet regularly for those weekend long runs. Even if they're not going the full distance, maybe they can tune in for part of your workout. Another tip is to make at least one workout each week a special occasion. It's easy to run out the door on your usual course, but travel to some scenic location where each run becomes a trip of exploration.

Approximately 750 people signed up for a class that I teach to prepare people for The LaSalle Banks Chicago Marathon, and I'm convinced that it was because class members knew they could show up on a Saturday morning and find 50 to 100 others to run with. A lot of the major marathons do have classes, and a lot of the larger cities do have training groups or running clubs. Hooking up with one of them may spur you on to greater glory.

Runner's High

Q: When I run and push past a plateau, I experience a sensation of a flood being released from the center of my body outward. It's not in any way painful, and if I focus on the sensation, I become more lucid, and my running seems to become easier. What is happening?

A: People don't talk about it as much lately, but 10 to 20 years ago, there was a lot of discussion about a so-called runner's high. It was that point in the middle of a run when a runner might begin to experience a feeling of exhilaration, what might also be described as a second wind. I say "might" because it wouldn't happen to everyone, or during every workout. Supposedly, this was one reason why we ran to experience this runner's high. Running, in one sense, became an addiction.

Scientists claim that the act of exercising releases some endorphins into the brain, as sort of a natural drug. The endorphins tranquilize the brain, supposedly taking some of the edge off the pain we feel as we run. My experience is that runner's high is more than that. When you're out running, you leave the cares of the world behind you. You relax. Your form begins to smooth out after you've warmed up. At least until the point when fatigue sets in, you start feeling pretty good. You are most likely to experience this runner's high between 30 and 40 minutes into an hour-long run. Regardless of whether runner's high is real or not, it does motivate many of us to keep running.

Why I Run

Q: I'm doing a speech on running and would very much like it if you would tell me why you like to run.

A: As a full-time freelance writer, I sometimes spend my whole day where I am now: sitting in front of a computer. Running allows me that automatic hour-a-day to get into the fresh air and experience the real world. Otherwise, the only time I'd get out might be to go to the mailbox.

Besides that, I'm good at it. I've won world and national titles and set world and national records. I have a big ego, otherwise I wouldn't be mentioning those facts. But those are the excuses to keep running. Throw the championships aside, and I still would run.

Today, the temperature was relatively warm for winter. Little wind. A storm yesterday had pounded flat the Lake Michigan beach across the street from where I live: a perfect surface for running. After working all day, I sneaked out just before sunset for a 40-minute run. It was too cloudy to see the sun go down, but on many of my late-afternoon runs, I experience just that. In the summer, I see the sun rise while I'm running across the manicured lawn of a golf course.

Life couldn't be better.

You never see the sun rise or set while you're seated in front of a computer.

Technique

Maximize Performance and Minimize Injuries

- Proper Form
- Runs Like a Duck
- Noisy Runner
- Stride Length
- Numb Toes

- Realistic Stretching
- Funny Arm Swing
- Best Pace
- Increasing Speed
- Running Downhill

While stationed in West Germany during the mid-1950s and training with a U.S. Army team, I attended a track meet in the town of Furth. I was not yet fast enough to deserve an invitation to participate, so I watched from the rail as Emil Zatopek ran the 5000 meters.

Zatopek was the greatest distance runner of his era, perhaps of any era, even though his many world records have long since been bested. The great Czechoslovakian athlete won gold and silver medals in the 10,000 and 5000 at the 1948 Olympic Games in London, then returned four years later to win both those events plus the marathon at the Games in Helsinki.

Zatopek was a classic example of why no runner should feel self-conscious about running technique. He ran hunch-shouldered, his fists clenched, his elbows stabbing the air. His head bobbed from side to side. His face was a mask of agony as though running was no fun. Yet his stride was smooth, and he won that evening as he won so many victories on and off the track. Banished from the Czech army and stripped of his commission because of his support of those antagonistic to the communist government,

Zatopek eventually regained his status among his people, and he had never been forgotten by those of us who love track and field.

The memory of Emil Zatopek running in Furth remains vivid in my mind, and I still invoke his name while advising runners not to worry about how they look when they run. Could a knowledgeable coach have made Zatopek a more efficient runner by smoothing his upper-body movements? Could a pair of orthotics allowed even faster world records? I doubt it, and what distance runner since has done better in the Olympics?

Still, people continue to ask questions about technique and—Emil Zatopek notwithstanding—I still try to provide answers.

Proper Form

Q: In golf, I can drive the cover off the ball because I have good technique. In running, I struggle. My whole body fights running. I have a strong body, but no endurance. How do you teach someone like me proper technique?

A: It's not easy, but it can be done. How did you develop your good golfing technique? Is it natural, or did you take lessons from a golf pro? Some golfers, such as Tiger Woods, seem to possess natural swings, but most need expert attention—otherwise, they never attain their full potential.

The same with another sport that I enjoy as a break from running: skiing. If you went to a downhill ski resort, you'd be smart to seek help from a ski instructor. Proper turning technique on the slopes can help prevent injuries. Most smart skiers understand that. One of the best tennis players in the world, Pete Sampras, works with a coach. Yet many runners—because running is such a simple sport—feel that they don't need lessons, or the instruction they do get revolves more around training schedules than technique.

Here are some general pointers on running form.

Footstrike. Most skilled runners land on their midfeet, but don't try to force your landing to what you think better runners do.

Stride length. How far you stride is less important than how fast you stride. Don't try to lengthen your stride believing that it will make you faster; the opposite may be true.

Carriage. Your trunk should remain more or less perpendicular to the ground. One of the world's best sprinters, Michael Johnson, is a straight-up runner. Carl Lewis also had a very erect carriage.

Arm carry. Your arms move in rhythm with your legs. They should swing forward more than sideways, with your elbows in and your hands cupped (rather than clenched).

Head position. Look 10 meters down the road. The head anchors the body. Resist looking down at your feet, particularly when running uphill.

To develop better technique, you probably need the attention of a coach. They're not easy to find, although more and more coaches are beginning to turn their attention to adult runners.

I suggest that you consider attending a running camp. Before sending your deposit, ask if you will be able to receive individual instruction related to technique. Some camps are better than others in providing critiques and videotaped analysis.

You could also consider employing the services of a running professional, just as you might a golf pro. (For more information on finding a coach or a camp, see "Stuck on a Plateau" on page 19.)

Runs Like a Duck

Q: I have a five-year-old son who is starting to get involved in sports. My son has always run awkwardly, but I figured that it was just his age. He moves his arms real fast and doesn't bend his legs enough. My brother says that he kind of runs like a duck, and so he doesn't run very fast. Are there some basic things I should be showing him?

A: Leave him alone. Children run the way they do because they run the way they do. It's natural. And it's usually because of the way their bodies are put together. By teaching him a form that works for adults, you may be doing him more harm than good.

If you leave your child alone and he continues to run, sooner or later, he will probably develop somewhat better form. If he's still running when he reaches puberty, his form will change entirely because his body will change. And if that means running like a duck, so be it. If everybody were meant to break 10 seconds for 100 meters, there would be no reason to run track meets anymore.

Noisy Runner

Q: Most other runners seem to make very little noise when their feet hit the ground, but I make this slapping sound with my shoes when running. Should I try to run more quietly, or should I just run loud and natural?

A: Every now and then, I'll be running in a race near a foot-slapper like you. Don't be self-conscious about it. People run differently for varying reasons. One of those reasons is biomechanics: how the various parts of their bodies fit together.

My only concern would be that the foot-slapping might be from some natural muscle imbalance, or form fault, that causes you to run "unnaturally." Most runners normally impact the ground at three times their body weight. If you're impacting the ground much harder, it may cause you to be more susceptible to injuries. That's worth checking out for preventive reasons.

Is there some coach or experienced runner you can ask to check your running form? Are you running smooth and straight despite the noise? A visit to a sports physician may confirm whether or not your feet are in balance. Fleet Feet Sports, a Chicago-area running store, uses a TV camera attached to a treadmill to analyze foot form as an aid in recommending which shoes to purchase. "We use it as a double check," says assistant manager Jason Para. "If we see someone with obvious problems, we may refer them to a podiatrist." Even a friend with a video camera may offer clues as to whether or not your form needs correction.

Now comes the tough choice, because if you don't have a record of injuries, you may not want to change: If it ain't broke, don't fix it. Some very fast runners had poor form. As long as you're happy running, who cares how much noise you make?

Stride Length

Q: I run about 20 to 30 miles a week and just completed my first marathon in 3:57. My personal record for the 5-K is 19:20. My problem is that I have a very short stride. When I try to run with a longer stride, it is very uncomfortable and my times are slower. I also am very inflexible. When I try to do a sit-reach (touch my toes) using straight-leg form, I don't come within 6 inches of my toes. Are the two problems related?

A: Why try to run with a longer stride? It won't necessarily make you a faster runner and could slow you down. A short stride can be very efficient for the marathon and also can protect you against injury, since you won't impact the ground as hard.

Ned Frederick, Ph.D., a biomechanist scientist from Exeter, New Hampshire, has done extensive tests involving stride length in his laboratory. Dr. Frederick believes that most runners reach their own "perfect stride length" naturally. Some years ago, I visited Dr. Frederick's lab while researching a magazine article. Through a series of treadmill tests, Dr. Frederick determined my natural stride length, then had me run at a constant speed to the beat of a metronome to force me into varying lengths. He determined that I was more "economical" when I used a slightly longer stride. I asked if I should work to lengthen my stride. "Not necessarily," said Dr. Frederick. "You may have adapted a short stride for various reasons." He cited injury prevention as one possible reason and, indeed, I have had a career with relatively few serious injuries.

As for inflexibility, the last I heard, they awarded medals for crossing the finish line after some 26 miles, not for touching your toes. There are a lot of reasons why people can or can't touch their toes that have nothing to do with their abilities to stretch. One is that they are female (looser than males). Another is that they may have short legs and/or long trunks. I once met Gaston Roelants of Belgium at a race in Europe. He appeared to have legs that came up to the bottom of his chin. Roelants won the Olympic gold medal in the 3000-meter steeplechase, but I'll bet that he would have flunked a toe-touching test.

Numb Toes

Q: I have been running for a very short time, averaging 2 to 3 miles a day. I have a high instep and believe that I have bought the correct type of shoes to compensate for this. When I run hills, however, my toes often become numb. I also tend to land on the front of my feet. What is the cause and resolution to this problem?

A: Having a high instep might be considered somewhat abnormal and could contribute to future injuries, so you were wise to take this into consideration while selecting shoes. Inserts, which can be purchased at a relatively low cost at the drugstore, may also be helpful. If injuries do occur when you increase your mileage, you may need to be fitted for orthotics by a podiatrist.

It is possible that in running up an inclined surface and landing on your forefoot, you cause some cutoff in circulation to your toes and extra trauma to the feet. Also, as a beginner, your forefoot muscles may not yet be fully conditioned.

I don't normally like to recommend form changes for runners I can't see in person, but the next time you run hills, try shortening your stride. Think of yourself as downshifting in a car to get up a steep hill. You also might try massaging your forefoot before and after days on which you run a hilly course. Another contributing factor could be shoe fit, since too-tight shoes can impair circulation. If numb toes continue to bother you, see a podiatrist.

Realistic Stretching

Q: I know that I'm supposed to stretch, but I'm confused as to how to do so, what stretches work best, and what is a realistic length of time to hold each stretch. And what is the most efficient way to stretch, allowing me more time to run?

A: Yours is a common concern. Most of us are runners, not stretchers. Although we recognize that stretching may help prevent injuries and promote flexibility, we view stretching as something that delays doing what we enjoy.

The best time to stretch is after you run, because the muscles are warmer, thus more pliable. But most of us probably need to do some limbering up just to get moving. So a balanced stretching routine would include a little stretching before, and a lot more after, running.

The faster you plan to run in a workout or in a race, the more you need to stretch. Thus, if you're heading out the door for an easy 4-miler, you can probably cheat and wait to stretch later. Starting your workout by walking a brief distance may be enough. If you plan to run fast 400s on a track, however, you need to warm up by jogging then stretching. Sprinters give more attention to prerace stretching than marathoners.

How long should you hold each stretch? Jonathon Fowles of Waterloo University in Ontario, Canada, researched that subject and discovered that in a 2-minute stretch, you achieve 55 percent of your relaxation in the first 15 seconds, then a further 25 percent relaxation in the second 15 seconds with diminishing results as you continue. "Thirty seconds of stretching is better than 15 seconds," says Fowles, "but each additional 15-second increment, though still good, contributes relatively less to increasing muscle length in a single session."

Adherence can also be a problem. A study at Duke University in Durham, North Carolina, had athletes doing up to 15 stretches, holding each stretch for 30 seconds and repeating four times. The athletes failed to improve flexibility and had more injuries because they failed to follow the stretching prescription. "The athletes saw it as too much," explains Fowles. Each addition in time resulted in diminished adherence by the athletes.

Based on that and other research, Fowles recommends selecting four or five stretches and holding each stretch for 15 seconds. Begin by stretching one limb, then stretch the other one, and repeat. Here are five important stretches for runners.

Heel hold. Stand beside a wall for balance, grab your leg at the ankle and pull the heel up toward your butt. Keep your pelvis forward. (No bending at the butt.) This stretches the quadriceps muscle.

Side bend. Stand beside a wall for balance and cross your left foot over your right. Bend from the waist and allow your left arm to slide down the side of your body. This will stretch your right iliotibial band and will help prevent knee pain.

Stair drop. Stand with the balls of your feet on a stair and allow your heels to drop against gravity. This exercise stretches the gastrocnemius muscle in the calf and the Achilles tendon. To stretch the soleus muscle, bend slightly at the knees and repeat.

Deep lunge. Move your right leg forward, foot flat, with about a 90-degree angle between the upper and lower leg. Your left leg should be back, with the knee down, and the heel off the ground. Hover with your hips low in that position, using your arms for balance if necessary. Keep your chest high. Lean backward for more of a stretch. This stretch lengthens the hip flexor muscles and buttock muscles of the opposite leg. "This is very important for recreational runners who sit at their jobs and allow these muscles to shorten," says Fowles.

Hurdle. Sit on the ground with your right leg forward and your left leg to the side in a modified hurdler's position. (Your left knee should be pointing away from your body; the foot of that leg should be near the knee of your right leg, what might be called a half-lotus position.) Stretch by allowing your chest to fall forward. Don't allow your back to curl or you'll fail to stretch the hamstrings, the purpose of this stretch. "This is also a very important stretch for desk-bound joggers," adds Fowles.

Moving directly from stretch to stretch, you should be able to complete this stretching routine within 5 minutes. To improve your flexibility, you can hold the stretches longer or add different stretches. But the most important thing is to find a stretching routine convenient enough to guarantee that you will do it.

Funny Arm Swing

Q: My main sport is soccer and to keep balance while frequently changing direction, I wave my arms. It has become a bad habit, and I even do it sometimes when I go out for a jog. Will this slow me down? How can I fix this form fault?

A: Swinging your arms out of the normal rhythmic matter probably will slow you down slightly, but I wouldn't worry about it since your main sport is soccer. If your main sport were running, you would probably want to focus on relaxation and maintaining a smooth gait, which eventually would help you eliminate your bad habit.

Perfect arm form should have you running with your elbows bent at about a 90-degree angle and swinging evenly waist high. Your hands should be cupped slightly. Think of yourself as scratching the top of your hipbones without quite touching them. You don't want excessive crossover as your arms swing in front of your body, but what qualifies as "excessive" differs from person to person. Some individuals carry their arms higher or lower than other runners, and they should not be told to change as long as this feels comfortable. The arms obviously need to swing in natural rhythm to counterbalance the stride. Distance runners, however, should use little effort to control their arms except when trying to accelerate.

Best Pace

Q: How do you determine your best base pace? Beginning in March, I started to speed up my base pace and have gone from 9:30 to 8:15 miles with no injuries. I feel that I can go faster over the next six months. I currently am running 20 to 25 miles per week.

A: You determine your best pace through experience. Train a lot. Race a little. Pretty soon, you'll find what pace is comfortable in training and how fast you can run in a race without running out of energy before the last mile.

It takes time. As a new runner, don't be in a hurry to learn skills that have taken some of us a lifetime. One way to speed the process is by purchasing a heart rate monitor that gives you feedback on how hard you are pushing yourself at various paces. Most runners find it comfortable to run most of their workouts at 65 to 75 percent of their maximum heart rate, what I would call an easy pace. In moving from 9:30 to 8:15 miles, you may be pushing yourself into a higher pace zone. This is not necessarily bad unless you overdo it.

Increasing Speed

Q: I am a 39-year-old mother of three, and I've been running since I was about 19. I ran through all three pregnancies except for maybe the last few months. My problem is, although I can easily run 6 to 8 miles a day, I'm not a terribly fast runner (9:00 miles). How can I increase my speed and still enjoy the run?

A: In order to improve your speed, you have to run fast during at least some of your workouts. One way to do that is to run shorter distances and/or program rest between hard (fast) workouts. If you've been running 6 to 8 miles a day, seven days a week, that's close to 50 weekly miles—a lot of running. Try cutting your distance in half and running at a faster pace. If your workout for the day is only 2 miles, you should be able to run that shortened distance at 8:00 pace, or maybe faster. If you broke that 2 miles into 400-meter increments (8 × 400), you could probably run faster still if you rested a few minutes between each fast 400.

To increase speed, you need to think like a racer, whether you participate in running races or not. That means you need structured workouts that involve warming up, stretching, wind sprints, interval training, repeats on the track, and strength training. In other words, the type of training that competitive athletes use to improve their speed.

One method to improve speed is to do bounding drills, a series of skipping and hopping exercises that can improve your strength and flexibility. Some coaches refer to these drills as plyometrics, and entire books have been written on the subject. You need to be cautious using these drills, however. Some drills (such as jumping on and off boxes) can be dangerous, particularly for adult runners and even for young runners.

Here's a safe drill you might try. It's called Fast Feet, and it was taught to me by Bill Bowerman, the former track coach at the University of Oregon in Eugene, who was a football player in college and also coached football for a time after graduation. Bowerman used the drill first with football players, then sprinters, but found that it worked for distance runners, too, since speed and strength are basic to all sports.

Standing erect, move your feet as fast as you can, not getting more than an inch or two off the ground, and not moving forward along the ground. Stay up on your toes. Move your arms in rhythm to your feet, but with very little motion, close to your body. The drill is difficult to describe in print, but actually quite easy to do.

Another bounding drill that I favor is simply skipping for short distances. If you attend track meets featuring experienced athletes and hang around where the sprinters and hurdlers warm up, you can learn other drills simply by watching. Bounding drills can help improve your speed, although they are best practiced under the supervision of a knowledgeable coach who has a good understanding of the principles of dynamic flexibility and who can also prevent you from doing too much.

Except for the very gifted, speed is not easily acquired. You have to work at it. So it becomes a question of whether or not you are willing to put forth the effort to increase your speed.

Running Downhill

Q: What is the proper technique for running downhill?

A: Hills vary in their steepness, so there is no single best technique that will get you down quickly and safely. With shallow hills, you can increase your speed and pass runners with less efficient technique, but on steeper hills there exists the danger of going so fast that you lose control and waste energy. If the ground is rough—as in a cross-country race—you may fall.

Here are some tips for running downhill.

1. As you start downhill, tilt your body forward, beginning at the waist. Make a conscious effort to shift positions so that your trunk remains perpendicular (90-degree angle) to the ground. How much you tilt, thus, depends on the angle of the hill.

2. When you do this, your speed will increase naturally. To cope with this speed, raise your knees and lengthen your stride. (Raising your knees and lengthening your stride will require extra energy. This is one reason why you will not regain all of the time you lost going uphill.)

3. Maintaining balance as your speed increases is not easy. If the ground is uneven, you will need to focus on technique. One way to maintain balance is to allow your elbows to rise

up and away from your body. (Think of yourself as a tightrope walker using a pole for balance, with your arms being the pole.)

4. To cushion the shock of the descent, land more on the front of your feet rather than on your heels.

The most important tip is to practice these techniques. Running downhill becomes tougher toward the end of a long race or run, when fatigue makes concentration more difficult.

Running uphill, of course, takes different techniques. If you can improve your uphill technique (and hold back a little) so you do not reach the peak of the hill exhausted, it will make it easier to run faster on the down side.

Training

Secrets of Success

- Milo and the Bull
- Farther and Faster
- Quantity
  versus Quality
- Morning Runner
- Intervals
- Rest
- Hill Repeats
- Tempo Runs

- Fartlek
- Clydesdales
- Heart Rate
  Calculation
- Getting Out of Shape
- Altitude Effects
- Overtraining
- Tracks
- Dogs

Training is a foreign word to many runners, most of whom simply want to run. Whether a mile or 10 miles a day, they only want to head out the door, spend the required time running through the streets and parks or indoors on a treadmill and finish with smiles on their faces.

Only when they begin to enter 5-K races and encounter the world of personal achievement do they realize that they have been "training" without realizing it. They also realize that to continue their improvement, they must begin to alter their training. At first, increasing commitment (either mileage or time) guarantees improvement. But as in many activities, runners eventually reach a point of diminishing returns, where training not only has to increase in volume and intensity but also has to increase in sophistication.

Runners who began their careers on high school teams usually learned how to train from their coaches. Those whose routes into the sport of running were from another direction often ask me questions or turn to books or friends for advice. I even get questions from school-age runners, particularly in the off-season.

Training properly can not only make you a faster runner but also it can make you a healthier runner, which in turn will contribute to not just fast times but good times.

Milo and the Bull

Q: I have recently begun a running program. I cover 4 miles about three times per week. I would like to increase my mileage without injury and want to run 10-K and beyond. With those goals in mind, how often should I run and how many miles each time?

A: There is no magic formula for increasing mileage, but consider the legend from ancient Greek times of Milo and the bull. Milo of Croton had ambitions of being an Olympic champion in wrestling, so he began by lifting a bull when it was only a calf and weighed very little. Each day, the bull gained weight, and Milo lifted it atop his shoulders. By the time the bull reached maturity, Milo had gained in strength and went on to victory in the Olympic arena.

Distance runners follow the lead of Milo when they increase their training a little bit each week, if not each day. Four miles a day is probably an ample training load if your only goal is to finish a 10-K race. But as your fitness increases, you may want to stretch your longest distance to 5 to 6 miles, if only once a week. Like Milo lifting the bull, you will improve your endurance.

The other approach would be to increase your weekly mileage by running more often. Instead of running three days a week, increase the frequency of your training to four, five, six, or even seven days a week. At the top levels of our sport, elite athletes run twice a day (morning and evening), and some do triple workouts.

I don't recommend such excessive training even for those with Olympic aspirations, but running more miles is not the only route to improvement. Vary those workouts. Instead of running 4 miles every day, run 5 to 6 miles one day and 2 to 3 miles the next. The days on which you run fewer miles become your easy, or rest, days. Or, you may want to alternate your running with other fitness activities such as walking, cycling, or swimming. That approach is known as cross-training.

There are many ways that you can train with only your imagination to limit you.

Farther and Faster

Q: I have run for 18 months but have not been able to progress beyond running 2 to 4 miles at 10:00 pace three times a week. I can't seem to go any farther or any faster. What sort of program should I use to get to the next level? I would like to be able to run 6 miles, three or four times a week.

A: One way to improve is to gradually build your mileage: going from 5 to 10 to 15 to 20 miles a week, and so forth. That's known as developing a base. While you're doing that, you can also focus on the quality of those miles, attempting to develop your ability to run those miles progressively faster. One way to achieve a faster pace is to run shorter distances. This is known as building speed.

Here are two ways in which you can improve your distance and your speed.

Distance. On one of your 4-mile days during the week, begin to gradually increase your distance. Run 4.5 miles. To cover this extra mileage, slow down from your usual pace to 11:00 or 12:00 miles, or even walk in the middle of the workout if necessary to go the extra distance. The following week, go 5 miles, then back to 4 miles the third week. Then move to 5.5 miles, and finally, 6 miles in similar slow progressions. If this progression seems too difficult for you, try adding a quarter-mile instead of a half-mile to your longest run each week. Use this distance workout one day a week.

Speed. On one of those 2-mile days, include some running at a slightly faster pace. On an out-and-back course, jog the first mile easy—even slower than your usual 10:00 pace. Turn around. Run back at a slightly faster pace (9:00 mile). Keep this up for 1 minute, then slow your pace (11:00 mile) to recover. Run slowly for 1 minute, then speed up again. Run 4 × 1:00 fast/slow in this manner, then finish by jogging the final distance, if any remains. Use this speed workout one day a week.

Most runners at the Olympic level train by combining base with speed training. They may run faster than you, but the training principles are the same. You don't need to train with the same volume or intensity as an Olympic athlete, but you can improve your ability to run faster if you train using a similar pattern combined with one more important item: rest.

Try this variation in your running routine and see if it improves your ability to go farther and/or faster. Once you accept the idea that every workout does not have to be the same distance run at the same speed, you are on your way to becoming a serious runner.

Quantity versus Quality

Q: I have heard a lot of talk about the quality of training versus quantity of training. Some training programs emphasize mileage buildups as one way to improve fitness. Others emphasize speed training as the most effective approach. I have a friend who favors quantity. Last year, he logged 341 days (out of 365) in his training log. To me, this is the route to burnout, since I only run five days a week to allow me time to concentrate on other activities. Which approach is best?

A: I'm not going to declare a winner in the argument between you and your friend, since I think that each of you has the right approach. He obviously has come up with a training system that works for him, and you have a system that works for you.

It appears that your friend averages only one day off every second week. You average two days off every week. Why should either of you change unless you have some specific and urgent goal like qualifying for the Boston Marathon or getting ready for some specific race where you want to post a fast time?

If you or your friend want to achieve success with your running schedules, you each need to include both quantity and quality in your routines. In fact, what I usually tell runners who are stuck on a plateau is to do something different, regardless of what that something different might be. But you don't always want quantity and quality at the same time. Why not embark on a program where you focus for several months on quality (while cutting back on quantity), then do the reverse. Go for a period where you do follow your friend's lead and run almost daily. Variety often is the secret to long-term success. Your friend should heed this message, too.

Morning Runner

Q: I'm 28 years old and I have been running for the past 8 years. I run 10 to 20 miles each week. From reading practically everything that you and Dr. George Sheehan have written, I know (biologically speaking) why running in the morning is more difficult than running in the afternoon for most people. It is for me as well. Because of my schedule, however, it's better for me to run in the morning. Will I ever get used to that?

A: Individuals seem to divide into two categories: morning people or evening people. I'm the former. I'm often up at 4:00 A.M., particularly in the summer. On warm days, I usually run just as the sun is rising, to beat the heat. Winters, I prefer to run just before noon. But as a full-time writer, I have a flexible schedule that permits me to set my own schedules for work and play.

I'm not sure that we ever fully adapt. Whether we are morning or evening people may be deeply imprinted in our biological makeup, perhaps at birth, perhaps because of what happens after birth.

I recently participated in a study into circadian rhythms directed by Patrick J. O'Connor, Ph.D., of the department of exercise science at the University of Georgia in Athens. During the study, I was forced to remain awake in a windowless room for 28 hours. It was no fun, but I managed to make the time go faster by watching Fred Astaire and Ginger Rogers videos.

Dr. O'Connor suggests that runners may obtain maximum performance benefits by working out in the early evening, when many circadian rhythms are at their peaks. In other words, if you peak biologically at 4:00 in the afternoon, you should be able to build muscle better by training at precisely that time.

This isn't an iron rule, and Dr. O'Connor proposes that we can modify our behavior somewhat. In other words, even if you are an evening person, you can train yourself to compete well in the morning, certainly a necessity since most road races start early. Dr. O'Connor suspects that most elite athletes are so focused that they can train or race well regardless of time of day. Based on my own running experience, I agree.

Research also indicates that mood improvements follow exercise regardless of the time of day the exercise is performed. "While it may be more difficult to get up and run in the morning," says Dr. O'Connor, "you will still feel better afterward."

At some point, you simply need to make a rational (as opposed to biological) decision as to whether you want to run in the mornings or evenings, based partly on your personal preference and partly on what your work and family situations force you to do.

Intervals

Q: I am a 50-year-old male who consistently runs 8:00 miles. I want to be able to run a 7:00 mile within six months. What is the best way? Should I run fast 400s?

A: Yours is seemingly a very simple question, and I could give you a very simple answer: Either train longer or train faster. But cutting 60 seconds from anyone's time resists simplistic solutions. Sophisticated training may be necessary.

Before suggesting a training program, I need to know more about you. Have you been running only a few months, or have you been running many years? Is the limit of your distance that 1 mile run in 8:00, or do you run that pace in longer workouts? And most important for anyone past the age of 30: What is the state of your physical health? If you haven't had a full physical exam (including possibly a stress test) in the last two years, you need one before embarking on any training program of which the aim is to improve performance. The reason is that in seeking to cut your mile time, you need to start doing speed training, and that will put extra stress on your cardiovascular system. That's okay if you don't have heart disease—and actually will help prevent heart disease—but it can be risky if you haven't had a recent physical exam.

Assuming that you are in good health, and the limit of your training is that 1 mile a day, I would begin by gradually extending the limit of your mileage over a period of three to four months. You need to build an aerobic base before you can begin speedwork, the interval training program that I am about to outline.

In the final two to three months of your six-month training plan, go to the track once a week and do some interval training. Run 4 × 400, walking during the interval between each 400. (That's where "interval training" gets its name.) Go back in succeeding weeks and do 5 × 400, then 6 × 400, 7 × 400, and 8 × 400. Run these 400s at 8:00-mile pace, or 2:00 per 400, what some coaches would call race pace. Resist the urge to go faster at this point. The most important goal is consistency week after week.

Then, having reached a maximum of 8 × 400 in 2:00 each, each following week, run the 400s slightly faster: 1:57.5, then 1:55, then 1:52.5, aiming toward a goal pace of 1:45, or the pace you would be hitting if you ran a 7:00 mile. The way to do this more easily is to begin cutting the number of repeats, going backward the way you came: 8 × 400, then 7 × 400, 6 × 400, 5 × 400, and then 4 × 400. Your final goal would be a workout where you run 4 × 400, walking between, with each 400 in 1:45. Put those four quarters together in a continuous run, and you'll have your 7:00 mile.

I don't guarantee that you'll be able to achieve that goal any more than I could guarantee that a 5:00-miler could drop to 4:00 using the same schedule, but the principle of gradual overload remains the same.

Rest

Q: I am a 44-year-old male. It seems that if I run every day, I do not recover enough to feel strong. How many rest days should I take per week? What is your advice on the amount of training days, and the intensity of the workouts, for a man my age?

A: It really varies from person to person. When I was your age, I sometimes trained twice a day, up to 100 miles a week, to get ready for the World Veterans' Athletics Championships. But I don't necessarily recommend that routine for everybody, nor could I maintain that level of training today in my sixties.

For some runners, a day where they run an hour at an easy pace qualifies as "rest." Others need total rest: no running. And maybe two days of rest. Everything is relative to your own level of fitness and motivation. Having said that, I would suggest that for runners serious about their training, two or three hard days a week might be appropriate, coupled with two or three days of running easy, coupled with one or two days of rest. That doesn't necessarily add up to a week, but people differ in their abilities to absorb training and in how much rest they need between hard sessions.

Hill Repeats

Q: When you see "6 hills" on a training schedule, such as those designed by Benji Durden, what should you assume is the distance, duration, and incline of the hill? And how would you do that workout on a treadmill?

A: Your question refers to the marathon training schedule by Durden, which first appeared in the August 1993 issue of *Runner's World*. During the base preparation period, Durden recommends that runners do a series of hill repeats once a week. The schedule proved very popular with our readers, and I later invited Durden to design an expanded version for my book *How to Train*. The following is from that book: "Once a week, Durden's runners head for the hills—or track. He begins with a buildup of repeats on a hill with a 4 to 6 percent grade that takes about 90 seconds to run. (If you don't have a hill of that height or length, do the best you can.) Starting with 3 hill repeats, the runner builds to 8 or 9 repeats, then switches to the track."

Converting that workout recipe to a treadmill is simple. One of the beauties of treadmill running is that you can control all variables, so set the treadmill at a 4 to 6 percent incline and crank up the speed so that you are running near maximum effort for 90 seconds. I can't give you a precise setting because it will differ from runner to runner depending on the level of fitness, but you should run the hill repeats at 90 percent of your maximum heart rate.

One of the advantages of hill training is that it builds the quadriceps muscles, which allow you to lift your legs off the ground. As most marathon runners who have hit the wall can tell you, it is often the quads that go at 20 miles. You suddenly discover that you can't lift your legs to maintain a steady pace and must resort to an ever-slowing shuffle. Another advantage of hill repeats is that there is less impact running uphill than running downhill, or even running on the flat (because the ground comes up to meet the descending foot). As a result, you can train harder on an incline with less damage to the muscles.

Although an incline of 4 to 6 percent may not sound like much, it is worth noting that the incline on Mount Washington, site of a popular New England uphill road race is 8 percent. Treadmill manufacturers permit settings up to 12 to 15 percent, but few runners can maintain momentum very long on inclines that steep.

Tempo Runs

Q: I'm about to turn 15, and I have been running seriously for about 2½ years. My fastest mile is 5:03; my 5-K, 17:25. I have done different types of speed workouts, but I am looking for something new to try. Could you suggest a good workout for me?

A: How about tempo runs? This is a workout guaranteed to raise your anaerobic, or lactate, threshold, which will allow you to hold a fast pace for a longer period of time.

A tempo run is one in which you change tempos, or speeds, in the middle of the workout. Jack Daniels, Ph.D., track and cross-country coach at the State University of New York at Cortland, may not have been the first to coin the phrase, but he certainly helped popularize the current focus on this kind of workout through his writing.

Suppose you are doing a 40-minute run. You begin easily, a warmup jog almost, then at about 10 minutes into the workout, you begin to switch tempos and gradually accelerate until you are running at a pace perhaps 80 to 85 percent of your maximum heart rate. You hold this fast pace for 15 to 20 minutes, then relax and finish the run at a slower pace. Dr. Daniels recommends that the midworkout pace be as fast as you can run all-out for an hour, or somewhat slower than 10-K race pace for most people.

Because tempo runs rely on perceived exertion to dictate pace (you listen to your body), the risks of overtraining are lessened. Plus it's fun to run fast. When I'm training hard, I usually like to do at least one tempo run a week, usually in some scenic area featuring soft-surface trails.

Fartlek

Q: I see the term *fartlek* in many training schedules. What is it?

A: Fartlek is a Swedish word meaning "speed play." This form of training was invented by Coach Gosta Holmer, whose prize pupils, Gunnar Haag and Arne Anderson, set world mile records back in the 1940s. Fartlek consists of fast, medium, and slow running over a variety of distances, depending on the terrain.

In a typical fartlek workout, you pick some landmark, such as a tree or a bush, and sprint to it, then jog until you've recovered. Select another landmark that is a shorter—or longer—distance away, and run to it at a faster—or slower—pace. The distance and pace are up to you. The most important skill for this drill is listening to your body. It's a very creative form of training best done in the woods. As University of Oregon track and field coach Bill Dellinger once said, "It can be the easiest or toughest workout you do all week."

Clydesdales

Q: I am 6 feet tall and once weighed 295 pounds. I took up running to lose weight and pared down to 224 pounds in 15 months, completing my first marathon in just under 5 hours. I'm still losing weight, but at a slower rate. I had been overweight all my life, so I want to keep running and maintain my somewhat slimmer self, but I'm concerned about injuries. The problem is that most of the training advice is directed toward people who are smaller and lighter than I am. What training advice can you offer?

A: You're right. There is very little in the way of specific training advice for "Clydesdales," the name that heavier runners use to describe themselves. An increasing number of races offer special Clydesdale categories with special awards to encourage runners such as yourself. Clydesdales are generally defined as male runners over 200 pounds and female runners over 140 pounds, but that may vary from race to race. Then there are "Super Clydes," men over 225 pounds and women over 155 pounds.

Not trusting my own skinny perceptions of how Clydesdales should train, I consulted with several running friends who are active on this Web site. While conceding that the same rules and training programs that work for runners my size don't entirely apply to them, they were unable to come up with much in the way of specific training recommendations. A hard 10-mile run (as described on a training schedule) is a hard 10-mile run no matter how much you weigh. You may not be able to run it as fast if you are 224 pounds versus 142 pounds, but you still have to get out and run.

Nevertheless, because the impact of feet striking the ground is higher for Clydesdales, you do need to restructure your training. Rest days are much more important for Clydesdales. Cross-training (alternate activities such as cycling, swimming, or walking) is more important. Equipment is important, but fortunately, most of the shoe manufacturers now offer extra-duty shoes. Keith Stone of Winston-Salem, North Carolina, who helps coach other Clydesdales, suggests that since heavy runners who make training errors suffer more serious injuries than light runners, they need to be more cautious. Whereas, light runners may be able to safely follow an 18-week buildup of miles toward a marathon, Clydesdales should consider extending that buildup for a longer period (say 27 weeks) so that the increase is more gradual.

What it comes down to is that Clydesdales must substitute brain for brawn while training as runners.

Heart Rate Calculation

Q: I started running several months ago and obtained a heart monitor to help me in my training. Based on the 220-minus-my-age (40) formula, my maximum heart rate is 180. Thus, my aerobic level (70 to 80 percent) should be 126 to 144 beats per minute. But during most workouts, at what I consider an easy 9:30 pace, my heart rate tends to rise into the mid-150s. When I slow down to keep within the 70 to 80 percent range, I have to run slower than I enjoy. How can I train more effectively to maintain a steady heart rate, yet increase my speed?

A: The problem is that you are using a formula to predict your heart rate, and formulas don't work for everybody. Another formula, considered more accurate by some researchers, is 200 minus half your age. Coincidentally, for those who are 40, the predicted number is the same (200 – 20 = 180), but after that, the numbers grow apart. I have a very low resting pulse and maximum heart rate, as measured accurately during stress tests, and the formulas don't work for me. They also didn't work for a talented young female runner I coached, who had a very high heart rate.

The only way to be sure of your maximum heart rate is to take a treadmill stress test where you run to exhaustion. Another way that works for more experienced runners is to run in a 5-K race wearing a heart rate monitor. Check your monitor in the last 200 meters as you sprint for the finish line. Or, run an 800 on the track, walk for a minute, and run another 800 full speed, before fully recovering. The maximum heart rate you hit at the end of this workout should be close to your actual maximum.

Since you are a newcomer to the sport and probably never have done speed training, I don't recommend this approach for you. It takes focus and concentration to be able to safely push yourself to the point where your heart won't beat any faster. I don't recommend anyone your age, who conceivably might have undiagnosed heart disease, to sprint flat out in an attempt to reach his maximum. If you do this on a treadmill under the supervision of a doctor, he can stop the test if problems develop.

Formulas aside, you most likely have a slightly higher heart rate than the formulas predict. That being the case, adjust your target zone upward and see how your training goes. As you get in better shape, you may actually find that your target may shift, which is normal. There are no formulas or approaches that work best for everybody. Inevitably, experience is the best teacher.

Getting Out of Shape

Q: How many weeks of *not* running would it take to get out of shape once you're in shape?

A: It depends on your definition of "out of shape." Some 2:10 marathoners might consider themselves out of shape if their times had sunk to 2:15.

It is true that your physical conditioning will deteriorate at some prescribed rate if you don't exercise. It doesn't happen overnight, though. It might not happen in two or three days, but after two to three weeks, you will begin to experience declines between 7 to 15 percent of several important exercise-related functions, including max VO_2 and lactate threshold. You no longer would be able to run that 2:15 marathon.

Studies by scientists such as Edward F. Coyle, Ph.D., at the University of Texas in Austin, have suggested that after a period of detraining, you have to train for two days to regain the fitness you might have lost by one day of inactivity. In other words, if you stop running for 6 weeks, it will take 12 weeks to regain your previous level of fitness. This is one reason why it is recommended that when a runner suffers an injury that prevents him from running for any length of time (such as a stress fracture), he finds an alternate activity to minimize the fitness loss and speed his return once the injury is healed.

Altitude Effects

Q: I'd like some advice about altitude training. I used to be a competitive skier and worked at ski resorts for 10 years. For the last 3 years, I've lived in San Francisco. I'm still active, but when I go back to the mountains and ski with my friends, I'm out of breath and my heart's pounding. What is the quickest way to increase my heart/lung capacity? I mountain bike, run, and skate a couple of times a week, but high altitudes now leave me beat.

A: Your problem has nothing to do with heart/lung capacity; the secret is in your blood. When you return to high altitudes, your blood loses its oxygen-carrying capacity. You don't have a sufficient number of red blood corpuscles, so they exhaust themselves trying to supply oxygen to your muscles, temporarily compromising your level of aerobic fitness.

It will take about 72 hours for your blood to bottom out and three weeks for it to build back up. In between, you will get that out-of-breath feeling. Part of the problem is psychological in the sense that you may have forgotten what it feels like breathing around 10,000 feet. When I visit my favorite ski areas, I know that I'm going to have to struggle for breath not only on the slopes but also while sleeping at night.

Cut back on your ski time. I know that you want to get maximum use from your vacation time, but if you pace yourself in the mountains (as you might in a marathon), you'll suffer fewer problems. Ski a full first day when your blood is still at peak, but leave the slopes an hour or two early on the second day, and ski only a half-day (or take a full day off) on the third day. By that time, you will have begun to acclimatize, and you'll be able to ski more comfortably the rest of the week. This advice also holds true for people running, biking, or hiking in the mountains. Go slowly until you acclimatize.

Another factor is that you've probably lost some of your technical edge while living in the shadow of the Golden Gate Bridge. Your old friends probably can ski, not necessarily better than you, but with greater economy of motion because that's all they do. So they actually may be using less oxygen than you.

Relax and invite them to go running with you the next time they hit the Bay Area. Believe it or not, they'll find running in your environment (thick air) as difficult as you find skiing in theirs.

Overtraining

Q: What exactly is overtraining? How do I know if I am overtrained, and how can I avoid it?

A: I define overtraining as doing more than the optimum amount to ensure maximum fitness. You train so hard that you become fatigued, and your performances start to slide. Judging from the slogans on the backs of T-shirts that I see at high school cross-country races, a lot of runners (and their coaches) believe that more is better. Such is not always the case. A rather obnoxious commercial that aired frequently on TV showed a mountain biker who trained so hard that she ran into a tree and knocked herself out. Overtraining is like running into a tree.

Knowing what overtraining is and avoiding it are two separate items. Prevention is not easy, particularly since some of our most successful runners get where they are because they were highly motivated. Todd Williams is the perfect example. Williams is the only American distance runner who qualified for the finals of the 10,000 meters at the 1992 Olympics and 1993 and 1995 World Championships. He thought that with just a little more training, and a little more dedication, he could be on the medals platform at the 1996 Olympics in Atlanta. Instead, he blew up in his qualifying race and failed to finish. With the 20/20 vision of hindsight, Todd now realizes that he overtrained.

Here are some symptoms to guide you.

- Elevated pulse rate before getting out of bed (assuming you take your pulse each morning)
- Restless sleeping
- Lack of appetite
- Your weight drops below normal (this will actually make you slower, not faster)
- Frequent colds and the flu
- Sluggishness while running
- Minor injuries that seem to take longer than usual to heal; the same with sore legs
- Deteriorating performances

Of course, by the time many of these symptoms appear, the damage has been done.

To avoid overtraining, take regular breaks, get plenty of rest, eat a nutritious diet, don't race too often, and keep a training diary so if you do crash into that tree, you'll know what not to do next time. Todd Williams now knows, which is why I'm hoping to see him on the awards platform at the Olympics in 2000.

Tracks

Q: I currently run on an indoor track at a health club, where 7½ laps equals 1 mile. Are all outdoor tracks at high schools the same distance? I would like to run at the local high school now that the weather is warmer. How many laps would equal a mile?

A: Many of us who have been in the sport for many years—and who participated in track at the high school or college level—forget that all knowledge is not shared equally. Here are some basic facts related to the track world.

Outdoor tracks. Most outdoor tracks are 400 meters long, converted from 440 yards after high schools and colleges began running metric distances. (Notice that I said "most." A few outdoor tracks are odd distances.) Four hundred meters is only marginally shorter than 440 yards, a few tenths of a second on the clock. Four × 400 meters equals 1600 meters, just short of a mile. The similar distance run most frequently in other countries and in the Olympics is 1500 meters, the so-called "metric mile." Cut the length of one turn off a mile, and you have 1500 meters. As a competitor, it always struck me as much more sensible to run 1500 meters rather than the mile, because you start on the backstretch with an entire straightaway ahead of you before hitting a curve, but for some reason, high school coaches stubbornly cling to the outdated 1600 distance in their track meets. Antediluvian attitudes is one reason why the sport of track and field has declined in the United States.

Lanes. Most tracks have painted lines circling the track, used for running distances such as the 200 and 400 meters, where runners stay in lanes. The starts are "staggered," so that if you run in lane eight, you don't run farther than the runner in lane one. Some tracks require "joggers" to use the outside lanes, forcing them to run extra distance per lap. (This seems like an unfair penalty to hand people who usually are slower to begin with, but it makes traffic flow more smoothly. And it prevents excessive wear and tear on the inside lane, which makes athletic directors, who invariably are not runners, happy.) If you examine the lane markers at the starting line, you usually can determine how much extra per lap you run in the outside lanes. If not, ask the resident track coach for help.

Courtesy. Different tracks have different rules, but track races are run counter-clockwise, so that's usually the way everybody runs on tracks. (If you want to run in the opposite direction, choose a far outside lane.) The inside lane generally is reserved for faster runners when they are running for time. They have the right of way and sometimes will yell "Track!" to clear joggers from their paths. If you are running at a slower pace for time, however, or doing a timed interval workout such as 4×400, you have the right to hold that inside lane. Runners coming from behind should go around you to the right (outside). That's better than you trying to move out of their way and possibly causing a collision. In fact, don't assume that you should move if passed by faster runners. Once done with your timed run, you *then* need to move to an outside lane to continue walking or jogging at a slower pace. Be sure to look over your shoulder before doing so in case someone is passing. And never cross a track without looking both ways any more than you would cross an expressway blindly. Rules may vary from track to track. Normally, common sense prevails. If you have any questions, again ask the local coach. Or run in the far outside lanes until you figure out the traffic patterns.

There are some advantages to running on tracks. You're out of car traffic. You're usually in a public area, thus safer. You're less likely to get hassled by dogs. You can tell exactly how fast and how far you run. Some tracks are hard and/or poorly maintained, but most are softer than running on concrete. Unfortunately, too many schools lock their tracks, preventing use by outsiders.

Dogs

Q: Do you have any advice about how to handle dogs that dart out from yards and chase and yip at you? I've considered water guns, throwing rocks, tossing dog biscuits, and even changing my running routes. Yesterday, a medium-size puppy startled me when he came charging through the bushes onto the street after me. Now I have an irate dog owner ready to run me down in his sport-utility vehicle. No matter what course I select, there always seems to be at least one or two dogs barking and baring teeth.

A: Sooner or later, every runner who likes to run the roads— particularly back-country roads that take him past farmyards—needs to develop a strategy for dealing with dogs. First of all, you can't be afraid of dogs, or at least you don't want to *show* your fear, because dogs can sense this, and it will incite them to attack even more.

Fortunately, most dogs are cowards who will retreat if you display some show of aggression—although I use this as a last resort. My initial strategy is to ignore dogs as much as possible. Pretend not to notice them, even though they are growling and yapping and heading your way. If dogs see that you're not interested in them—or the property that they are trying to protect—they often will lose interest in you. Dogs are turf-protectors and have a defined idea in their minds as to the borders of their turf. Usually, this is the yard, their green space, but their turf also may encompass sidewalks and encroach into the street. It's usually a good strategy to cross to the other side of the road to make sure that you're not invading the dog's turf.

If the dog is accompanied by an owner (who may be entirely insensitive to your problem), it's usually a good idea not to pass between the dog and that owner. If the owner is a child, be especially cautious because dogs have usually been taught to protect children. If the dog owner tells you, "He won't bite," don't believe him. Many times, the next words out of an owner's mouth are, "That's unusual. He's never bitten before."

At some point, you may need to confront the dog to escape unbitten. Remember what I said about dogs being cowards. They're more likely to bite you from behind because they fear that you'll hit them if they attack from the front. So play on the dog's fear. Wheel around.

Point at the dog sternly. Shout "Stop!" This may cause the dog to stop, or even retreat somewhat. Use this break to continue running, even if it means running backward. The farther you can get away from the dog's turf, the less likely he will continue his attack. Another strategy is to reach down and pretend to pick a rock up off the ground to throw at the dog. In cases where I'm approaching a dog that I suspect (or know from past experience) may cause me trouble, I'll look for a stick a hundred or so meters away that I can carry while passing the dog. The dog won't want to be hit by that stick and so will be less likely to go after you.

Still, the best strategy remains ignoring the dog as much as possible. But all dogs are different; what works with one won't work with another. I received several dog bites early in my running career but have not been bitten since I developed the above strategies. I hope that they work for you.

Cross-Training
Supplement Your Running Routine

- **Weight Training**
- **Power Lifting**
- **Cycling**
- **Adding Other Activities**
- **Swimming**
- **Cross-Country Skiing**
- **Equivalent Exercise**

- **Spinning**
- **Snowshoes**
- **Duathlon**
- **Marathon to Triathlon**
- **Triathlon to Marathon**
- **Hates Running**

When is switching to another sport cross-training, and when is it merely play? If you jump into a pickup basketball game or play two hard sets of tennis, are you cross-training or participating in some exercise that might increase your chances of injury and prevent you from running?

Cross-training as a term, as a way of training, and as a philosophy crept into the athletic public's consciousness in the early 1980s, simultaneous to the development of the triathlon as a popular sport. Triathlete Sally Edwards, who wrote a book on the subject, is generally conceded as having been the first person to use the term.

The cross-training theory—at least as it applies to runners—suggests that you can only reach a certain level of fitness by running, and that if you add other sports with the potential to improve your aerobic fitness (bicycling, swimming, cross-country skiing) or muscular strength (weight lifting), you can rise to an even higher level of achievement. Cross-training also proves useful while recovering from an injury or as an alternate form of training for those who are susceptible to injuries if they run too many miles.

At some point, cross-training for runners collides with the law of specificity that suggests, logically, that the best way to train as a runner is to run. But in the meantime, cross-training has become a very useful alternative exercise for most runners.

Weight Training

Q: I am a 16-year-old runner between cross-country and track. Should I weight train? What are the best lifts? I also want to know how to improve drastically.

A: I don't know about improving "drastically." Would you settle for improving "gradually"? Regardless, I contacted Bob Williams, program coordinator at Sports Medicine Center, Providence St. Vincent Medical Center in Portland, Oregon, to see if he could suggest some strength training exercises for young, and adult, runners. Here are the areas of the body that runners should strengthen—particularly during the time between seasons.

Abdominal area. It's very important, says Williams, to strengthen your trunk. Hang from a pull-up bar and pull your knees to your chest slowly, working up to three sets of 10 to 15 repetitions. Or, do the same number of crunches: with calves resting on the seat of a chair and your back flat on the floor, lift your shoulders.

Quadriceps. With weights on your shoulders, do half-squats, lowering yourself down to about a 70-degree angle. (Make sure that your feet are at least shoulder width to optimize proper balance.) See if you can begin with 40 pounds and work up to 75—although this will vary depending on your basic strength. A second exercise would be lunges with a barbell on your shoulders. Take one step forward and lower your back knee to the ground. Do three sets of 8 to 12 repeats for either exercise.

Hamstrings. With weight on your heels (preferably using a machine), lift your heels to your buttocks. Start with 10 pounds and work up to 30 to 40 pounds, doing 20 to 30 reps and up to three sets. Or you can use a rubber tube, which you can tie to a door, putting a loop around your foot. Face the door, keep your leg stiff, lift your foot, and bring it backward away from the door. Do 10 to

15 fairly fast reps until fatigued. Recover and do the exercise again.

Upper body. For your shoulders and chest, do bench presses. Start with an easy weight with which you can do three sets of 20 to 30 reps. Gradually increase the weight over a period of time. For biceps and forearms, do double-arm curls.

The best time to do strength training is either on days when you don't run or on easy days when you don't run hard. Save your strength training for after the run rather than before. Also, don't overlook stretching exercises before and during your weight work. For a light warmup before lifting, do two sets of 10 to 15 push-ups, trunk twists, and circular swings.

Power Lifting

Q: I ran my first 5-K recently, and I loved it. I read somewhere that lifting weights would help me to a better PR (personal record), so I started working out with a powerlifter friend. Thus far, I've gotten much stronger and can feel the power in my strides, but I'm also putting on some pounds (about 15). Is it okay to continue lifting as I proceed with my running routine?

A: I'd stay away from power lifters if you want to improve as a 5-K runner. Typically, power lifters use very heavy weights, which almost from necessity have to be lifted slowly. Heavy lifting can cause you to bulk up, plus it puts extra strain on the knee joints, particularly if you're doing any deep lifts. Most distance runners are better off training with somewhat lighter weights, which allows them to maintain a quick-lift tempo, better suited for the type of speed needed to run fast.

Also, while strength often equals speed, there comes a point where too bulky (antagonistic) muscles can interfere with your ability to carry that speed much farther than sprint distances. It's no coincidence that the runners capable of winning marathons do not resemble Arnold Schwarzenegger. Fifteen pounds of extra weight—even muscle—has to be carried with each stride.

Don't abandon the weight room, but keep a healthy distance from your powerlifting friends. It's okay to meet them at the gym, but don't copy their lifts. As the running season approaches, you may need to back off some from your strength training if you want to perform your best at 5-K distances.

Cycling

Q: I'm a 39-year-old male and have been running for about a year. I run about 20 miles a week, running every other day. On off days, I ride a bike. How can I better my times for the 5-K and 10-K? My best times are 22:01 and 49:23, respectively. Should I abandon my bike riding and increase my running days? Or is there a way I can combine these two exercises in my training?

A: It seems that you already are combining bike riding and running fairly successfully. You didn't tell me, though, whether on those cycling days you were simply going out and spinning or whether you had your head down on a 10-speed cranking 20 mph.

Whether or not you have given the subject much conscious thought, you are training for health and fitness. I know that you'd like to improve your times—as would we all. And you should continue to improve for several more years by doing little more than maintaining the same routine.

At some point, however, you may bump into the law of specificity that suggests the best training modality for running is running. Cycling can serve as an effective cross-training exercise and will help with your aerobic base, but there's no substitute for running day after day.

So it gets down to how much you enjoy riding your bike. My recommendation is to pick a period during the year—maybe two to four months—when you become more serious about your run-training, perhaps pointing toward a specific race. During this period, eliminate some of your biking days and substitute running. While upping your running mileage, do it gradually so as not to court an injury. Then after the race season, cut back a bit on your running and get back on your bike, either outdoors or in the gym. You'll find that you can rest your body (somewhat) while maintaining aerobic fitness, getting ready for the next period when you shift back into your running mode.

This technique is called periodization by those who design training schedules. Experiment with this form of cross-training for a while, and you should succeed in lowering your 5-K and 10-K times.

Adding Other Activities

Q: I am a 17-year-old high school runner. This summer when I am training to help our team defend the cross-country state title, I want to increase my mileage to around 60 miles a week for two to three weeks in July, then slowly lower that mileage to between 45 and 50 miles during the season. I also want to incorporate some cross-training into the mix but am unsure of how much biking and swimming I should do. What biking or swimming workouts are equivalent to running 3.5 miles at 7:00 pace? I would like these workouts to take the place of running twice a day. I want to run in the morning and bike or swim in the afternoon.

A: First of all, don't do anything radically different without consulting your coach. Obviously, your team has had success, and you don't want to experiment with different training strategies that might cause you (and the team) to go backward. So discuss what I am about to say with your coach.

Having said that, the training equivalent of 3.5 miles at a 7:00 pace would be maybe twice that distance at 12 to 15 mph on a bike (but it depends on what kind of bike). Maybe about a half-hour of biking. In the water, maybe 20 to 30 minutes of swimming, but it depends on how efficient a swimmer you are.

You realize, of course, that I'm guessing. But then you've (wisely) chosen to use cross-training as an add-on, or substitute, exercise for what would be an easy running workout.

My feeling is that you should not train hard either biking or swimming because you don't want to develop antagonistic muscles to those you use for running. You don't want to turn into a triathlete. Triathletes usually compromise their running abilities by teaching themselves to compete in three events at the same time. A little cross-training is good; a lot may make you a slower runner. Use the second workouts mainly to loosen your legs, not to develop speed or strength. That means "spinning" on the bike and easy "stroking" in the water. It's easy to go out and train hard swimming or biking because you're using different muscles, but you don't want to turn an easy running workout into a hard cross-training workout. So if you can train at the same degree of easy effort you might have used in that second run, you'll be okay.

Swimming

Q: Is swimming detrimental to running? I have been able to run 5-Ks under 18:00, but since starting to swim three or four days a week (in addition to running three or four days), my times have gotten worse.

A: It's hard to measure performance from week to week, since outside factors such as course difficulty and weather, even how hard you're training, can affect times. I'm not willing to pull the plug yet on your swimming pool.

I wouldn't say that swimming is detrimental to running, but you do develop other muscles while swimming that won't help you as a runner. Swimming is an upper-body sport; running is a lower-body sport. If you swim a lot and develop muscle mass in your shoulders, you'll gain weight, which could slow you down. Also, energy put into swimming is energy robbed from more specific run-training. I've often felt that swimmers develop more body fat for both buoyancy and warmth, but exercise scientists claim that may be a myth.

Swimming is an excellent form of cross-training. It can help build and/or maintain cardiovascular fitness while you are injured or while you're resting between hard days. But taken to its extreme, hard swim training will make you a better swimmer and detract from your running performance. I doubt that's true in your case, but at least be aware that you need to balance different training regimens to achieve your racing goals.

Cross-Country Skiing

Q: When heavy snows hit last winter, I all but replaced running with cross-country skiing in preparation for a 50-K ski race. With a great running base already in place, I figured that I could keep my endurance up simply by skiing, so I mostly skied during the six weeks before the 50-K and did no long runs. On race day, I fell short in endurance and dropped out at 40-K. Was I mistaken to abandon running for skiing? I'm a novice skier who does well to cover 10 to 11 kilometers in an hour.

A: I may get in trouble with some "won't-change" runners with this answer, but I consider cross-country skiing an even better sport than my first love, running. The main reason is that it's a total-body fitness sport. It exercises both the upper and lower body. Cross-country skiers compete using two techniques: the "classic" diagonal stride with skis kept parallel in groomed tracks and "skating," in which they take sideways strides across a packed trail, similar to the motion used in ice skating. Skating is much faster than classical skiing, but I prefer the latter. You use your muscles more like you use them in running.

Runners should also be wary—to answer a portion of your question—of doing nothing else but skiing during the winter, but not for the reason you mentioned. Nordic skiing will get your cardiovascular system in great shape, but when you return to running, you're at risk for injury if you haven't kept your (specific) running muscles tuned, too. If you do ski exclusively during the winter, be cautious making the switch back to running when the snow melts.

Now, the point of your question. You didn't tell me whether in your six weeks exclusively on skis you were doing any long ski workouts, similar to those done running. If not, there's where you fell short, since you may not have conditioned your (specific) ski muscles for an event that was going to last 5 hours or more.

Another point: You wouldn't have considered six weeks sufficient time to get ready for a running marathon. So six weeks may not have been enough to ready those upper-body ski muscles. Usually in the fall, I begin doing more strength training to ready myself for the ski season. The bottom line: Do some strength exercises outside the ski season and keep at least some of your running up outside the running season.

Incidentally, put the American Birkebeiner on your must-do list for a year or two down the road. It's Nordic skiing's equivalent of the Boston Marathon. For entry information, contact the American Birkebeiner Ski Foundation, P.O. Box 911, Hayward, WI 54843. Learning to ski certainly takes the edge off long, cold winters, and I strongly endorse the sport as an activity for runners during the cold off-season.

Equivalent Exercise

Q: What is the conversion rate for biking and swimming to running miles, and does it change with the intensity of the effort?

A: Yes, but I can't offer you a conversion chart, and I'm not certain that I would trust a chart if one were available. There are too many variables related to time, effort, and even muscular differences. Some people bike more efficiently than they run, and vice versa.

One of the best studies comparing the value of one exercise versus another goes back three decades. The bestselling book *Aerobics*, by Kenneth H. Cooper, M.D., offered points to describe different levels of exercise. Dr. Cooper devised the system while in the U.S. Air Force, having been assigned to determine a way for astronauts to get in shape for the rigors of outer space. His solution was basically simple: run, swim, or cycle for so many minutes and you scored a certain number of points. How many points you scored in a week, month, or year determined your level of fitness. People love to keep score, so Dr. Cooper's aerobics point system proved instantly successful.

Comparing some exercises to Dr. Cooper's charts, I discovered that if you ran 5 miles in an hour, swam a mile in about 45 minutes, or cycled 20 miles under 2 hours, you'd earn 10 aerobic points for each exercise. For stairclimbing, you would need to work out on one of those machines for 30 minutes, climbing 90 flights of stairs with your average heart rate about 135 beats a minute to score 10 points, says Dr. Cooper.

Actually, point scores vary under the Cooper system depending on how fast you run, swim, or cycle. You need to have the charts in his book in front of you to effectively compare exercises. Also, are you swimming the breaststroke or the more efficient freestyle? Are you riding a comfortable (but slow) mountain bike or a 10-speed racing bike made out of a lightweight alloy and featuring snap-on pedals and aerodynamic handlebars? And what resistance do you use on that stairclimbing machine?

Dr. Cooper's original system was based on oxygen consumption expressed in milligrams of oxygen burned per kilogram of body weight per minute (ml/kg/min). Various other systems depend on calories expended during exercise, which relate to a variety of variables, including body weight, intensity, and duration. In lecturing to groups of runners and others interested in fitness, I know that this is about the point where everybody's eyes go blank. It sounds reasonable to me, however, that if you were to swim or run or bike or climb stairs for the same length of time (say, 30 minutes) with your pulse (as measured by a heart monitor) beating at the same level of intensity (say, 70 percent of maximum), you could be said to be exercising at about the same level.

Dr. Cooper's aerobics point system was great for motivating people to start exercising. *Aerobics* and its 13 sequels are available in 41 languages and have sold more than 30 million copies worldwide. The running boom and booms in other fitness sports can be traced back to its publication in 1968. Yet as a result of those booms, we now have many more ways to exercise. For example, I doubt that Dr. Cooper realized that the roller-skating he might have done as a kid would resurface in the 1990s as trendy inline skating. With the profits from sales of *Aerobics*, Dr. Cooper funds a research group at his Aerobics Center in Dallas, but even his staff of sports scientists can't keep up with all the new exercise machines coming onto the market.

Spinning

Q: What do you know about Spinning? There are two gyms in my area pushing it as the "ultimate" cross-training exercise for runners. I hate bikes, even the recumbent ones, but my trainer said that Spinning offers a new approach and I will get a better workout than with running.

A: I don't necessarily agree with your trainer that you'll get a "better" workout than with running, but you'll get a somewhat "different" workout.

Spinning, according to cycling coach and exercise physiologist Edmund R. Burke, Ph.D., is the technique of pedaling rapidly in low gears. "This reduces the forces your muscles and joints must transmit and results in less wear and fatigue," says Dr. Burke.

"Spinning places the demands of cycling on your heart and lungs, where you want them," Dr. Burke says. He identifies the essence of Spinning as fluidity.

That was always my approach to indoor biking, long before Johnny G., Spinning's "inventor," coined the term. I always pedaled with very low resistance. Yes, you can get a tougher workout by cranking up the resistance to simulate the amount of effort it might require for you to pedal up a steep hill. You can also pop out of the saddle and do one-minute "burns" to condition your quads, but this may or may not make you a faster runner.

I use bike training on my off days, its purpose being to help me recover before my next hard running workout. I'll jump on an exercise bike in the basement and pedal for anywhere from 10 to 30 minutes. Or, I'll go for an easy bike ride outside with my wife and enjoy the scenery. In both of these cases, I'm not working very hard, and I am improving my mind as much as my body, burning a few calories at the same time.

Used in this sense, Spinning can help loosen your muscles much in the way that swimming loosens your muscles. One mistake some runners make when they jump on a bike on off days is that they punch the resistance lever on the indoor bike, or use too high a gear on the outdoor bike, and thus train harder than if they were jogging at an easy pace on what was supposed to have been a day of rest. Thus, they fail to recover for their next hard running workout. Bicycling is an excellent way for runners to cross-train, but you must use this alternate exercise judiciously so as not to compromise your running training.

Snowshoes

Q: I live in New England, right near a golf course and some off-road trails. I'm interested in trying out snowshoeing as a way to cross-train. Can you give me some advice about starting out, and on equipment?

A: More and more runners have begun to discover snowshoeing as a form of optional winter training. Conversely, manufacturers have begun to manufacture shoes designed for running in snow as opposed to crossing deep drifts. Snowshoe races have begun to attract runners in the northern states. Many of the better ski stores now carry snowshoes, but make sure that you purchase narrow shoes for racing. If the salesperson doesn't know what you're talking about, find another store.

Once you get the snowshoes on your feet, you'll be surprised how easy it is to walk or run on them. The learning curve for a fit runner is about 30 seconds. Just start running! You can wear boots, but I just wear my regular running shoes. You may bang your ankles until you get used to the movements. If so, use ankle pads.

Barney and Janis Klecker train regularly on snowshoes, and at one time, Barney manufactured snowshoes. Barney is the American record-holder for 50 miles; Janis won the 1992 U.S. Olympic Marathon Trials. The trials were held midwinter, so much of her prerace training was on snowshoes. As for training, Barney Klecker recommends running on snowshoes no more than three times a week. He feels that if you train on them more often, it may cause your stride to shorten. One advantage of wearing snowshoes is that there is little impact. Barney and Janis found that they could do a hard snowshoe run and come back the following day and run hard on the roads. In fact, after one summer stress fracture, Janis rehabbed by running on snowshoes on the golf course.

I highly recommend snowshoes for winter cross-training. In fact, I feel sorry for y'all down south who can't take advantage of this activity.

Duathlon

Q: I have an extensive athletic history in different sports. I have competed in track, soccer, mountain biking, and volleyball, although mostly running. My goal for this summer is to compete in a duathlon (running and biking). What kind of training regimen do you suggest for someone with this goal but limited training time?

A: Let's consider what you need to do in general terms to get ready for a sport that features running and biking. I'd focus on your weakest event, which I suspect may be biking. Begin by taking time to learn bicycle-riding techniques, which many runners switching to multisport events overlook. Position on the bike is particularly important, and your bike needs to be set up properly. You want to be positioned not merely for maximum power but also for relaxation.

Split your training into three phases: running, biking, and days when you both bike and run. This final phase is important to get you used to transitions. Since most duathlons feature the bike ride sandwiched between two runs, on one day run before you bike; on another, bike before you run.

Since you have limited time, confine your workouts to less than an hour, except for one longer workout on the weekend. Train five or six days a week. Here's a possible schedule.

Monday: Run
Tuesday: Bike
Wednesday: Run/Bike
Thursday: Bike
Friday: Rest
Saturday: Bike/Run (long)
Sunday: Bike (short) or Rest

The details are up to you and depend on your level of physical fitness. Don't be afraid to modify the program depending on your work schedule.

Marathon to Triathlon

Q: I will soon finish my third marathon in 10 months. I want to try something different and will switch to triathlons for the summer. I plan to start with a mini-triathlon that includes a 5-K run, then build to longer events. This is my first year running after a period off. I have dropped my 10-K pace from 9:30 to 8:00 per mile by doing a combination of endurance (long runs), strength training, and speedwork (bike and treadmill sprints). Is there something that I should change, or emphasize, in my training as I switch to triathlons? I do intend to add additional miles with biking and swimming. Should I cut back on my long runs? Or try to increase my pace at longer distances?

A: Hold it! Before you plot this tremendous increase in training, take a couple of weeks off after that third marathon. Doing too much too soon is a sure route to an injury, particularly since you will find it easier to swim or bike than run those first few post-marathon weeks. Then, just when you think that you're recovered and ready to really crank up the tri-miles: Bang!

With this word of warning as prelude to your switch to triathlon training, you need to concentrate as much on subtraction as addition. In other words, cut old increments out of your schedule before adding new increments. If you're running 7 hours a week, don't add 7 hours of swimming and 7 hours of biking, or anywhere near that amount. You need to increase your hours of training somewhat for the triathlon, but that increase should be gradual just as the mileage buildup in marathon training is gradual.

Focus first on technique, particularly in swimming. Learning stroke basics is essential for success in the triathlon. If possible, work with a swimming coach. Presumably, you already have developed your endurance through marathon training. With this as base, work on your speed in the water and on the bicycle. Make swimming and biking your hard days. Run easy on days between to recover. Improvement will come fastest if you work on your weakest events first. The length of the triathlons you plan to do also may determine your type of training. And don't forget that the fourth element in the triathlon is the transition between events.

Triathlons are fun and offer a break from running. I went through a period of several years when I focused most of my training on the tri-sport. My wife (correctly) identified this as a midlife tri-crisis. But eventually, I returned my attention to running, and I'm happy to be back.

Triathlon to Marathon

Q: I participate in five or six triathlons a year. Running is my best leg. Nevertheless, trying to improve in running has been quite difficult. I am 43 years old and run 6 miles every other day with a long run on Sundays of 8 to 10 miles. I have no specific plan; I just get up early in the morning and run four times a week in addition to my swimming and cycling. I want to create a base to enable me to run a marathon in six months. A half-marathon in 1:45 has been my longest run both in running races and triathlons. Can you give me suggestion to redirect my training?

A: You need to remove some items from your normal triathlon training. Cut any swimming or cycling you do in half. In fact, cut back particularly on the cycling, since the muscles you develop in that sport work against your ability to run. (When and if you do cycle, simply pedal at an easy pace; don't train hard.)

Eliminate also any fast/slow training (speedwork) that you may be doing now for any of the other two triathlon disciplines. Speed training is very effective for improvement, but I'm next going to suggest a mileage buildup for the marathon, and you don't want to combine too much speed and distance. So remove the former; focus on the latter.

The key to your marathon training is going to be the long run on Sundays. You're already at 10 miles, so begin a steady progression that will get you to at least one long run of 20 miles three to four weeks before the marathon. No need to go fast. Pick a pace 1 minute or 2 minutes per mile slower than your projected marathon pace. Save at least one day a week for some training at that marathon pace. Plan on one or two days of rest, usually before and/or after your hardest workout of the week. It's okay to do some cross-training (bike or swim) on one or two other days, so you won't forget how it feels to be a triathlete, but don't overdo it on those days.

Hates Running

Q: I have started to train for a triathlon. I have always hated running, but I know that I will have to do some to prepare. I have been working out in a gym an hour a day for almost one month now. I break up my hour with 30 minutes on machines, the rest of the time on free weights. I love the results and am looking forward to the triathlon season beginning soon in Florida. Could you recommend a way to start from scratch, with a surefire strategy for dealing with the boredom and pain of running?

A: Boredom? Pain? You hate running? What can we do to change your mind?

First, get out of that gym and say hello to the outside world. You'll have to move outdoors eventually because that's where they hold triathlons. There are some great running trails in Florida, from the beach at Daytona to the gator swamps near Gainesville. Try to make each run a special experience in a scenic area. Go somewhere where you won't get bored.

Be sure to start slowly. Even though you may be in great shape from your gym work, running (or biking or swimming) uses different muscles than weight training. Walk, jog, walk until you're capable of running continuously. Think like a beginner to lessen the chance that you will get hurt.

7

Marathon
The Classic 26-Mile Challenge

- **First Marathon**
- **Speedwork**
- **Longer Runs**
- **Realistic Goal?**
- **Minimum Mileage**
- **Training Errors**
- **Breaking 3 Hours**
- **Too Much Too Soon**

- **Weights and Running**
- **Marathon as a Training Run**
- **Hills and Flats**
- **Crashing**
- **Final Long Run**
- **Postrace Syndrome**
- **Boston**

It is the distance running event: the marathon. It is the event by which many runners define themselves and measure their mettle. To have finished even one marathon is a singular achievement, an accomplishment of which to be understandably proud. That's the T-shirt you keep, maybe even to frame and hang on the wall with your race number, certificate, and finishing medal.

For some runners, one marathon is enough. For others, they continue battling the classical 26-mile, 385-yard distance in a quest for personal records (PRs), seeking the best marathon they can run. For a number of more gifted competitors, running fast enough to qualify for Boston becomes a goal worth pursuing.

Marathons are among the best organized of running events. They need to be because their courses cover so much territory with intersections that need to be guarded and water stations that need to be manned by hundreds of volunteers. More than most races at shorter distances, marathons tend to be productions encompassing entire weekends, with expos featuring vendors and celebrities signing autographs and pasta parties where the eating of spaghetti becomes a ritual feast.

While most experienced runners run frequent 5-K and 10-K races with minor changes in their regular pattern of workouts, running a marathon involves Training with a capital T. It's a campaign that lasts 18 weeks or more and features a mileage buildup and taper carefully designed to get the participant to the starting line in the best possible condition for success.

Once the finish line is crossed and the ribboned medals are hung over the marathoners' shoulders, they walk stiff-legged to the refreshment area, clutching a blanket around their shoulders, proud in the accomplishment and wondering, will I ever feel any better or any worse than this?

Not all runners run marathons. One survey of **Runner's World**'s 450,000 readers elicited the response that only 15 percent of them had run a marathon in the previous year. Still, we all respect the marathon and those who run it and often think, "Maybe next year will be my marathon year."

First Marathon

Q: I'm 39 years old and have been running a little over a year, about 30 to 35 miles a week. My longest runs have been 10 to 15 miles, and my times in all events have been improving. My training partner wants me to run a marathon with him in four months. Am I ready?

A: There's no question that you're ready physically; the only question is whether or not you're ready psychologically.

You would have no trouble making the jump from the half- to the full marathon. With four months between now and your goal marathon, I could point you to any one of a number of training schedules, including an 18-week program I designed for the class I teach with Brian Piper and Bill Fitzgerald for The LaSalle Banks Chicago Marathon. If you followed our directions (the important one being to start training slowly), you'd float to the finish line.

Running that first marathon is a special experience, like getting married, having a baby, or earning a Ph.D. degree. Don't jump into your first maraton too soon, or with too little thought, simply to please a friend. My initial reaction is that you probably should wait until you're ready to do a marathon on your terms at the right time and in the right place. You could accompany your friend to the marathon and support him in his efforts. After you've experienced the event as a spectator, decide when and where and maybe even *if* you want to run your first marathon.

One of the major attractions of the marathon is not only the race itself but also the training that leads up to the race: those 18 weeks of meeting with fellow runners (if you train with a group) for what becomes almost a ritual long run on the weekend. The buildup. The final 20-miler. The taper. The weekend with its pasta party. That's all part of the marathon experience. Don't enter into this contract lightly. Make your first marathon a very special event and, yes, it is a lot like planning a wedding.

Speedwork

Q: I am a 30-year-old born-again runner who hasn't trained for 10 years. I am up to rotating easy 4-mile and quicker 2-mile runs during the week, and up to 7 miles on Saturdays. How rapidly should I increase my miles if my ultimate goal is to run a marathon? Also, I am awfully slow. Should I worry about speed yet?

A: It sounds as though you are following a good program. I don't recommend that you push into the netherworld beyond 25 weekly miles too rapidly. I'd hold at 25 for a while to make sure that you consolidate your gains, then consider adding one or two workouts a week where you do some speed training. Here's a 2-mile workout you can try that my old coach Fred Wilt used to do.

Go to a track and run eight laps (3200 meters). The first four laps are jogging. Run the next 200 (half a lap) fast, followed by 200 jogging. Repeat this three times, for a total of four laps. It's a quick speed fix. It can either be very difficult or very easy, depending on how hard you push the 200s. Once you're used to the routine, you can explore other types of speedwork, and maybe start thinking about doing that marathon.

Longer Runs

Q: I want to run a marathon. I can now complete a 5-K with no problem. My time was 27:28 at the last race I ran. I don't know how to progress toward longer distances because all I can think about when I run is finishing. Past 30 minutes of running, I am tired and ready to stop. How do I cross this barrier?

A: You can cross the barrier by very gradually increasing the length of your longest run. To do so, you need to do two things: run slower, and rest the day before and the day after. I recommend that beginners spend at least a year gradually conditioning themselves so that running is normal, natural, and fun. In your case, you probably need to achieve a level where you can do that 30-minute run comfortably, stopping when you want to rather than when you have to. The two suggestions I've just offered above will help you with that.

Once you become comfortable running a half-hour (which for you translates to about 3 miles), you can begin increasing your distance somewhat over a period of weeks. Go 3.5 miles, then 4.0, then 4.5. Or increase with quarter-mile increments. Take your time building distance. Don't be afraid to step back a week to gather before the next upward push. Nobody's looking over your shoulder grading you on your effort, although you might consider joining a class or training with a local club of joggers for group support. It's amazing how much easier it is to run talking with others than it is to run solo. As many years and as many miles I have run, I still find that to be true. At some point, it will be time to test yourself in a 10-K race, a distance of about 6 miles.

Having finished that first 10-K, and with your weekly training mileage up around 15 to 25 miles, then it may be time to consider doing a marathon. Once you make the decision to go, it then becomes only a matter of picking which first marathon to do and selecting a training program that will help you achieve your goal. Most of the major marathons in large cities have training classes that help runners prepare for the race. Because of the support you will get through group dynamics, you should consider enrolling in one. The Leukemia Society of America also runs a Team in Training program to prepare runners for different marathons around the world.

If you have to train on your own, select a good training schedule and see if you can recruit friends to do at least some of the long runs with you. There is a lot of support available for runners interested in completing their first marathons. If you can tap into this support network, it will make it much easier for you to cross the barrier.

Realistic Goal?

Q: I will soon be 47 and have run off and on for 10 years—more off than on. I recently dropped 40 pounds to 190, and I run about 20 to 22 miles a week. I would love to run a marathon. Is this a realistic goal, and if so, how do I get there?

A: Certainly, it's a realistic goal. A lot of people with less background than you have gotten there. What you need to do now is pick a specific marathon as your goal. Each January, *Runner's World* publishes a schedule of U.S. and international marathons. (The list also is available at www.runnersworld.com.)

In choosing your first marathon, you should consider one of the two following options.

1. Run a local marathon. Staying near home guarantees you support from family and friends when you run. You'll also save on travel expenses.

2. Run a big marathon. It's more comfortable if you're a first-timer running in a big (5,000 runners or more) marathon, because you'll have more company on the course, regardless of how slowly you run.

Hundreds of thousands of people finish marathons each year in the United States. Hopefully, you soon will be one of them.

Minimum Mileage

Q: What do you feel is the minimum number of miles I would need to run a week to get to a sub-4:00 marathon?

A: I don't know enough about your basic ability or how long you have been running or how many miles you are currently running to specifically answer your question. Some individuals have enough natural talent that they can train for three weeks and jump into a race and run that fast. (Often it is because they carry a basic level of conditioning over from another sport.) Other individuals could train the soles off their shoes and never crack 4 hours.

Based on those runners who enroll in the training class that I teach in Chicago, most beginners can finish by peaking around 40 miles a week (including one long run of 20 miles that same peak week). That doesn't mean that they average 40 miles every week of the program, but the progression is aimed for them to reach that mileage level.

The more experienced marathoners in our class who seek to improve their times hit a peak mileage between 50 and 60 miles a week, usually running two or three 20-milers in the course of their training. World-class marathoners regularly train at more than 100 miles a week, week after week of daily double workouts. When I was running my fastest marathons, that was the level of my training commitment. I had to spend many years building my training to the point where I could both reach and maintain that level. If you misjudge and do too much (and I did on several occasions), the crash can be very hard.

While researching a previous book on marathon training, I surveyed more than 100 coaches who felt that 55 miles a week was needed for success in the marathon. We're talking personal-record territory. What is the minimum number of miles you need in order to break the 4-hour barrier? It depends a lot on those factors mentioned above. We all differ in our abilities to perform.

Training Errors

Q: I just ran my first marathon and was very disappointed when I had to hobble the last half-dozen miles because of cramps in both quads and my right calf. I did three 20- to 22-mile training runs at my marathon pace of 9:00 per mile with absolutely no problems. I ran my training runs indoors on a padded track, and the marathon was on concrete. Could that have been the reason why my legs gave out on me?

A: Here are examples of some of the training errors that you may have committed.

- You trained too hard and too much. Running three long runs at 20 to 22 miles was probably two too many for a first-timer. You certainly peaked too soon and were fatigued from overtraining when you went to the starting line. Usually, I recommend that first-timers only do a single long run of 20 miles.

- You ran the long runs too fast. Elite athletes run their races faster than 5:00 pace, but none that I know run anywhere near that fast during their long runs; if they did, they'd break down. They might run workouts of 20 to 30 miles at 5:30 to 6:00 pace, and while that sounds incredibly fast to midpack runners, consider how much faster they run in a race. Yet I frequently encounter midpack runners who run as fast or faster than they expect to run in the race itself. And they break down. The purpose of the long runs is to condition the body to get used to running for long periods of time and to burn fats along with glycogen to preserve the latter. If you run your long runs too fast, you defeat that purpose, and risk overtraining.
- You ran those runs on an indoor track. A friend of mine used to run up to 20 miles on a 16-laps-to-a-mile indoor track and eventually needed a hip replacement. Running on a track is okay for speed training and some short runs, but to run long you need to get out on the roads so you're not constantly going around turns, which puts extra stress on your leg muscles.

Another problem might have been insufficient nutrition, but I'm inclined to suggest that the three previous training errors contributed the most to your downfall.

Don't be discouraged. Everybody makes training errors. Learn from yours and approach the marathon with more respect the next time you run it. As Bill Rodgers once said, "If you run enough marathons, you'll learn that the race can humble you." Now that you've been humbled, you can go on to greater glories.

Breaking 3 Hours

Q: I'm interested in breaking the 3-hour barrier in a marathon. I've run two marathons, one five years ago in 3:28.58 and one three years ago in 3:07. Although I'm a fairly consistent sub-40:00 10-K runner, my mileage threshold is about 45 miles a week. I'd like to properly prepare for a race in about three months and give myself a chance at 3 hours. Any suggestions?

A: Your past performances suggest that you are capable of breaking 3 hours. The secret is totally focusing your energy on a single marathon and spending six months or more training toward that goal.

I recommend forgetting about a marathon in three months and planning now for an all-out attempt in six months.

Select a marathon where course and probable weather conditions are likely to come together to offer the best chance for you to run your best. Try to pick a flat course. I'm biased toward Chicago since it's my hometown, but there are a number of good marathons that offer the potential for fast times. You'll need to do some research to determine which marathon is best for you.

Then carefully plan your training. What elements worked best for you when you set your previous PRs? That's probably the type of training you need to consider now. I'd suggest a gradual buildup since that limits the risk of overtraining. In the early months of your training, you might want to try some races at short distances to work on speed and test your fitness, but consider them mostly as training opportunities. Use the winter for easy running to build an endurance base. Spring and early summer are good times to do speedwork.

Three to four months before your planned marathon, shift training gears from speed back to endurance, but with more of a vengeance. Begin a buildup that will be gradual enough to bring you to a maximum of 55 weekly miles a month before the race. I know that's more than the 45 stated as your threshold, but I'm hoping that intelligent training can get you there.

If you train right and keep monitoring your training to guard against injuries, you should have a good shot at achieving your goal.

Too Much Too Soon

Q: I just turned 50 and have been training for several years now. I started training five months ago for my first marathon and have four more months until the race. I want to qualify for Boston and need a 3:30. My 5-K times are under 20:00, my 10-K time is 41:00, and I've done a half-marathon in 1:36. I currently run 6 to 7 miles easy on Mondays, Wednesdays, and Fridays, with interval training Tuesdays and Thursdays. Saturdays, I alternate between a 10-mile tempo run in 70 minutes or a long run, now up to 18 miles. Last weekend, I ran that distance in 2:19 and felt good. Everyone tells me that once you hit the 20-mile mark in a marathon, you're halfway there. Hearing that makes me feel uneasy. Am I on schedule for a 3:30?

A: You're ahead of schedule, in fact, too far ahead. At the pace you're training, you might not make it to the starting line. I checked the prediction charts, and a half in 1:36 suggests that you should go the full distance in 3:20. (Your 5-K and 10-K times project an even faster finish, but it doesn't always work that way.)

The problem is that you are doing 18-milers four months before the race. Sure, you're talented, but will you be able to keep up that pace without suffering an injury? Seven-time Boston champion Clarence DeMar once told two-time Boston champ Johnny Kelley, "You have to run 20-milers to finish a marathon, but you can't run too many of them." That advice rings true a half-century later.

Also, you're running your long runs too fast. If I calculated correctly, you ran your last 18-miler at 7:35 pace, which would get you to the marathon finish line in 3:20. Yes, you can run that fast now, but particularly because you do speedwork, I suggest that you slow the pace of your long runs. I normally advise runners to do their long runs 1 minute to 2 minutes slower per mile than their planned marathon race pace. You don't need to run much faster than 9:00 pace on the long runs. If you're feeling good, pick up the pace toward the end, and that will help you do the same in the marathon itself.

Consider your ultimate goal. If you hope to qualify for Boston, take a more conservative route.

Weights and Running

Q: I am training for a marathon, and along with the weekly long runs and track work, I cross-train with weights. For legs, does lifting count as a heavy day, an easy day, or something totally different altogether? I keep the weight relatively low and the reps high and have found tremendous benefits as a result. I'm not sure when to put lifting into my weekly routine because I worry about overtraining.

A: I go with "something totally different altogether." Like you, I've always felt that the best approach for distance runners was to use light weights and high reps. You're much less likely to bulk up that way and add weight from "too much" muscle. If you're interested in fast running times, you don't want to be carrying muscle that isn't going to help you run faster.

There's also the danger that developing the "wrong" lower-body muscles might inhibit your running. Consider, for example, the overdeveloped quadriceps muscles among Tour de France riders. Some of the better bicycle racers have quads so overdeveloped that they literally overlap their kneecaps. Okay for biking; bad for running.

I use strength training less to run fast or to look good at the beach and more for maintaining my lean body mass. If you're interested in good health, as opposed to performance, you definitely need to do some strength training. This is particularly important as you age and also important for women as a hedge against osteoporosis.

But I've noticed that on days after I've trained hard using free weights, my legs are dead for the next day's run. And often my knees are sore. That's one reason why I'd be cautious about too much lifting, particularly during the buildup for the marathon.

My recommendation is that you decrease the amount of your strength training as the marathon buildup continues, and particularly as you reach the climactic long runs near 20 miles. For the same reason, I usually advise marathoners to remove some of the speedwork from their program. The mileage buildup in marathon training puts enough stress on your body, so you don't want to stress it more with too much cross-training, speed training, or weight training. Do the strength training on one of your off days when you don't have a hard running workout scheduled. After completing the marathon, and after several weeks of rest to allow your body to recover, then you can get back to more serious weight lifting.

Marathon as a Training Run

Q: I am planning to run a marathon as a long training run. My PR last year was 3:17, but I recently ran a half-marathon in 1:21, and I aspire now to break 3 hours. I ran one 20-miler three weeks ago, but most long runs have only been about 16. Any suggestions on how to approach a marathon as a training run?

A: I frequently use organized marathons (or other long races) as training runs, and so do other smart runners. One reason is that there's plenty of support along the course in the way of fluids. Also, streets are blocked from traffic, you have the company of other runners, and you get accurate mile splits.

There are two approaches to marathon training runs: Go the full distance but much slower than your usual pace, or run a fast pace but with a planned drop out short of the finish line.

It depends on the marathon you choose as to how far you go. I ran

Chicago last year and exited the course at 10 miles and cut through the Loop so I could see the winners finish. I've also done planned exits at Twin Cities at 13 and 20 miles with someone picking me up by car. While I always remove my number the minute I step off the course, unfortunately, not everyone does the same. Rosie Ruiz's 1980 Boston "victory" is the most notorious example of someone crossing the line without having run the full distance.

I would be less inclined to use marathons for training runs if there were more road races conducted at distances between the half- and full marathon. One of my favorite races was the 30-K because you stop just short of the wall. I won a national title at that distance when younger, and on another occasion, set a masters record that lasted longer than it should because you rarely see 30-K races anymore.

If you do use a marathon as a training run, I strongly suggest that you register and not run as a bandit. You're using the race's services, and so you should pay. When I do training marathons, I always start toward the back so as not to get in the way of serious marathoners, and if crowds are thick at the first few water tables, I run by so as not to block those going all the way.

Hills and Flats

Q: I'm training to run my first marathon: Los Angeles in three months. I've been doing one hill workout, one tempo run, and one long run per week. The other days, I run easy or cross-train. In about five weeks, I plan to move into a speed phase with 800-meter repeats. I also plan on racing one 10-K and two half-marathons before the marathon. I've been doing my long runs on trails in the mountains. Seven miles up with about a 4,500-foot elevation gain and 7 miles down. The run takes me approximately 3½ hours, and I really love being out there. I wouldn't mind doing a longer run, but I was told not to exceed that time for a long run. Should I switch my long run to a flat course where I can pick up the pace and cover more distance, or is my current program all right? If it is all right, do you think that I risk injury if I gradually increase my long run to 5 hours or more? I would like to someday run ultras.

A: It sounds as though you've been inspired by the training ideas of Benji Durden, a very good coach who works out of Boulder, Colorado. If you asked Durden, he probably would tell you that the Los

Angeles Marathon doesn't have any hills the size of those you train on, so you need to get out on the flat for most (if not all) of your long runs during the next three months. Runs over terrain that steep are good for your muscles and mind, but you need more specific race-related training. Despite your high level of fitness, you won't be able to realize your full potential unless you practice the rhythms necessary for running on flat terrain.

Beginning immediately, start doing your long runs on the flats every other weekend. On the other weekends, continue with your mountain long runs. Six weeks before the race, eliminate the mountain runs entirely and stick to the flats. I'd also stay away from any grossly steep hills during the final three-week taper. You will, of course, have shifted from hill repeats to 800 repeats (presumably done on flat terrain), so you will have gradually added more and more flat running to your training mix to get ready for what you'll find in Los Angeles.

At this point, I see no advantage to running longer than 3½ hours. Save those 5-hour workouts for if and when you decide to train for an ultramarathon. Concerning those long, flat runs, Durden would tell you that there's no particular advantage to running them fast. Keep the pace 1-minute- to 2-minutes-per-mile slower than the pace you plan to run the marathon. Since you are doing 800 repeats and tempo runs during the week, that's more than ample speedwork. You don't want to wear yourself out by turning your long runs into mini-races. From the sound of your training, you should be ready to run a great race. All you need is a little work on the flats.

Crashing

Q: I recently completed the Boston Marathon and am now two-for-two in "crashing" during the second half. In both marathons, my second-half time was 6 minutes slower than for the first half, although my overall time did improve in the second one. The 10-K I raced in the middle of my Boston preparation suggested that I should have been able to break 2:40. I truly did not feel like I was pushing the first half at Boston. But once again, the wheels fell off. Do I need to train better, or should I accept the fact that maybe I was not meant to run 2.40?

A: Despite posing as an expert on all matters pertaining to the marathon, I failed to finish my first three races at that distance. Two of those DNFs (Did Not Finish) came at Boston, when I ran with the leaders well past the halfway point. In the third one, at Culver City, California, I led the race much of the way before being passed at 20 miles. My problem was that I was trying to win the races, not finish them. I have more success coaching first-timers to finish marathons because I advise them to plan a race pace a half-hour slower than their predicted times. Nobody offered that advice to me before my early marathons, although I wouldn't have listened anyway.

You ran faster at Boston than you did at your first marathon. If you want to break 2:40, you need to keep training, and keep trying. In your next marathon, try a more conservative beginning. Run the first few miles slower than 2:40 pace, then gradually get into a groove that would bring you past the half slightly slower than 80 minutes. See then if you can hold that pace and improve upon it in the final miles. Running "reverse splits" (such as 81 for the first half, 79 for the second) is not easy, but you might try that strategy to see what happens. And if that doesn't work, try again.

Eventually, I got my act together and won four marathons overall along with other age-group victories. Keep trying and sooner or later, you can achieve similar success.

Final Long Run

Q: I'm training for my first marathon. I am logging three 6-mile runs during the week and a long run on Sundays. Having increased my long runs by 1 mile a week, I currently am at 17 miles. I plan on continuing that trend until I conclude with a 22-mile run two weeks before the marathon. Is two weeks enough time to recover after a 22-mile long run? I've heard that you should run at least one 22-mile run before a marathon.

A: Twenty miles is the longest workout in my training class in Chicago. In Portland, the classes organized by Warren and Patti Finke with Bob Williams's help use 22 as the ultimate long run. In Dallas, Robert Vaughan focuses more on time rather than distance, with 3 hours being his upper limit. Jeff Galloway takes people to 26 in his classes but has everybody walk 1 minute out of every 10, not only in workouts but in the race itself. Bill Wenmark sometimes takes experienced marathoners to 31 before Twin Cities or Grandma's Marathons. We all coach marathoners somewhat differently, but basically, we all believe in a steady mileage buildup with a taper starting two to four weeks before the race. Yes, we disagree somewhat on the taper, too. Ultimately, the precise distance probably does not mean that much as long as you believe in what you are doing.

Can you recover in two weeks after a 22-mile run? Yes, but why don't you allow yourself some extra room and taper for three weeks? A pattern I recommend for experienced runners is to do two or three 20-milers with seven, five, and three weeks to go before the marathon, running "setback" workouts of 12 miles on the weekends between. Whichever pattern or final distance you choose, don't get yourself into trouble by pushing the final weeks too hard. That's when all sorts of bad things can happen because you'll find yourself on the edge of over-training from the cumulative mileage.

Remember that it's not the length of that final long run that counts, but all the good training you did leading up to that final run.

Postrace Syndrome

Q: I just finished running my first marathon, and I'm not sure where to go from here. When my mileage was high, I didn't do much in the way of weight training or stairclimbing, but I'm back to those routines. I want to continue running and find a happy medium between running and other exercises, but my motivation is low and I feel stuck. What do I do now?

A: A lot of first-time marathoners suffer from what I heard Joan Benoit Samuelson, 1984 Olympic Marathon gold medalist, refer to in a talk at the carbo party before the Chicago Marathon as "PMS." She asked how many people in the audience had suffered from PMS, and only a few women shyly raised their hands. Joanie laughed and said, "I'm talking about post-marathon syndrome!" After that, a lot of men stuck their hands up, too.

It's not uncommon. You invest a lot of energy, both physical and emotional, into training for your first marathon. Maybe a week after finishing, you look around and say, "Is that all there is?"

You don't necessarily want to contemplate running another marathon—at least not yet. Your body is still tired and may need three to six weeks to recover. Your mind may need even more recovery time since you've run out of goals. Relax. Every marathoner sooner or later encounters PMS. Hit the weight room. Get back on that stairclimber. Or find some new routine. Put in some miles, but not necessarily as many or as hard. Eventually, you will find a new goal—maybe even another marathon.

Boston

Q: How can I enter the Boston Marathon? If I have no racing experience, can I apply right away?

A: Without racing experience, you normally cannot enter the Boston Athletic Association Marathon. This oldest of continuously run marathons (founded in 1897) is an event that is restricted to marathoners who have met strict qualifying standards. You need to run at least one previous marathon in a reasonably fast time to gain entry. This is one of the reasons why Boston is so unique. It is also somewhat of a status symbol to be accepted to join the field at the starting line in Hopkinton. It shows that you have achieved a certain level of excellence among your running peers. You might compare it with being able to break 100 in golf or score a 200 game in bowling.

The entry standards established by the sponsoring Boston Athletic Association (BAA) begin at 3:10 for men 18 to 34 and 3:40 for women the same age. After age 35, add 5 minutes for every five-year age group. Thus, the standard for a 35-year-old male would be 3:15, the standard for a 60-year-old male would be 3:40. It's an achievable standard, but it's not easy. That's why those who have gained entry to Boston wear their shirts proudly. For the 100th anniversary, the BAA held a lottery open to all runners and allowed 38,000 starters; in normal years, approximately 10,000 get to run the race.

The BAA allows a limited number of runners who raise money for designated charities to enter each year. If you want to run Boston, I suggest that you run at least a few marathons to see if you have the basic ability (and dedication) to qualify for the race. If not, you might then consider the charity route.

For more information, send a stamped, self-addressed return envelope to the Boston Athletic Association, P.O. Box 1999-A, Hopkinton, MA 01748. Request an entry blank. The post office box number usually matches that of the year of the next race. Thus, in the millennium year, it will be P.O. Box 2000-A.

Racing

Take Your Running to the Next Level

- **First 5-K**
- **Respectable Time**
- **Half-Marathon**
- **Race Taper**
- **Last Meals**

- **Starting-Line Jitters**
- **Drinking Technique**
- **The Next Step**
- **Downtime after a Race**

Dr. George Sheehan, the late *Runner's World* philosopher, once said that the difference between a jogger and a runner was an entry blank. Not everybody is inspired to enter a running race, or beyond that, to enter frequent races. Surveys suggest that, increasingly, the readers of *Runner's World* are more interested in health and fitness than setting personal records and winning age-group prizes. Nevertheless, most runners enjoy participating in an occasional 5-K or 10-K race and sometimes gearing up for a marathon. Many others might race if they realized how much fun most long-distance races are.

My first race was a 660-yard run as a sophomore member of the track team at University High in Chicago. (I placed third and scored a single point for our team.) I had joined the team mainly to win a letter sweater and define myself as an athlete. As the season progressed, I improved as a runner, and Coach Paul Derr bumped me up to the varsity to run the mile.

I didn't run my first cross-country race until my freshman year at Carleton College. Between my junior and senior years in college, I entered my first road race: the 1952 National Amateur Athletic Union 15-K Championship, which started in Jackson Park, only a mile from my home on the South Side of Chicago. I might say that I finished in the middle of the pack, but there was no "middle-of-the-pack" in the 1950s. Probably fewer that two dozen runners appeared for that race. Even into the early 1970s, most American road races had fewer than 100 entrants. The running boom (inspired partly by Frank Shorter's gold medal in the 1972 Olympic Marathon) would soon change that.

Today, the first racing experience of most runners (who didn't compete in high school or college) is a mega-event with entrants in the thousands, even tens of thousands. San Francisco's Bay to Breakers regularly attracts 60,000 or more runners, and in March 1997, I participated in the Round the Bays race in Auckland, New Zealand, where 80,000 participated in the world's largest running event. The racing scene had undergone a major transformation since I first ran track. Standing next to me on the starting line at Round the Bays was a woman pushing a baby carriage. (We both finished somewhere in the middle of the pack.)

Whether from a desire to own a distinctive race T-shirt or not, many joggers eventually become runners by entering a road race. Despite what George said, I'm not sure that there is much of a distinction between the two groups these days. We're all runners at heart, even if some of us have more T-shirts. I get a lot of questions from high-schoolers hoping to improve performance and earn that still-prestigious letter sweater, but also from adults who don't quite know what to expect at that first 5-K.

First 5-K

Q: In the past, I could not even jog for a minute without running out of breath; then I started biking. One day, I tried jogging on a treadmill and made it to 15 minutes. Now I can run for 20 minutes at 5.5 miles an hour, and I have lost 30 pounds. A friend is determined to get me to run my first 5-K only a month from today. Is that enough time, and if so, what is the best way to train for the race?

A: No sweat. You're there already. I could push you out the door right now, and you could finish that 5-K.

If you're running 20 minutes on a treadmill at 5.5 mph, that's a little over 10:00-per-mile pace, so you're already covering close to 2 miles in your workouts. The 5-K is 3.1 miles. Once you get to the race and have a number pinned to the front of the race T-shirt that you will be handed at the registration table, and with the excitement of having all those people around you, you'll fly that extra mile.

You're probably nervous because you've never run in a race before. I've got news for you: at least one third of the people on that starting line have never raced before either. Just to be safe, you might run a few more minutes longer on the treadmill on several occasions before your coming-out party. Doing several 25- to 30-minute workouts will add to your confidence.

Other than that, all I can say is enjoy the experience.

Respectable Time

Q: I am a new runner who runs 3 to 4 miles a day. I entered my first 10-K race recently and loved it! The day before the race, I felt like I should be doing something to ensure that I would finish in a respectable time. Then I found myself wondering, "What is a respectable amount of time?"

A: World-record-holder Paul Tergat of Kenya runs the 10-K in 26:27.85; the rest of us are followers in his wake.

Respectable? I think that finishing a 10-K is respectable for a beginning runner like yourself. You won't find me handing out any disrespect to runners, regardless of their speeds.

There are various world records, national records, state records, club records, and age-group records, but the only records that count are personal records (PRs).

It seems to me that since you've just finished your first 10-K, you've just set a PR. Congratulations. How many other runners can say that they equaled your achievement the last time they ran a 10-K?

Don't worry about respectable times this early in your running career. To finish is to win.

Half-Marathon

Q: I am interested in running a half-marathon in six months and would like some advice. All of the training information I have found is based on your PR for the 5-K or 10-K, but I have yet to run any races. I currently run 2 to 3 miles, five days a week, at a 10:00-per-mile pace. I realize that I have to increase my mileage, but what else do I need to do? I would like to run a few races prior to the half-marathon, but what schedule should I follow?

A: You're on the low end of mileage for finishing a half-marathon comfortably, but you have ample time to build to a point where you can comfortably complete one. You're now running 10 to 15 miles a week. Suppose we increase your weekly mileage by less than a mile a week. That would bring you to the starting line running around 30 miles weekly. That's more than enough.

Less important than total mileage each week, however, is the distance of your longest run. Gradually build yourself to a point two to three weeks before the race where you can run 10 miles at an easy pace. You can do this by adding a mile to your longest run every other week. Once you get into the race itself, inspiration should carry you those extra 3 miles.

You could enter your first 5-K anytime. After all, you run 3 miles in practice. Schedule two or three races between now and your half-marathon just so you can get used to the racing scene, but don't race much more often. In a month or two, try a 10-K. Races at 15-K or 10-mile distances are tougher to find, but one of those would offer you a final test two to four weeks before your goal race.

Don't worry about pace. Not all training schedules are pace-based. Many are based on distance, or effort. If you put in the mileage between now and the race, you should have little trouble meeting your goal.

Race Taper

Q: I am 26 years old and have been running for a little over a year now. I ran my first half-marathon recently and qualified as a member of a Brooklyn team to race against the four other New York City boroughs to see which borough is number one. This race in September comes in the middle of training for the New York City Marathon in November. I would like to know a tapering program for the race without interfering with my marathon training.

A: Since the September half-marathon is just a semi-important race en route to the more important marathon, I suggest that you use a half-taper. Normally, I suggest that runners include some races in their marathon training programs as a test of pace anyway. The half-marathon is an excellent race distance for this purpose.

Maintain your normal training schedule until three days before the half-marathon. At that point, cut your training in half, both in intensity and mileage. Assuming the race is Sunday, on Thursday do your usual workout, but not as far. Friday, just do some easy jogging. Saturday, do nothing, so that you will go into the half-marathon well-rested.

It's important to alter your training after the race as well as before. Run easy for two to three days afterward before jumping back into your marathon training program. If your body tells you to rest more, listen.

All of this adds up to nearly a week of easy running, but you won't lose your edge. Racing the half-marathon will help with your preparations. If you were to race too often, however, it could detract from your marathon training, which is why I recommend that you run only a few races.

Last Meals

Q: What is a good choice of food the night before a race and right before the race?

A: A familiar joke among runners is that your prerace meal should taste good going down, taste good coming up, and look good on the sidewalk. Hopefully, if you follow my advice, it won't come to that.

Food choice depends partly on the race. If you're talking a 5-K or 10-K race, or any of the shorter distances run in track meets, you don't need extra energy other than what you might get from your normal dinner. Before a marathon, make certain that your muscles are well-stocked with energy-rich glycogen, which is why a meal rich in carbohydrates works best. (Foods high in carbohydrates include rice, potatoes, breads, fruits, vegetables, and pasta.) That's one reason why marathoners usually have spaghetti the night before a marathon.

Having said that, you would not want to try anything exotic (lobster) that might be likely to upset your stomach the night before even a short race. You also would not want to eat (or drink) so much that it might keep you from sleeping well (although even that might not necessarily affect your performance). For that reason, pasta is a good choice even before short-distance events. Unless it is a very important short-distance race and I'm eating out, I usually just order whatever appeals to me on the menu—even a burger and fries.

As for the race-day meal, if it is a short-distance race early in the morning, I'll usually go to the line without taking any solid food rather than forcing myself to get up early to eat breakfast. (Figure that it takes 3 to 4 hours to digest your food.) For a marathon, however, I will make an extra effort to get up early—even if it means getting up at 2:30 A.M. for juice, toast, and coffee before the Honolulu Marathon with its start at 5:30 A.M.

Afternoon races, such as high school track and cross-country meets, present a slightly different problem. During the several years that I coached high school teams, I discovered that school cafeterias do not always provide the best food choices for athletes, nor do those young athletes make the best food choices themselves. In that case, it's best to have a good breakfast and a light lunch, even if you need to brown-bag it.

Other alternatives for prerace nutrition include sports drinks or energy bars. They won't necessarily give you more of an energy boost than a well-balanced meal or snack eaten 3 to 4 hours before, but some runners feel more comfortable if they have something in their stomachs. (For events lasting longer than an hour, you may need to refuel during the run.)

Eventually, it comes down to experience. Sooner or later, after you've eaten enough prerace meals, you discover what works best for you. So experiment.

Starting-Line Jitters

Q: I'm a sophomore in high school and am about to start the cross-country season. I've had a good summer of training 40 miles a week for most of the summer with only a few rest weeks. One thing that troubles me is the mental aspect of running. Sometimes before a race, I get so scared that I wonder if I can even move my legs when the gun goes off. What can I do to allow me to relax more and help my concentration so I can have a great season?

A: A certain amount of prerace nervousness is natural. It's tied into the body's natural instinct to "fight or flee" when confronted with danger. You should be able to tap into this system to psych yourself up for your most important races.

I've never been a great practice runner in the sense of being able to record fast times in trials. But put me in a race—particularly one where I need to do well—and I find an extra gear. I've often surprised myself by my ability to achieve times in competition that I could never achieve when only racing the stopwatch. Nervousness is part of every runner's prerace mental preparation, although I admit that some runners handle this better than others.

You don't need to go into every race frightened or nervous. These three strategies will help you with your mental game.

Training. Getting in good shape by training properly will boost your confidence in your ability to perform. Knowing that you will run well will take some of the edge off your nervousness. Running a couple of good races at the beginning of the season to confirm your fitness also will make you feel more comfortable about late-season races, the ones that count.

Experience. As you continue to race and become accustomed to the racing scene, you will find that this allows you to relax. This is true for adult runners as well as for high school runners. Familiarity breeds confidence.

Routine. One way to relax is to have a specific warmup routine that you use before each of your races. It's like having a checklist in which you, say, jog a mile or two, stretch, go to the bathroom, run a few strides, stretch, rest, jog a bit, then go to the line. Whatever your routine, warming up the same way each time will both help you relax, as well as occupy your time during the final nervous hour before you race.

Don't relax too much. A certain amount of tension is essential to success. It's one way the body knows that it is in a race instead of in a time trial. If you're in good shape and scared standing on the starting line, think of how scared your opponents are of you!

Drinking Technique

Q: I will be running my first 10-K in a few weeks. When I run a 5-K, I grab a cup at the only water station, take a gulp, lose the rest, and move on. In a 10-K, especially on a hot day, I know that I will need to drink more. Is there any special technique to use for drinking on the run?

A: If I'm running next to you, it's okay if you splash some water on me—but not the replacement drink. (It's sticky.) Here are some tips that will help you get through the water stations.

Look left. If they are handing out water on both sides of the road, go to the left. Most runners are right-handed and favor that side.

Go long. Check to see how far ahead the water station continues. Sometimes, it is easier to grab at the end of the line of tables rather than the front. That's taking a slight risk, since if you miss, or if someone grabs the last cup just as you are reaching for it, you may need to continue unrefreshed.

Check the contents. Make sure that you know what they are handing out. Often, there is water at the front and a replacement drink at the end (or vice versa). Sometimes water will be on one side, the replacement drink on the other. This may be obvious because of signs or different-colored cups or because the volunteers are shouting, but sometimes it is not. Know what you're grabbing, and don't splash the contents of the cup over your head until you're sure.

Grab and cover. If you don't want to slow your pace, grab with one hand and instantly cover the top of the cup with the other to minimize spillage. It takes practice to drink while in full stride, and you may spill more than you get inside of you. More of a problem is that you can gag on water gulped down too fast.

Walk to drink. To ensure that you get enough fluids, walk through the water stations and drink as you go. Walking will also enable you to drink more than one cup. One strategy is to take the replacement drink first, then wash it down with water to remove any aftertaste from your mouth. I once checked to see how much time I lost walking through water stations and it was only 7 seconds per station. That adds up to less than a minute lost during a marathon, and you'll probably make up more than that time by staying cool.

Seek assistance. If you don't want to lose even those 7 seconds, find someone to hand you a plastic bottle filled with your favorite fluid. Technically, having someone hand you a bottle is cause for disqualification, but unless you're running near the front of the pack, nobody will know or care. (Most elite athletes have fluid in bottles on tables provided by the race management, which they must grab unaided to stay within the rules.)

When I was younger, I wouldn't drink in a 10-K or in the last 6 miles of a marathon, figuring the water wouldn't get absorbed into my system fast enough to do me any good. On those occasions, I'd throw the water on top of my head rather than drink it. Now that I'm older, and slower, I drink in 10-K races and in those last miles of the marathon.

As for etiquette, look behind and around you before heading for the refreshment station to make sure that you don't cut off another runner. Running in the Midland Run in New Jersey, two women suddenly darted diagonally across my path, almost tripping me (and themselves). My pet peeve is runners in races who dart and weave without regard for others around them.

Run enough 5-Ks and 10-Ks and you'll soon get the hang of it. Drinking at the water stations is not that difficult a technique to master.

The Next Step

Q: I just successfully finished my first 5-K in 31:14. I ran the whole way and still felt strong at the end. Now I'm confused as to how I should resume my training. What do I do next?

A: You probably should relax and savor your victory for a while. Make sure that you are well-rested after your first competitive effort. Even running a slow pace, you may suffer some sore muscles compared with after your regular workouts.

Once the thrill of victory has faded, then it's time to consider new goals. Moving up in distance might be one possibility. You could train for a 10-K race, or you might want to remain at the 5-K level and see if you can run that distance progressively faster. Since you are a beginner, you are guaranteed almost continual improvement. As others who have been running for a while can tell you, the closer you get to your potential, the more difficult it becomes to improve. But that could be years away.

There are two basic ways to improve: run longer or run faster. A third way would be to combine both. For someone like yourself, a fourth way would be simply to continue what you're doing. No need to be in a hurry to move off your plateau. When you no longer are running significantly faster times each race or workout, then you can consider altering your training. Then is the time to add speedwork or hills, or both. You might consider heading to the track for interval training or into the woods to run some fartlek workouts, and you'll begin to learn the value of a tempo run with a speed buildup in the middle of the workout as opposed to simply going out and running the same pace day after day. You also might see the value of attending a running camp or hiring a coach. There are many tricks to improve your ability as a runner, but for the present, be content at having finished your first 5-K.

Downtime after a Race

Q: I am a 61-year-old runner who just completed the New Bedford Half-Marathon in 1:55. I took one day off and tried running easily for a few days but felt awful. How much rest would you recommend after running a half?

A: It varies from runner to runner. Certainly, those of us in the upper age categories need more rest after all-out efforts than do high-schoolers. How far and hard you run also affects how you feel afterward—and how fast you recover. Recovery after a 5-K might take a day; recovery after a marathon might take a month.

Craig Virgin, an Olympian and two-time world cross-country champion, once commented that 10,000 meters on a track was equal in stress to two or three road 10-Ks. Having to concentrate while going around in circles for 25 laps took much more out of him than running a road race. In contrast, running a road 10-K was like a birthday party. Hilly road races, however, are tougher on the body than flat road races. Downhill courses, such as the Boston Marathon, require more recovery time because of the impact on the muscles. Uphill courses actually are easier on the body. One year, I ran the uphill portion of the Pikes Peak Marathon (setting a masters ascent record) and discovered, to my surprise, that I could do sprints on a grass field the next day. The Comrades Marathon in South Africa, with a 2,500-foot altitude difference between start and finish, alternates the course's direction each year, and most runners feel the "up" year is easier than the "down" year because of less pounding.

There's one rule of thumb that suggests that you need one day of recovery for every mile run in a race. Another rule of thumb, promoted by veteran runner and writer Joe Henderson, suggests one easy day, and no racing, for every kilometer run in anger. I ordinarily don't go along with rules of thumb since we're all different, but in your case, this would mean backing off training for a couple of weeks before going full speed again. (That is, 13 days for the 13.1 miles you ran, or 21 days for 21.1 kilometers.)

The important point is that when we race, we usually stress the body more than through normal training. The excitement of racing makes us run harder and faster. So relax. The way you feel is a natural response to the extra stress you put your body through during that half-marathon.

Injuries

Prevention and Treatment of Aches and Pains

- **Postvacation Blues**
- **Training while Injured**
- **Chafing**
- **To Run Again**
- **Sore or Injured?**
- **Hot or Cold?**
- **Running through Pain**
- **Plantar Fasciitis**
- **Stomach Cramps**
- **Achilles Tendinitis**

- **Ankle Sprain**
- **Calf Injury**
- **Shinsplints**
- **Compartment Syndrome**
- **Runner's Knee**
- **Hamstring Injury**
- **Iliotibial Band Injury**
- **Progressive Pain**
- **Dangers of Stretching**
- **Break from Training**

A question frequently asked of me at appearances is "How often have you been injured?" Or, a variation: "What was your worst injury?"

The answer to the first would be: not often. A few nicks and chips here and there, but nothing to interrupt a running career that has lasted a half-century. The worst running injury I suffered was a pulled knee ligament in 1969. I had just completed a hard interval workout at the track with some high school runners on a cool evening, and we stood chatting for a while after the final 400. Finally, someone said, "Let's jog a few laps to cool down." I felt a sudden stabbing sensation in my knee. I couldn't even get my foot off the ground!

I feared surgery, but several months away from running provided a miracle cure. My knees often get sore after a hard workout, but I'm still running after all these years. On one other occasion, I suffered a stress fracture in my lower leg. That occurred at the end of the Trans-Indiana Run, during which 10 otherwise sane individuals, including myself, ran the length of the state of Indiana (350 miles) in 10 days.

So why would someone who gets injured so infrequently be qualified to answer questions about injuries? Probably because I've been fairly successful in avoiding those injuries. One reason for my success is good biomechanics. I don't have any major impediments to my stride that put me at high risk. But I've also learned a few things about injuries over the years. One is that the best cure for most injuries is rest, although many runners don't like that option.

The injury I get the most questions about is shinsplints. Most of them are from beginners whose muscles have not yet adapted to their new fitness routines, or high-schoolers who go out for track in the spring without having run much in the winter. Shinsplints are painful, but rarely fatal to a running career. The second largest problem area is the knee—more precisely, the connective tissue around the knee.

I'm usually nervous responding to questions about the knee, back, or other areas of the body where the wrong advice could aggravate the problem, since I believe in the approach to healing originally suggested by Hippocrates: "First, do no harm." As I frequently point out, I do not have a medical degree. Even if I did, often an injured runner should be treated in the offices of a qualified sports doctor, usually a podiatrist or orthopedic surgeon, the two medical specialists best trained to treat running injuries.

Alas, not all doctors are equal, nor do they all understand running injuries. They do not always realize that "stop running" is not the option we want to hear. If we all were biomechanically perfect, and if we never overtrained, we would rarely suffer running injuries. But the world doesn't work that way, so I try to offer the best advice I can.

Postvacation Blues

Q: I've averaged 40 miles a week over the past year. I recently took a week off from running while on vacation. When I returned home, I became extremely sore after an 8-mile workout and felt very tight in the back of my left leg just above my knee. The following day, while on a 3-mile run, I felt something pull in the back of my left leg (just above the knee). This injury occurred 25 days ago. I took a week off from running, and I've only run nine times since then, but the back of my knee still gets extremely sore when I run. I feel fine while walking, and the leg doesn't bother me while stretching. Any thoughts about it?

A: It sounds to me like you pulled a muscle or tendon and probably need the intervention of a sports medicine specialist to tell you what the exact injury is and to recommend specific treatment. I would be cautious doing any more stretching until your injury is diagnosed, since stretching can aggravate an injury if you're constantly tugging on the muscle or tendon. Sometimes the best approach is total rest. After the injury heals, you can start a stretching routine to prevent reinjury.

Without knowing all the details, I'm not convinced that the injury was entirely due to that 8-mile run, or the fact that you took a week off. You wouldn't have lost muscle fitness that fast. Maybe it was something else you did on your vacation. A lot of running injuries are caused by activities other than running, and past injuries from other sports sometimes play a part. If you drove 700 miles before the 8-miler, muscle stiffness from sitting cramped in a car could have been partly responsible. If you had been engaging in other activities while on vacation, the injury might have begun there. Injuries often occur because of multiple causes.

What happened to you might serve as a warning signal for others. It's not a good idea to train too hard immediately after even a short layoff, particularly if you were engaged in other activities.

Training while Injured

Q: I recently went on an easy run of 3 miles. The next day, I had pain in my right foot. Two days later, I went to the doctor, was diagnosed with a stress fracture in my heel, and now, here I sit with a cast from knee to toe on my right leg. How can I avoid losing my base fitness? I can't walk very well, and I think that cycling is out. I have been told that I must wear this cast for three to five weeks, and then it will be some time before I can begin to run again.

A: Your options are limited. Sometimes doctors put casts on runners because they know that's the only way they can stop those runners from exercising too vigorously and reinjuring themselves. Even cross-training can be a curse when runners are eager to begin exercising again. I would check with your physician before beginning any exercise routine that might put extra stress on your injury and impede rehabilitation.

Once the cast is off, you should be able to engage in other activities. Aquarunning is the best rehabilitative exercise for most running injuries because you can use a life vest to float in the deep end of the pool and mimic the running movements. Other exercises can be done in the water without the vest as your heel begins to heal more completely.

If you have access to a gym, see if there are some machines that allow you to isolate the upper body. But be careful which machine you use. Rowing machines would seem to offer one possibility, but the legs still come into play. Your best bet is to work with a physical therapist who can assess your injury and offer specific training routines. Maintaining fitness will not be easy with your leg in a cast, but you do not want to maintain it at the risk of lengthening your rehabilitative time.

Chafing

Q: I experience chafing between my legs when running more than 5 miles. I wear normal (floppy) running shorts. Do I just need to keep running and build up calluses? Are there any lotions available?

A: You do not want to develop calluses between your legs. Lotions (from petroleum jelly to various products designed to eliminate chafing) will work, but they eventually rub off and leave you naked around the 18-mile mark. If you race, many of the longer races thoughtfully provide lubricants at aid stations, and you certainly can carry your own, whether in a packet pinned to your shorts or smeared onto your race number before starting.

I never used to have problems with chafing, either between my legs or beneath my arms, until one winter when I gained a few extra pounds. Suddenly, I had a chafing problem. Losing those pounds eliminated the problem, but runners don't have to be overweight to experience problems with chafing, particularly on long runs.

Consider purchasing the type of hip-hugger (or half-leg) shorts similar to those worn by cyclists, but without the padded crotch. You'll continue to rub, but it will be nylon against nylon. Hopefully, that will cure your problem. Long tights also work for the same reason.

To Run Again

Q: I'm a veteran marathoner, 44 years old, who also plays volleyball and tennis. I tore my anterior cruciate ligament (ACL) playing volleyball and just last week underwent ACL reconstruction surgery. I'm unable to find any other runners who have had this surgery, since it's not really a runner's injury. At my age, is it conceivable to even think that I'll ever get myself back into long-distance running? I'm already working with a physical therapist and am prepared for hard work.

A: I wish that I could look into your knee and give you the answer you want to hear. Your physical therapist has had much more experience with similar injuries than I, but even he is not going to make promises he can't deliver.

Your age does work against you somewhat. And yours is a difficult injury to a critical joint. *Anterior* means "forward" and *cruciate* means "crossing." The anterior cruciate ligament crosses in front of the knee and helps stabilize it. Runners normally don't tear this ligament unless participating in another sport, such as volleyball, basketball, or tennis, that requires sudden shifts in direction. Will you be able to run more marathons? Only time will tell. You may need to confine yourself to shorter races, or maybe even no races. Increasingly, though, surgeons have found improved ways to repair and rehabilitate knees, so hope for the best.

A word of caution to others who enjoy participating in sports that use different muscles than running. If you go to the tennis court without having picked up a racket in a month, you probably are more vulnerable to injury than someone totally out of shape. That's because you've conditioned your body to run in a straight line, but not sideways. Jumping up and down, as in volleyball, can also prove risky. But a bigger problem is that by being in excellent aerobic shape, runners often can stay in the game longer than those less physically fit.

Jack H. Wilmore, Ph.D., an exercise physiologist at Texas A & M University in College Station and a former 2:58 marathoner, tore his meniscus in a weekend volleyball tournament. "I was in my third or fourth hour of play because we kept winning," recalls Dr. Wilmore. "I went up to block a spike and came down wrong." After a year of rehabilitation on a bike, he returned to running, but 6 to 8 miles is now his limit. "My knee lets me know if I go too far or too fast," he says.

Runners be warned: Quit early or risk being carried off the court. Be particularly cautious in other sports if you're at peak training. Running 20 miles on Saturday and grabbing a tennis racket on Sunday is a very bad idea.

Sore or Injured?

Q: How can you differentiate between sore legs and injured legs? I've heard that with sore legs, you can run through the pain, provided that you have taken a day or two off for rest. But if you are injured, you need to take more time off. My legs hurt when I begin to run for about a mile, then they feel better. This started when I began to increase my speed training for an upcoming 10-K.

A: So-called "sore legs" (or sore muscles) might be classified as a temporary injury. You tear the microscopic muscle fibers by stressing muscles during a hard workout. This happens most often when you do a workout involving speedwork to prepare for a 10-K. These tiny muscle tears hurt, just like your finger would hurt if you cut it. Over a period of hours and days, the tears heal, and the muscles no longer feel sore.

Try this test: Stand completely still. Do you feel any pain? Now move. Do you feel anything? In a lecture at the American College of Sports Medicine's annual meeting, Priscilla M. Clarkson, Ph.D., of the University of Massachusetts in Amherst, commented: "One interesting aspect about sore muscles is that they only feel sore when you move them." Dr. Clarkson suggested that soreness usually develops 24 to 48 hours after exercise, then the muscles gradually return to baseline. "The swelling that accompanies soreness will decrease your range of motion," noted Dr. Clarkson, "and there will also be a decrease of strength." That is why smart coaches recommend that runners alternate hard and easy days in training. Yes, some of the soreness will begin to dissipate if you warm up with a mile of jogging, but if you continue to ignore your sore muscles and train hard, you may slow the rehabilitative process that permits you to gain strength and speed.

Incidentally, there's no truth to the belief that muscle soreness is caused by lactic acid, which develops in the bloodstream during anaerobic exercise. Lactic acid normally disappears within 30 minutes after you stop exercising. Resist any advertisements for products that promise to speed lactic acid removal. "Massage, ice, and anti-inflammatories can only partially alleviate soreness, which eventually goes away on its own," says Dr. Clarkson.

A so-called injured leg also might involve a muscle tear, but usually to a more specific part of the body, such as the Achilles tendon or hamstring. It may take weeks to months for a severely torn muscle to heal, and if you hurt yourself badly enough, the injury may be permanent. Some parts of the body don't regenerate themselves, or they may require surgery to achieve even a partial repair.

Another way to tell if you're injured or merely experiencing sore muscles is to determine how much of your body feels sore, or hurt. If both your legs feel equally sore, you're most likely experiencing the soreness that comes with overuse. If you can point to a specific point on one of those legs, it's more likely an injury.

In either case, it's never a good idea to run through pain. Pain is a signal to your body to slow down, and you ignore that signal at your own risk.

Hot or Cold?

Q: What is better for sore muscles and achy joints, heat or cold? How can you make an ice pack that is convenient and reusable?

A: Cold is better immediately after exercise to reduce swelling, particularly in the case of an injury. Heat works best before exercise to warm the injured muscle so that you can exercise it with less risk of making the injury worse.

Various rubs can be useful for warming muscles before a run. Use your hands to spread the rub over the injured area and massage the muscle to get the circulation going. This may help you warm the muscle so that you can do some training, but beware of products that may mask the pain and cause you to make the injury worse. Also, you don't want to use heat immediately after you injure a muscle because it will increase the swelling.

Once the swelling has gone down, you can use heat to help speed the healing process. Soaking in a hot tub or applying a hot-water bottle to the injured area may help increase circulation, but don't overdo it. Sometimes, just doing nothing and allowing the injury to heal itself is the best recourse.

A cheap and easy way to make a cold pack is simply to take a paper cup, fill it with water, and put it in the freezer. After the water freezes, you can peel back the paper to rub ice on the injury. Or, go to the drugstore and buy a reusable gel-filled ice pack. They last forever; I've used the same one for years.

Marlene Cimons, runner and health writer for the *Los Angeles Times*, recommends a bag of frozen vegetables as another option. "Frozen peas or corn are best because of their small size and uniformity," suggests Cimons.

Running through Pain

Q: I know that you're not supposed to run through pain, but how much pain must you feel before pulling out of a workout, or not starting the workout at all? Aren't there some cases when it's okay to go ahead and run, accepting that running is not always pain-free?

A: Some runners have more tolerance for pain than others—and this can get them in trouble. Others, if they weren't willing to accept some pain, would never run at all. Most of us run through a certain amount of pain because we discover that by warming up properly and starting slowly, we can minimize it.

"It is almost always advisable to take an extra day or two off from exercise if you experience pain related to your running or walking," explains Michael J. Helms, D.P.M., an Indianapolis podiatrist. "Sometimes it is okay, however, to continue training at a reduced level when you have pain or soreness in your legs or feet," he adds. Dr. Helms offers some specific guidelines.

Yes, you can run if:

- The pain is mild and goes away as you run or walk.
- The pain does not cause you to limp, even slightly.
- The pain shows signs of improving from day to day as you continue to run.
- The sore area is not at all swollen.

No, you should not run if:

- The pain or soreness that you feel is present throughout your workout.
- The pain worsens the farther you go.
- The problem causes you to limp or alter your gait in any way.
- The problem is getting worse from day to day.

I frequently suggest to runners with injuries that they see a sports doctor, either an orthopedist or a podiatrist. Unfortunately, many injured runners delay seeking medical care because they are afraid (often with good reason) that the doctor will tell them to stop running. Dr. Helms has been running and racing on the track and roads for more than a quarter-century. His advice is worth heeding.

Plantar Fasciitis

Q: I had plantar fasciitis last year and, as a result, only ran two marathons. I took the rest of the year off from long-distance running since it hurt too much to run. It has now been nine months since my diagnosis, and despite the fact that I can run and do speedwork, the dull ache after workouts reminds me of the plantar fasciitis. The ache goes away with ibuprofen, but I know that ibuprofen can mask a lot of pain, and I'm afraid of reinjuring myself. I stretch before I run, but is there anything else I can do? Will this ever go away completely?

A: You've already done most of the right things. I, too, would be cautious about reinjury, particularly since you're a serious runner if you normally run more than two marathons a year and include speedwork in your training.

The plantar fascia is the tendon that connects the heel with the toes. Plantar fasciitis most commonly manifests itself as sharp heel pain, almost as though you had stomped on something with your foot and broken your heel. The pain actually dissipates somewhat as you run, then returns the next morning. Steven Subotnick, D.P.M., who is in private practice in Hayward, California, says that the injury is very prevalent in that area because runners do a lot of running in the hills above the city. Pushing off while running hills is a common cause of plantar fasciitis. So is speedwork.

Perhaps part of your problem is that you can't relax long enough to allow the injury to fully heal. If you can figure out a routine that will combine at least some hard training with other exercises (cross-training) that do not stress the injured area, you might be able to obtain relief. Add extra rest to the mix, at least to get yourself over the hump. Try to think of what activities on your part stress the plantar fascia most, and see if you can eliminate them. Certainly, that would include speed training that forces you to toe off more than normal and also running hills. That's right: everything I tell people to do in other sections of the book if they want to run faster. That's running's Catch-22.

I used to get plantar fasciitis about once every four years, mainly because my main event was the 3000-meter steeplechase. It was less the shock of landing and more the stress of pushing off to clear barriers and the water jump. In one of my bouts with it, I switched as much of my training as possible to running barefoot on golf courses or the beach. My theory was that with no shoes to cushion the blows, my body would be more sensitive to what the foot was doing as it touched the ground. Barefoot running worked for me, and I still believe that runners should include some barefoot running in their training to help strengthen their feet. Stanford University distance runners do about 2 miles of barefoot running a week, and the school won both the men's and women's NCAA cross-country championships in 1996.

Here's a good stretch: With knee bent, ankle flexed toward you, grab your toes with one hand and pull them back toward your ankle. Hold for 15 seconds, relax, then repeat. Another good stretching exercise for plantar fasciitis is toe rises, which are done by standing flat-footed and rising up onto your toes. Arch supports or orthotics may help, but those are best prescribed by a podiatrist. To strengthen your plantar fascia, pick up marbles or golf balls with your toes or grab a towel with your toes and pull, then grab some more.

One other tip: Do not get out of bed barefoot in the morning, or even in the middle of the night. Put your running shoes beside the bed and put them on before standing up. Early morning is when you can really stretch the tendon and do the most damage. Another treatment is to wear a boot on your foot so you can't stretch the plantar fascia while sleeping. That sounds like a radical treatment, but it apparently works in severe situations, according to reports from podiatrists.

Stomach Cramps

Q: What is the best way to avoid side aches? My usual run is 5 miles. Sometimes, I feel fantastic; other times, stomach cramps stop me. I've tried changing my diet, but that doesn't seem to help. Any ideas or tricks of the trade that I should know about?

A: My first reaction would be that you're eating too soon before running, or that you're eating the wrong foods, but you seem to have considered that. It's still possible that you have some dietary intolerance. Many people are lactose intolerant, but don't know it. Try keeping a food diary to see if there is any one food you eat on days when you have side aches.

Here are some other coping strategies.

Change breathing patterns. Belly breathing sometimes works.

Change pace. Speed up. Slow down. Anything to change how you're running.

Concentrate. Focus on the cramp. Try to wish it away.

Dissociate. Try to think of anything but the cramp.

Massage. Rub the offending muscle, toward the heart.

Strengthen your muscles. Sit-ups. Crunches. Lifting.

Side aches can be caused by a variety of culprits—including appendicitis—so I hope that you find a method to make them go away.

Achilles Tendinitis

Q: I have suffered from Achilles tendinitis in one foot for more than a year. Despite physical therapy, the injury won't heal. I now run 2 to 4 miles every other day. The tendon feels fine while I run, but the next morning, it's tight again. I use heel cups, stretching, and ice. Lately, my other tendon has begun to bother me. Do I need to stop running until the pain is completely gone? Is there a risk of building up scar tissue? Is the key to healing to go slow and for a short distance? What about biking, exercise machines, or walking?

A: Achilles tendinitis is hardly a life-threatening injury, but it can be very frustrating because curing the problem often takes so much time. I've suffered Achilles tendinitis on several occasions, although fortunately, not a serious case. One friend, Gordon Dickson of Hamilton, Ontario, suffered chronic tendinitis, and although he competed in the Olympic Games for Canada and placed third in the Boston Marathon, it limited his effectiveness as a runner.

The Achilles tendon connects the calf and the heel and is the largest tendon in the body. Since tendons are denser than muscles, they don't heal as rapidly, and blood circulation is relatively poor. One problem is that the injury feels worst when you get out of bed. After you begin to move, it feels better. When you run, it may feel better still. It's afterward that the tendon really begins to hurt. Because of this, runners continue to run through and past pain and, eventually, may turn an acute injury into a chronic one. Scar tissue will continue to build as you continue to run. Eventually, surgery may be the only solution.

Tendinitis is an inflammation of the tendon (swelling, redness, soreness), so ice and anti-inflammatory medication can help with initial symptoms. But you probably need to stop running immediately so as not to aggravate the problem more. Walking or other forms of cross-training may allow you to continue exercising. If you use an exercise bike, do so with your heels (not toes) on the pedals. If you swim (or aquatrain), do so using other muscles. My initial impression is that exercising on a cross-country ski machine might aggravate the injury as much as, or more than, running. With any cross-training exercise, pain should tell you whether or not it works. You want to find ways of training that do not bring the muscles of the lower leg (and Achilles tendon) into play.

There may be various reasons why you would injure your Achilles tendon. Your feet may overpronate, that is, roll too far inward as you go through the running motion. They may be flat or have high arches, and worn-out shoes (particularly at the heels) may also cause the problem. Speed training and/or running hills could stress the Achilles tendon, and training errors—such as running too far, too fast, or too often, or suddenly increasing your training—can cause a problem.

Heel lifts in your shoes may help and so may arch supports. Eventually, the runner may need to obtain orthotics, or shoe inserts, from a podiatrist. Here are two stretches for the calf muscles that help lessen Achilles tendon injuries.

Wall leans. Place one foot perpendicular to, and several inches from, a wall. Place your other foot as far away as possible with your heel on the ground. Thrust your hips forward, which will stretch your lower leg muscles. Hold for 10 to 30 seconds and repeat by switching leg positions.

Heel drops. Stand with your toes on a step or other raised surface with your heels overlapping the edge. (Allan Levy, M.D., whose *Sports Injury Handbook* served as source for much of the above information, describes this as similar to if you were going to do a back dive off a diving board.) Lower your heels, stretching the backs of your lower legs. Hold and repeat.

These stretches are also suggested for runners who are troubled with tight calf muscles. Because the calf muscle is most responsible for providing forward motion when we run, it could be said that the wall lean and the heel drop are the two most important stretching exercises.

Stretching and other temporary solutions such as ice and anti-inflammatories are only helpful to a point in curing Achilles tendinitis. Anyone suffering from chronic symptoms of this injury needs to visit a sports doctor, probably a podiatrist. The doctor may prescribe cessation of running and/or cross-training. If an MRI (magnetic resonance imaging) examination shows excessive scar tissue, or a heel spur, as the cause of the irritation, surgery may be necessary.

Ankle Sprain

Q: I suffered a third-degree sprain in my ankle about 1½ years ago. I completely tore the ligament that helps lateral movement, so now I only have two out of the three ligaments. How can I go about running again without suffering a lot of pain in my ankle?

A: Very cautiously! Do stretching and strengthening exercises for your ankles, and be very prudent when choosing running surfaces.

Running normally does not cause ankle injuries, mainly because running is a straight-forward and repetitive exercise, particularly when compared with football, basketball, or other sports where ankle sprains are more of a problem. Still, runners often run on uneven surfaces or roads with potholes. Step in one, and you may have a sprain. Most sprains that involve no tearing or fracturing heal quickly; others may require surgery.

The immediate treatment for sprains is RICE: rest, ice, compression, elevation. Stretching exercises include using a balance board. (You balance on the board, flexing and unflexing the muscles around the ankles as you shift positions.) Or you can do band exercises in which you tie a rubber exercise band around your feet, pushing and relaxing. Another is to sit on a chair and, with one leg in the air, use your big toe as a "pen" to write the alphabet in the air, moving your ankle to form the letters. Still another is to sit on a counter with a weight looped over your toe and lift it by using your ankle. Elastic ankle bandages can offer temporary support, but I'm unenthusiastic about long-term use since it is more important to strengthen the ankle so you can prevent future injuries instead of immobilizing it.

One podiatrist offers some advice and an additional exercise: "This exercise will build up muscle strength, coordination, and the nerve impulses from your ankle to your brain (to reduce ankle sprains). Standing in a doorway, balance on one foot for 15 seconds (barefoot). Repeat several times for each leg. Work up to 45 seconds over several days. Then start back at 15 seconds with your eyes closed. If you lose your balance, grab on to the door frame. When you achieve 45 seconds with your eyes closed, you can move your arms back and forth as you would in running. Once accomplished, you should be ready for the trails."

Some podiatrists, however, do caution runners against running on unstable surfaces. While that advice probably makes sense for those who have already sprained their ankles, or have unstable ankles, the rest of us *should* be running on those kinds of surfaces to prevent ankle injuries. Don't rush out into the woods today if you're not used to running trails, but running regularly (or occasionally) on soft and undulating surfaces can help strengthen your ankles. Then when you do hit the occasional pothole, you're less likely to get hurt. If you do turn an ankle, however, do what the doctor says.

Calf Injury

Q: I'm a 44-year-old male and have been running 20 miles a week for the last 15 years. In the last 2 years, I have experienced moderate to severe pain in the back of my mid-calf region in both legs. Any idea what is causing this, and is there a cure?

A: One of the problems with aging is that we encounter little twitches, such as the calf injuries now bothering you, which sometimes cause us to limit our training. After recovery, we discover that we can't quite return to our previous level. It's as though we had been forced to step to a lower level. That's one reason why our times slow as we age. But that's a philosophical statement beside the point of your question, which relates to tight calves, not uncommon even among younger runners. What caused this to happen? Perhaps there was some incident that you may or may not remember that caused extra stress on your calves, and you still haven't recovered from it.

Do you keep a training diary? If so, go back and check the kind of workouts you were doing—both in the area of volume and intensity—before your injury. Was their some training error you made that predisposed you to injury? Was there a too-fast mileage buildup, perhaps to get ready for a marathon? Were you doing a lot of speedwork without sufficient rest? There might even have been other factors—such as stress on the job, or a recent viral infection—that could be one of the reasons for your injury.

Have you seen a sports doctor for a proper diagnosis? Perhaps you have some biomechanical imbalance that can be overcome with inserts or orthotics, although orthotics are expensive and should be considered only as a last resort. If you are the type of runner who lands farther forward on your foot—a "toe" versus "heel" runner—you may be more prone to calf injuries. Well-muscled sprinters often can move fast because of their biomechanical talents, but sometimes get in trouble if they try to go long, or long and fast.

The same stretching exercises (wall leans and heel drops) suggested on page 107 for Achilles tendinitis also work for the calves since those tendons attach to the bottom of the calves. Stretching the calves is important because if your calves are inflexible, they can cause you to become injured in other areas of the leg or foot. In addition to Achilles tendinitis, you can also develop plantar fasciitis and/or shinsplints from tight calves. This is why you often see smart runners leaning against walls before and after 5-K and 10-K races.

If you still can't lick the problem of tight calf muscles, you may need to modify your training routine by running less or substituting cross-training on alternate days. A visit to a podiatrist's office might result in a better diagnosis and cure.

Shinsplints

Q: What is the best thing to do for shinsplints?

A: Shinsplints are a common problem among runners, particularly beginning runners. Sports doctors dislike the term *shinsplints*, which they consider too vague. "To me, shinsplints is a nondiagnosis that doesn't tell me anything," complains Joe Ellis, D.P.M., in his book with Joe Henderson, *Running Injury-Free*. "Shinsplints can describe almost anything related to leg pain. You might as well say that you have 'foot splints,' 'knee splints,' or 'back splints.' All this term tells me is the general location of the pain, not its cause."

Dr. Ellis claims that what most people consider shinsplints covers five related lower-leg injuries: 1) tendinitis of the lower leg, 2) inflammation of the bone covering, 3) stress fractures, 4) nerve irritation, or 5) compartment syndrome. Despite what Dr. Ellis says, it's easier to use that term than to say "medial tibial pain syndrome." Runners usually don't know medical terms; they just know that the front of their legs hurt, most often toward the inside.

As a high school coach, I found that it was the freshmen and sophomores who most complained about shinsplints, not only because they were new to the sport but also because their bodies were still growing. The cause of their pain was often a muscle imbalance: the calf muscles overpowering the shin muscles. As they continued to train, the muscles became better balanced, resulting in diminished pain and finally a cure.

On one Sunday run with my running club, I discussed the problem with Debbie Frey, an assistant coach at Valparaiso High School in Indiana. Frey commented that too many youngsters spend 15 years engaging in very little physical activity. Then suddenly, they decide that they want to be runners and join the cross-country or track teams. Good decision, but their muscles are too weak to stand the stress of regular training. After a few weeks or months, they become injured. The same scenario occurs with adult runners, particularly females, who start to exercise in their twenties or thirties and do too much too soon.

Telling someone that his shinsplints will disappear as his muscles become better balanced may not be good enough for someone whose pain is very real right now. An inexpensive drugstore remedy is arch supports. If you visit a sports doctor's office, he most likely will prescribe the same remedy or, in more severe cases, orthotics. The same stretching exercises (wall leans and heel drops on page 107) recommended for Achilles tendon and calf injuries also help prevent, or relieve, shinsplints.

In the *Healthy Runner's Handbook* by Lyle J. Micheli, M.D., director and co-founder of the Sports Medicine Division at Boston Children's Hospital, with Mark Jenkins, Dr. Micheli offers the following recommendations for those who have (to use his term) "medial tibial pain syndrome."

- Stop running, but do not discontinue exercising.
- For the first 48 to 72 hours, administer an ice massage.
- For relief of minor pain, take acetaminophen or ibuprofen; for major pain, take aspirin.
- Refrain from running until you no longer feel pain on the inner side of the lower leg.
- When you resume running, choose soft surfaces and cut back your training.
- If symptoms persist, see a sports doctor.

For certain cases, I advise checking with a sports doctor sooner because what you believe to be shinsplints could be a stress fracture. If you feel the pain in your leg, or legs, while walking as well as running, that's a bad sign.

Beginning runners eventually become experienced runners, and when that happens, their shinsplints often disappear.

Compartment Syndrome

Q: I get a repeating injury to the muscle/tendon that can be felt next to the shin halfway between the knee and ankle: a sort of band that seems to attach to the bone. It becomes inflamed when I get to about 60 miles a week of running. I have tried very gradual increases in my mileage, but the inflammation still comes back. I have gone to several doctors, but the most they could do was prescribe anti-inflammatory medicine and rest. If I don't back off, it gets so bad that I literally can't walk. It isn't shinsplints, and it isn't a pulled muscle. I have had my form analyzed twice, and that doesn't seem to be the cause—

or so they say. I have tried different shoes, surfaces, and alternate exercises to no avail. Do I just keep searching for a sports medicine doctor who can help me?

A: Your search may need to continue, but your recurring injury might be some form of compartment syndrome, an injury that bothered distance runner Mary Slaney at one point in her career. It's not a common injury, but it can be very limiting if you have it. Imagine a rubber hose filled with water that expands and bursts when the temperature dips below freezing.

There are four separate compartments in the leg through which muscles, tendons, nerves, veins, arteries, and bones run. Each is wrapped within a fascia. Pressure caused by fluid buildup or muscles that enlarge (perhaps as a result of extra training) slows the blood flow and causes pain. Surgery is sometimes needed to slice the compartments and relieve the pressure.

I'm not suggesting that you suffer from compartment syndrome, but that's the first thing that comes to my mind. Since you apparently don't experience this problem until you get your mileage up to 60 miles a week, the obvious solution would be to never train more than 59 miles weekly. Unless you are an elite athlete trying to win an Olympic title, you should be able to achieve all of your goals within that mileage level.

If not, you may need to continue seeking the right doctor.

Runner's Knee

Q: Please explain runner's knee, and what can be done about it. Is that what they call chondromalacia patella? Is there a wrap or something that can be placed on the knee to allow one to continue to run without pain?

A: As the term is most frequently used, *runner's knee* refers to pain beneath the kneecap during exercise caused by excessive pronation of the foot while striking the ground. This foot fault causes and exaggerates the normal inward twisting of the lower leg, which in turn twists the knee. If you've ever seen slow-motion videos of what happens to the knees of even biomechanically efficient runners, you wonder how any of us can continue in this sport.

Excessive twisting causes the kneecap to rub painfully against the long bone of the thigh. As the rubbing continues, the bone rubs thin, causing a very painful chronic ache. Technically speaking, runner's knee is different from chondromalacia patella, which is a softening of the cartilage covering the underside of the knee and is also caused by bad biomechanics.

Runner's knee or chondromalacia patella should not be confused with various tears and strains of the ligaments and tendons surrounding the knee, which often are the result of a specific accident, such as a quarterback being blindsided by a linebacker. When that happens, the quarterback usually is sitting in an orthopedic surgeon's office the next morning being scheduled for surgery almost immediately. That's what is known as an acute injury, because it is caused by a single event.

The pains that many runners feel in their daily training are more often the result of a chronic injury, which occurs from repetitive-motion events over a long period of time. Runners, particularly those with bad biomechanics, suffer chronic injuries to the knee and the soft tissue around the knee. Because this pain develops gradually and runners often learn to adapt to it (using ice, anti-inflammatories, or wraps to relieve pain), they sometimes avoid visiting a doctor's office.

I get a lot of questions from runners suffering from knee pain. I don't consider runners more susceptible to knee problems than athletes in other sports, and there is little evidence that running even excessive mileage can cause degenerative arthritis (one bad rap that our sport gets), but the knee is a vulnerable joint. Sometimes knee pain suffered by runners is the result of activities not connected with their running—such as playing tennis or skiing or tripping on a rug.

I become very nervous answering questions about knee injuries, because the knee is a sensitive joint that can be stressed in many ways. I'm even wary of suggesting stretching or strengthening exercises to people with knee pain for fear that I will offer the wrong advice and cause them more pain. I'd rather have them be seen by a qualified sports medicine practitioner.

There are, however, two exercises that will strengthen the muscles around your knees. I learned about these from Vern Gambetta, former director of conditioning for the Chicago White Sox and Chicago Bulls and now president of his own consulting firm, Gambetta Sports Training Systems, in Sarasota, Florida.

Quarter squats. Stand on one foot, with the other leg behind you, arms to each side for balance. Do a quarter squat by lowering your body gradually, dropping in height not more than 6 to 12 inches. Start gradually, but work up to 10 repeats with each leg. You can do two other variations on these quarter squats. Hold your off-the-floor leg to one side as you squat. The other is to hold the leg in front of you.

Straight-leg lifts. Lie on your back. Keeping both legs straight, raise one leg 6 inches up, hold for 10 seconds, then lower. Repeat 10 times. Work up to three sets for each leg. When this is comfortable, you can add an ankle weight. Add weights as you get stronger.

Getting back to your original question: Yes, you can run out to the drugstore and buy a knee wrap, which will probably relieve pain—temporarily. But that's not getting at the cause of your problem, which most likely is some biomechanical imbalance causing your knee to twist excessively when you run. My recommendation is to see a sports doctor.

Wasn't there a TV ad where a mechanic said: "You can see me now, or you can see me later." The same pitch works for bad knees.

Hamstring Injury

Q: I am struggling with a strained hamstring and am wondering how long I have to put up with this. Is it foolish of me to try to run through this? I ice and stretch religiously and have lessened my training.

A: You are doing the right thing by icing, stretching, and modifying your training. Sometimes our bodies signal us to back off by twitching one of our muscles, such as a hamstring, but not everybody responds to body signals as well as others. It is a mistake to run through pain.

Here are two stretches for the hamstring.

Hurdler's reach. Sit on the floor with your legs outstretched and ankles together. Place your hands beside you on the floor, then gently slide them forward, keeping your back and knees straight and trying to bring your chest as close to your knees as possible. You can do this with both legs together, but a better approach is to focus on one leg, cocking the other leg so your knee faces outward and out of the way.

Knee grab. Lie on your back, legs straight, then bring one knee toward your chest, so it is at a 90-degree angle to your hips. Grab the leg behind the knee to keep the thigh stable and straighten your knee as far as possible, keeping your ankle pointed toward the knee. The opposite leg should remain straight on the ground, unless your back hurts.

Until the hamstring pull, or strain, disappears, you might be better off shifting all (or most) of your training into sports that stress the muscle less: cycling or swimming. Let pain be your guide as to how hard to push. One clue is whether or not the muscle feels better as you continue. If it feels worse, stop.

Proper warmup is important to avoid hamstring pulls. Jog easily for a period, then stretch all muscles, then begin to exercise very slowly. I prefer stretching after (or during) workouts rather than before.

Iliotibial Band Injury

Q: I recently returned to running after 18 months of suffering from IT (iliotibial) band problems in my left leg. After about four weeks of mild soreness of the sartorius muscle in my right leg, I ran a 3-mile race and two days later ran a 20-minute tempo run. The pain and soreness on the tempo run would not subside, and afterward, I was limping. Is it advisable to take prescribed or over-the-counter anti-inflammatories? And how can I keep this from becoming a nagging injury like the IT band problem? I am stretching more now than ever: 15 minutes, twice a day.

A: The sartorius muscle connects with the hip and tibia (lower-leg bone) and helps in bending the hip and knee. It's the longest muscle in the human body. The iliotibial band is in the same area of the body, running down the outside of the thigh from the rim of the pelvis to below the knee. The IT band provides lateral stability to the hip. Injuries to the IT band are difficult to diagnose, since pain can result either in the knee or in the hip, or in both areas. The pain comes on gradually, becoming worse each time you run. Each time you extend your leg, the tightened band rubs across the bone of the hip or the center of the knee, and it hurts.

Anti-inflammatories (and ice) can relieve pain, but I'm always wary about overdosing on even the mildest of drugs. Rest may be your most effective form of treatment. My recommendation is to stop running for at least 72 hours, then see if the pain remains when you start again. If it pains you to run, try walking. If after several more days of rest and/or easy walking and jogging, the injury does not show any improvement, you need to see your sports doctor again.

As for stretching a half-hour a day, that seems almost excessive. It's possible that by stretching too much or too hard, you may actually be aggravating your problem. As an experiment, stop stretching for a 72-hour period. See if that has any effect on your injury. It may not, and I'm not telling you to abandon stretching permanently, but it's worth a try.

Progressive Pain

Q: I'm 31 years old and have been running for about six years. A year and a half ago, I started to encounter problems with one hip. Nagging soreness would start about 5 to 6 miles into a run. I continued training but found the trigger point dropping from 4 to 3 to 2 miles, until finally, it was painful from the start. At that point, I took a month and a half off to recover. It didn't help. I sought the advice of a doctor, who was a marathoner. He suggested an insert in my right shoe to accommodate for a leg-length difference. He also told me to stretch. This didn't seem to help. The nagging pain continued.

I joined a health club so I could use its treadmill, and the pain retreated until I tried to push myself and run faster. Next, I shortened my stride, and that seemed to help. With a shorter stride, I can run longer, but I don't feel that I'm getting much benefit from my running. Also, any time I hit the trails or streets, the pain comes right back. I've now begun to feel the pain in my other hip. Sometimes, the pain shoots down to the back of my knee, causing a numbing sensation. I probably sound like a paranoid and hypochondriac, but my frustration level is getting the best of me. Any suggestions would be greatly appreciated.

A: Far from seeming like a paranoid or hypochondriac, you sound very rational. And you did everything right. You followed all the obvious strategies in seeking a cure, starting with rest, seeking medical help, stretching, and switching your training pattern—even your stride. To a point you succeeded, until you tried to raise your training level again (an understandable decision).

Desiring a second opinion, I discussed your case with Stan James, M.D., of Eugene, Oregon, the orthopedist who did the knee surgery on Joan Benoit Samuelson that led to her gold medal in the 1984 Olympic Marathon.

"The hip pain in the runner, particularly with radiating pain into the thigh, suggests the possibility of a low-back problem, even without actual back pain. This could also be a pyriformis syndrome (a small hip muscle that can sometimes irritate a portion of the sciatic nerve). A problem with the hip joint itself could be the culprit, or a chronic hamstring pull (up high) could also cause buttock pain." Although you already were seen by one doctor, considering the duration of the symptoms, Dr. James recommends that you consult an orthopedist.

Dr. James also recommends that runners suffering from back, hip, or other injuries should analyze their past running habits. "Most injuries are from training errors, which can be avoided in the future if you change your approach." Reducing mileage and intensity and substituting cross-training is one route strongly advised by Dr. James.

Dangers of Stretching

Q: I have been running for several years from 25 to 35 miles a week. One day not long ago, I started running and my knee was a bit sore. (I've never had knee problems in the past.) Halfway through an 8-mile run, I decided to give it a second stretch. After I was done stretching, the knee hurt so much I could barely walk. I iced the knee and have been resting it for almost a month. It seems fine until I try to exercise. Fast walking and running seem to hurt it. Could it be my running form?

A: A lot of people promote stretching as a means for avoiding injuries—and that's true to a point. But stretching too much, too hard, or at the wrong time can also cause injuries. I suspect that's what happened to you.

More than likely, you had slightly strained some tendon in or around the knee, possibly because of some hard training—or maybe for some reason totally unrelated to your running. You were on the edge of injury, and if you had taken a few days off, you might have never had a problem. But the knee was vulnerable. You thought that you were doing the right thing by stopping to stretch, and oops, you pulled something.

Regardless of my guess's correctness, you obviously are in pain and need to see a sports medicine professional who can feel the knee and tell you exactly what the problem is.

I doubt that your running form is the cause, but there may be some underlying biomechanical problems that will need correction. See what the doc says.

Break from Training

Q: I've been diagnosed with a stress fracture that is going to prevent me from doing any exercise for at least six weeks. I miss my daily running "fix," and I'm worried about losing fitness and gaining weight. What can I do?

A: Psychologist Jim Loehr, Ed.D., president of LGE Sport Science in Orlando, Florida, and author of *Toughness Training for Life*, offers some advice on how to maintain an upbeat attitude when you are unable to run.

Take time out. Use the injury to give your body and mind a rest. Relax. Don't fight the injury. Read a book. Spend more time with your children or spouse. Get caught up on your work. Return to running refreshed in spirit.

Rethink your training. What was the cause of the injury? Was it overtraining, or just bad luck? By figuring out why you got injured in the first place, you may be able to avoid it happening in the second place.

Get stronger. While rehabilitating, strengthen the wounded body part so that the injury won't happen again. Do some cross-training for total-body fitness.

Recharge your battery. It's easy to get in a rut while running. Time away from the sport will allow you to appreciate how much fun running can be. You'll enjoy running more when you return.

Re-examine your approach. Put running into perspective. Run too many marathons lately? Maybe it's time to shift your attention to shorter and faster distances. Or the reverse may be true. Maybe you need a period of time when you don't go near a starting line. Then again, pointing for a specific race may remotivate you. When you return, do something different.

Dr. Loehr recommends thinking of an injury not as bad luck, but as a breather: "an opportunity to reestablish balance in your personal and (running) life."

10

Feet and Shoes
Two Keys to Success

- Blisters
- Black Toes
- Morton's Toe
- Pronation
  and Supination
- Bunions
- Dry Feet

- The Old Soft Shoe
- Proper Fit
- Cross-Trainers
- Growing Boy
- Barefoot on the Track
- Shoes for Clydesdales

Feet, don't fail me now!" That used to be the cry of a certain comedian when escaping danger. Feet, unfortunately, frequently do fail runners. That's because the feet first contact the ground during the running stride and transmit the shock of landing (three or four times the body weight) upward through the ankles, calves, knees, thighs, hips, and even the upper body. It is because of what happens when the feet hit the ground that we get injured. If our feet, and the various bones and sinews emanating from those feet, function correctly, we suffer fewer injuries.

One way to limit ground shock, of course, is to purchase proper running shoes. Unless you plan to run barefoot (Abebe Bikila of Ethiopia won the gold medal in the 1960 Olympic Marathon unshod), your most important purchase as a runner is the pair of shoes you wear in workouts and races.

When people ask me questions about their feet, I usually suggest that they see a podiatrist, or foot doctor. Although orthopedists might disagree, podiatrists are the sports doctors of first choice for injured runners because of everything said above about ground contact causing injuries. Solve the problem at the foot, and you often can cure or prevent injuries to other parts of the body.

I don't receive many questions about shoes, mainly because **Runner's World** magazine has an advice columnist who specializes in providing information on running shoes, specifically which shoes are best for which runners. This colleague, Bob Wischnia, also supervises the frequent shoe reviews published in the magazine. The most comprehensive reviews are in our biannual "Shoe Buyer's Guide," usually in March and October.

Blisters

Q: I'm a beginning runner of about six months, doing 2.5 miles every other day. I'm developing calluses and blisters on the tips of some of my toes. Is this normal?

A: No, blisters definitely are not normal. I suspect that you may have narrow feet that slide forward in too-wide shoes and contact the fronts of the toeboxes. It is also possible that your shoes are too small, so check the fit. Some runners have biomechanical problems that cause their feet to impact the ground unevenly, although the first two reasons are more likely in your case. For treatment, consult a podiatrist.

Once you identify and solve the immediate problem, you can prevent future blisters by paying more attention to foot care. Your podiatrist can offer guidance, but Owen Anderson, Ph.D., editor of *Running Research News*, has some advice on the subject.

- Keep your feet dry, although foot powders may actually cause more friction.
- Wear insoles. Dr. Anderson suggests Spenco.
- Acrylic or polyester socks are better than cotton or wool.
- Shoe selection is important. Too-tight shoes may cramp the feet, whereas too-loose shoes may allow the feet to slide.
- Petroleum jelly reduces friction initially but, eventually, may cause more problems than it cures.
- The best bet may be moleskin, a covering that can be applied over the areas most likely to blister. It is available in most drugstores.

To this I would add that if you look in your shoe and identify the area that contacts the blister, you sometimes may find an imperfection that can be smoothed or removed.

Black Toes

Q: I just ran 16 miles for the first time. Everything was going great until about mile 14, when my toes started hurting. When I got home, I found that I have three black toenails. This has never happened to me before. What causes it and what can I do?

A: It never happened to you before because you never ran 16 miles before—at least in those shoes. Examine your shoes. You may have worn them out to the point where they no longer protect you. In fact, whenever you have blisters or problems with your feet such as this, the first thing you should do is look inside your shoes.

A lot of things happen when we press the edge of the envelope and train for a marathon, assuming that was why you were running 16 miles. Regardless, I'm going to suggest that one of three things may be wrong.

1. Your toeboxes are cramping your toes. (Shoes can shrink after you begin sweating in them.)
2. Your feet are too narrow for the type of shoes you wear, allowing your toes to slide forward.
3. Your feet swelled during the course of the long run, meaning the shoes no longer fit your feet as well as they did at mile 1.

In any case, you probably need a new pair of shoes and maybe a different style as well.

Your toes turned black because blood blisters formed beneath the nails. To drain the blood and relieve the pain, sterilize a needle and stick it through the nail and into the blister. I say that even though I would never perform the operation myself (even though I do with normal blisters). I would see my regular podiatrist and ask her to perform this operation. Her hands are steadier than mine, and I can close my eyes when she sticks the needle in my toenails. You'll heal much more quickly if you also get expert care, and your podiatrist may be able to suggest some long-range solutions after actually examining your feet—and shoes.

Morton's Toe

Q: I've had a terrible pain in the ball of my foot toward the large toes. I'm told that it's a form of tendinitis. I haven't run for five weeks. Now I'm running again and it seems okay, but it still hurts a bit. Ever hear of anything like this?

A: It sounds like you may have tendinitis or some similar injury. If someone diagnosed you as having that, I hope that he was a podiatrist or some similarly qualified sports medicine specialist and not merely another runner. What you have also could be a stress fracture, or it could be Morton's neuroma.

Look down at your foot and see if your second toe is longer than your big toe. That's Morton's foot, or Morton's toe, and reportedly 25 percent of the population has such a configuration, including me. The knuckles of my second toes rise above my other toes because they have been forced backward from contacting the front of the toebox. I've never had any major injuries because of this slight foot deformity. Runners with more pronounced deformities, however, can suffer problems, including nerve inflammation caused by pinched nerves, which is Morton's neuroma. Arch supports or orthotics might help. You probably do need to see a podiatrist for a more studied diagnosis, but in the meantime, you're back running after five weeks' rest. The question now is: Will the pain subside as you continue to run or will it return? If the latter happens, then it is time to take your case to a higher court of medicine.

Pronation and Supination

Q: I pronate severely. Over the years, running on and off, I have developed stress fractures in both tibia that simply will not go away. I now run with neoprene tubes around my shins to warm them and help with blood flow, and I have purchased some great shoes that control my feet. What would be a good program for me to use to get back to my 3 miles every other day? These fractures are really uncomfortable! Someone told me that I could have the scar tissue massaged away. Is that true and where do you go to get this done?

A: Before I answer your question, let me define what pronation is and how it differs from supination.

Pronation. When the outside of the foot contacts the ground, it rolls inward, which causes twisting in the lower leg. It's normal to pronate from the outside heel, across the bottom of the foot and toward the large toe, as the body moves forward until the foot is flat on the ground. Excessive pronation, though, can cause problems.

Supination. This is the opposite of pronation. After contact, the foot rolls outward from the inside of the heel, across the foot and toward the little toe. This foot movement might be considered less normal, and Joe Ellis, D.P.M., co-author of *Running Injury-Free*, believes that fewer than 2 percent of the population supinate. "Very few of them are distance runners," he says, "because their feet probably won't allow this type of activity."

If you pronate as badly as it seems—and I hate to suggest this—running may not be the sport for you. I'm assuming by now that you have been to a podiatrist who has prescribed orthotics but that they have not been able to cure your problem. And I would hope that whichever health experts you have seen suggested stretching exercises and told you all about ice and anti-inflammatories.

My suggestion is to modify your routine to encompass other fitness activities, limiting your running to a single, glorious day a week. Try cycling or swimming, and don't overlook the benefits of fitness walking. By blending walking and running, you might be able to find a better route to aerobic fitness.

Can scar tissue be massaged away? Massage certainly can help. I see a massage therapist every other week, but I'm not sure that would be enough for your problem. See if you can locate a good therapist who can give you 30-minute massages with the emphasis on your trouble spots. Hopefully, this will give you some relief, but unfortunately, there are some people who biomechanically might be better off in other fitness activities.

Bunions

Q: Bunions are my problem. I've been running only three years and the pain from both feet has increased over the last six months. A podiatrist recommends surgery. An orthopedist has suggested medicine to ease the pain, but it only helps a little. The recovery period from surgery is quite long, and I am very reluctant to do it. Can I overcome bunions and keep running?

A: I'm sure that you're not the first runner to suffer from bunions, nor will you be the first to overcome your problem. For those unfamiliar with the problem, a bunion is a deformity of the big toe that causes the first joint of the big toe to angle outward so that the tip of the toe points inward toward the smaller toes. A similar problem can affect the little toe. According to Lyle J. Micheli, M.D., director and co-founder of the Sports Medicine Division at Boston Children's Hospital, "Bunions are usually congenital, or genetic, though they may be brought on by an intensive running schedule."

My mother's feet were badly deformed by bunions, although I escaped her fate because I never attempted to cram my feet into high-heeled shoes that didn't fit properly. Despite Dr. Micheli's remarks, I don't believe that runners are more susceptible to bunions than those in other sports or those who don't run.

As for the cure, the standard treatment of ice, compression, and elevation may help relieve pain after your workouts. Anti-inflammatory drugs also may help, but this is really avoiding the issue. Eventually, it gets down to a decision as to whether you are willing to merely manage your pain or go for the surgery. That's a decision only you can make. You've done the right thing in consulting two specialists. It's now a question of which opinion you choose.

Dry Feet

Q: After doing a moderate amount of running, my heels are dry and cracking. What is the best therapy for this?

A: Dry skin is a problem that many runners must face, particularly in the winter. Inside air can become very dry, and the skin follows suit. Overdressing causes runners to sweat as much as on hot days during the summer, and the extra clothes trap moisture. Then gravity pulls everything down toward the shoes. If you notice that you finish each wintry workout with your socks soaking wet, that offers you a clue to a cure.

The first line of defense should be your socks. Light socks are best, and you should change them every day. Change shoes every day as well. Allowing your shoes 48 to 72 hours of rest lets them dry out. You also might try using talcum powder on your feet before you run to keep them dry. Standing in a hot shower for a long time after a workout may feel good, but it's not good for your skin anywhere on your body.

Once out of the shower, use a moisturizer on your feet: a light layer rubbed into the skin (not too much or your feet will slip in your shoes). You may want to reapply moisturizer several times a day to keep your skin soft.

The Old Soft Shoe

Q: I recently bought a new pair of running shoes, and I've noticed that whenever I run in them, my left ankle continuously cracks. It's been three weeks since I bought the shoes, and I've put about 75 miles on them, but the ankle is still cracking. Is this normal, and if not, could it cause any future damage to my body?

A: No, it's not normal, and you should try to determine the reason for the cracking sounds, particularly if you have not experienced this problem with previous shoes. Have you made any other changes in your routine, such as level of intensity or surfaces on which you run? My initial impression, as yours, is to fault the new shoes, but don't entirely rule out other causes.

Most likely, you have chosen a pair of shoes inappropriate for your particular running style or body configuration. My best guess is that your shoes are too soft and allow insufficient support, causing your ankle to twist (and crack) after the shoe first contacts the ground. A lot of runners seek soft (read "mushy") shoes under the mistaken belief that they are protecting themselves from injury by paying more than $100 for a high-tech product, when the opposite is true. Compare the firmness of your new shoes with previous pairs that caused you no trouble, assuming you still have them.

The fact that your ankle cracks may be for reasons other than foot-strike and may not cause future damage, but any twisting motion that begins below will eventually cascade up the leg, through the knee, and into the hips, leaving a wake of damage.

You should consider three sources for furthering your knowledge of shoe choice.

1. The store manager. The store may have sold you the wrong shoe. That's not necessarily the manager's fault, because his bright-eyed shoe salespeople should not be expected to analyze all of their customers' biomechanical problems (some, but not all). With 75 miles on the shoes, you probably won't be able to get a

refund, but you may get a better understanding of what went wrong with your choice.

When buying shoes in the future, it's a good idea to shop in a running store where the salesperson is someone who qualified last year for the Boston Marathon, instead of some teenager whose main sport is football or baseball. Be sure, also, that you try the shoes on in the store to make sure that they fit, and walk or run in them. Notice that I said "shoes." Try on both shoes since it's normal to have one foot slightly bigger than the other.

2. A podiatrist. It should be a podiatrist who runs and/or someone who knows and understands our sport. (Ask other runners for a recommendation.) He should be able to guide your shoe selection and let you know about any muscle imbalances that may need correction.

3. *Runner's World* magazine. Several times a year, the magazine publishes survey articles on running shoes, researched by Bob Wischnia. Bob works with Paul Carruzza, a shoe specialist who tests shoes for *Runner's World*. Nobody does a better job. The most thorough article by Bob and Paul usually appears in our special shoe issues in March and September. You can learn a lot about what shoes work for your type of foot and stride by thoroughly reading this issue. Since manufacturers constantly change model names and styles, it's not easy to keep up with the market, but Bob and Paul do a good job.

Proper Fit

Q: I am trying to lose 20 pounds, and I enjoy incorporating running into my walks. How long does it take for new shoes to feel right? I find that my foot falls asleep toward the end of my workouts.

A: Your shoes should feel right before you leave the store, otherwise don't buy them. One of the great myths is that you can break in a pair of uncomfortable shoes. It's not true. What gets broken in is your feet. Most of the reasonably priced shoes on today's market are well-designed and carefully manufactured. Most shoe companies realize that if they don't make good shoes, they won't sell a second pair to a customer, and there's more money to be made in repeat business than in one-time sales. So be fussy when you try shoes on at the store.

If your foot falls asleep, that suggests to me that you selected shoes that were too small. That's a common mistake made by runners, particularly beginning runners and women who don't want to admit that their feet are that big. The way running shoes are sized, you may need to choose a shoe a half- or full size larger than your normal street shoes. Determining the right size for your feet is essential if you don't want to have the problems you describe.

Cross-Trainers

Q: I'm getting ready to start running for the first time. I work at a department store and was able to get a pair of shoes at a good discount. When I got home, I discovered that they were cross-training shoes instead of running shoes. Can I still run in them?

A: You can as long as you don't run in them too far or too fast. Unless you've thrown away your receipt, I suggest that you exchange them for a pair of shoes specifically designed for running.

It's not a rap against cross-trainers, it's just that they're made for cross-training, which means those sports other than, or in addition to, running. The designers compromise some of the features that benefit runners or walkers, whose form of locomotion is straightforward. Cross-training shoes permit more sideway movement, like that found in racquetball or basketball. Cross-training shoes also work well if your principal activity is working out on a lot of machines at a health club, in which case you want your shoes to look fashionable as much as provide support and cushioning.

If you've already started wearing the shoes and can't take them back because they're scuffed, save them for those off days when you do cross-training or run only short distances. It's best to own and use more than one pair of shoes anyway. That permits you to alternate shoes, allowing them to dry out and regain their cushioning between workouts. Serious runners often have at least three active pairs of shoes, phasing out the oldest and most worn pair of shoes just as they are phasing in a new pair. Given that strategy, you can use a pair of cross-training shoes in your inventory, but you still need another pair designed specifically for running.

Growing Boy

Q: Since beginning to run about three months ago, I have found that my shoe size has increased one full size. An employee at a local shoe store told me that it could be the result of the constant pounding from jogging. Also, I think that my arches are falling as a result of running, even though I'm not that big at 6 feet, 160 pounds. I'm 24 and haven't grown in years.

A: Well, you're growing now, at least in the feet. It's not unusual for an individual's shoe size to increase after he starts to run, although an increase of one size does seem excessive. If you went to the gym and exercised on strength machines, you probably would expect your muscles to grow, so maybe you shouldn't be too fearful of some foot growth.

Three months is a short time, however. I suppose it's possible that your arches are falling, but why do you think so? Are your arches painful when you run?

For your own peace of mind, it's probably time to make an appointment with a podiatrist, whose advice I would trust more than that of an employee at a local shoe store. Even if nothing hurts, preventive medicine isn't a bad idea.

Take your running shoes so the podiatrist can check for excessive wear. Also take some of your older shoes to drive home the point that your feet indeed have grown. The podiatrist probably will tell you that they simply have spread to form a better platform for your running. Be wary if the podiatrist tries to put you into a pair of orthotics right away. They are expensive and can be an example of overkill if you're not yet feeling any pain.

Barefoot on the Track

Q: I recently went out of town and hoped to do some speed-work after my day's business. Unfortunately, when I unpacked, I realized that I had forgotten my running shoes. After talking it over with my training partner, I decided to run on the rubberized track barefoot. It was a lot of fun, and there are no apparent aftereffects. Was that a bad idea?

A: In 1972, I set an American masters record for the 5000 meters on the rubberized track at the Crystal Palace in London running barefoot. The record lasted nearly 25 years until it was broken at the 1997 Drake Relays by Steve Plasencia. So I don't think that it was a bad idea. You do need a soft track or some other soft surface such as a golf course to train safely barefoot.

Ethiopian Abebe Bikila caused a stir among the shoe companies when he won the 1960 Olympic Marathon in Rome running barefoot, and that was on pavement. That started a fad of barefoot running, and later during that decade, a high school in Indiana won the state cross-country championships with a team of barefoot runners. (The practice later was banned by the state high school association, perhaps worried about liability.) More recently in the 1980s, South African Zola Budd ran barefoot, then she received a contract from a shoe company and saw the wisdom of wearing shoes.

Theoretically, running barefoot (or in lightweight shoes) can allow you to run faster. Reportedly, the difference between a training shoe that weighs 11 ounces and a racing shoe that weighs 7 ounces can be as much as 40 seconds for a 10-K runner with a best time of 40:00; a marathoner would save a minute for every hour he ran. Given that data, the ultimate racing shoe may be bare feet. According to Thomas McMahon, Ph.D., the Gordon McKay professor of applied mechanics at Harvard University: "The spring of the arch of the human foot returns 70 percent of the energy that goes into it. Even a high-quality running shoe returns only 40 to 50 percent of the energy required to compress it in a simulated running step."

I ran a few races barefoot, although I don't necessarily recommend this for every runner; one reason we wear shoes is to encapsulate the feet to avoid injury. More runners, however, should consider doing at least some barefoot training.

At the 1997 American College of Sports Medicine meeting, I got into a conversation with Michael Fredericson, M.D., of the Stanford Sports Medicine Program. Dr. Fredericson works with the Stanford cross-country teams, which had both won NCAA titles the previous fall. Dr. Fredericson has the Stanford runners run at least 2 miles a week barefoot in order to strengthen their feet. One problem, he says, is that we cram our feet into over-cushioned shoes, sometimes with orthotics, and our foot muscles become weak. So keep up the barefoot running when you have an opportunity, but don't do it on concrete or in the winter. Done in moderation, barefoot running can probably help prevent foot injuries.

Shoes for Clydesdales

Q: As a 6-foot-4, 235-pound runner, what are the best types of shoes to wear for running?

A: Not being anywhere near your size, I contacted Keith Stone of Winston-Salem, North Carolina, who helps coach other heavier runners (known in runners' jargon as Clydesdales). My initial reaction from previous discussions with heavyweight runners was that more important than any training schedule was their footwear.

Stone agreed: "What I've discovered from working with other Clydesdales is that the same training techniques work, but training mistakes seem to be less forgiving. Because of the dynamics of biomechanics, each pound of upper-body weight provides 7 pounds of stress on the limbs of the lower body. Weigh 20 pounds more and it creates 140 pounds of pressure. That's why items like shoes are so important."

One of the early shoe-company pioneers, who retired a millionaire before age 40, once told me that runners should wear the lightest possible shoe that they can tolerate without getting injured. He said that despite the fact that the sales of light shoes, which cost less, would decrease the value of his stock options.

But that doesn't pertain to you. When visiting the shoe stores, you should skip past feather shoes to the shelf with the motion-control shoes, to use the name favored by *Runner's World* magazine in its biannual shoe buyer's guide. Motion-control shoes are defined as "the most rigid, control-oriented running shoes. Designed to limit overpronation (or slow the rate at which a runner overpronates), motion-control shoes are generally heavy but very durable and offer stability and maximum medial support." Yes, heavier shoes may slow you down in a 5-K race, but that's why they have separate divisions for Clydesdales.

11

Women
Be Your Best

- Estrogen
- Breast Cancer
- Old Wives' Tale
- Menstrual Cycles
- Amenorrhea
- Chafing Heart Monitor

- Safety
- Running after Pregnancy
- When You Gotta Go
- Fertility
- Stress Fracture
- Woman's Best Friend

Each weekend during the summer, when not traveling, I try to run with the Chicago Area Running Association's marathon training class. Two colleagues and I teach the class to prepare runners (many of them first-timers) for The LaSalle Banks Chicago Marathon, which is run in October. The class has been enormously successful, growing from 300 to 750 participants in four years.

Probably a majority of our class members are women. My wife, Rose, noticed this when she joined us one Saturday in August for a workout along the Chicago lakefront. Rose left early, walking, and saw our different pace groups both coming and going. "You have a lot of women in your class!" she told me later. It wasn't an accusation, but more a statement of fact. I confessed to her, "Yes, and a lot of them are young women." During my lectures I had noticed that many of the women sitting in the audience seemed to be in their twenties.

I'm not sure whether more women than men are running these days. The ratio of men versus women in road races remains two-to-one, perhaps because men seem more drawn to competition than women. Surveys of *Runner's World* magazine readers suggest that our audience has become increasingly more interested in health and fitness rather than the racing scene, and maybe that's because of a feminine influence. A few races do attract more women than men; Bloomsday in Spokane, Washington, is one example. Some races are designed exclusively for women, such as the Race for the Cure, which raises money to fight breast cancer.

If women predominate in our marathon training class, maybe it is because they realize that one way to improve is to take a class. Women also send more questions to my online "Ask the Expert" column than you would expect from America Online's predominantly male demographics. Most of the questions I get are not related to gender, but a few are about problems exclusive to women runners.

Estrogen

Q: I am a 44-year-old female going through menopause, and my doctor wants me to take estrogen therapy. Since I'm a nurse, I know most of the side effects. I am most concerned about how estrogen may affect my running. I usually do well in local races, having run 19:35 for a 5-K this summer.

A: Different people react differently to different drugs. Estrogen is no exception. Some women welcome the cessation of periods that comes with menopause. Others don't like the hot flashes or weight gain. Also to be considered is the effect estrogen might have on your risk factors for cancer, heart disease, and loss of bone density.

Your question arrived just as I was leaving for the annual meeting of the American College of Sports Medicine (ACSM). At the meeting, I was able to discuss the subject with several ACSM members, including E. Randy Eichner, M.D., of the University of Oklahoma Health Science Center in Oklahoma City.

Dr. Eichner suggested that there should be no performance loss and no gain if you choose to take estrogen. In taking estrogen, you are merely replacing what you normally would begin losing as you age. He noted that birth control pills containing estrogen have a neutral (or slightly positive) effect on performance for young women. There is an increased risk of cancer among some women who embrace estrogen therapy but a decreased risk for heart disease and osteoporosis. You should look to your family history to guide you in your decision. Currently, the benefits of estrogen therapy seem to outweigh the negative effects, but Dr. Eichner concedes that all the answers are not yet in. The one area where estrogen might affect performance negatively would be if it caused you to increase body fat, but presumably you would begin to notice any weight gain.

Breast Cancer

Q: I am a 35-year-old female who finished chemotherapy treatments for stage-two breast cancer about 14 months ago. My best times in the year or so before my diagnosis were 38:20 for the 10-K and 3:06 for the marathon. Since my diagnosis, I have worked back up to bests of 39:18 in the 10-K and 1:27:01 for the half-marathon. I plan to continue to train with the hope of returning to, or exceeding, my previous level. What am I doing to my immune system by training intensively? Do you have any information about the effects of training on the immune system and whether or not too much racing may trigger another bout with cancer?

A: One of the most knowledgeable individuals when it comes to the effects of exercise on the immune system (both positive and negative) is David C. Nieman, Dr.P.H., of Appalachian State University in Boone, North Carolina. Dr. Nieman became interested in the subject of colds and upper respiratory infections after he caught the flu at the peak of his training for a marathon. Surveying runners in the Los Angeles Marathon, he discovered an increase in upper respiratory infections both immediately before and immediately after the race that could be linked to high-mileage training. (Run more than 60 miles a week, Dr. Nieman discovered, and you risk compromising your immune system.)

So, intense training may be dangerous for someone with a history of cancer, although immunity suppression may be linked more to sudden change rather than mileage. Suddenly increase mileage and intensity and you may be at more risk. I'm not sure whether Dr. Nieman or I can offer definitive proof, but we suspect that if you gradually, and intelligently, increase your training to that 60-mile (or whatever) level, your immune system probably will not be impaired and you can maximize your chances of achieving a peak performance. That's simply smart training.

Laboratory studies with mice at Waterloo University in Canada, however, did indicate that strenuous exercise actually spread injected breast cancer cells through the body more quickly than in mice who rested or exercised moderately. Dr. Nieman conducted a study with eight women two years after they had been successfully treated for breast cancer. He had them exercise moderately (brisk walking, some resistance exercise) for two months, then measured the function of an important immune cell that does kill some types of cancer cells. "The two months of moderate exercise training did not enhance or suppress their function," Dr. Nieman concluded. In other words, moderate exercise ended up being a neutral factor regarding immunity, even while making the women fitter.

In continuing studies, Dr. Nieman discovered that when he ran male and female distance runners long and hard in the lab, their immune functions were suppressed for 3 to 12 hours afterward. He feels that this explains the increased risk runners have for colds and sore throats after heavy exertion. Whether or not this would have any bearing on the immune systems of post-cancer patients, he does not know. (Most cancer experts feel that the immune system probably has little to do with breast cancer; hormonal influences appear to be more important.)

Dr. Nieman concludes: "If the breast cancer is active and spreading, it may not be wise to exercise intensely. It may cause the cancer to spread through the body more. However, in a successfully treated patient such as yourself, I would have a hard time believing that hard exercise is going to negatively affect your survival rate. There is evidence that lean and active women have less breast cancer than sedentary, overweight women. I would surmise that vigorous exercise might lower the risk of reoccurrence in the same way that it prevents the breast cancer in the first place."

As to whether or not you should race, I see no reason why not. To be on the safe side, check with your doctor first. It's all a matter of odds, and they seem to be on your side.

Old Wives' Tale

Q: I've recently started jogging, and a few people have told me that it may harm a woman's internal organs. Is there any truth to this?

A: No, there's no truth to it. It's an old wives' tale—or, more properly, an old husbands' tale.

Joan Ullyot, M.D., wrote in her pioneering book, *Women's Running*, that if anybody had to worry about their organs being jostled by jogging, it should be males, not females.

So keep on striding. By the way, if anyone tells you that your uterus will drop, there's little danger of that either.

Menstrual Cycles

Q: I am training for my first marathon, and my training has gone well. The week prior to my menstrual period, however, I often become dizzy during my runs and feel very fatigued. My normal training speed is 8:00-miles, but before my menstrual period, I have difficulty running a 9:00 pace. Once I get my period, my energy improves over the week until I am back to normal. Unfortunately, the marathon will come during my tired week. Do you have any idea what may be wrong, or what I could do to avoid fatigue during the marathon?

A: Your symptoms are a lot more normal than you suspect. I consulted Diane Palmason, who runs a series of running camps for women in Colorado and British Columbia. She has created a training program for women to accommodate their menstrual cycles and often discusses this topic with women during focus groups.

Palmason discovered that there were considerable differences in the ways that women modified training to accommodate their menstrual cycles and that women often experienced a range of effects from month to month.

"The experience of lowered energy is not unique," she says. "In discussions about the effects of the menstrual cycle on running at our camps, for every woman who says 'no problems,' there are two others who will describe a variety of changes that directly affect their training and performances. The range of differences between women is significant, but premenstrual lethargy is quite common.

"At age 59, I have not been bothered by such symptoms for some time, but my partner, Maureen Custy, became aware that the levels of her iron stores (ferritin) drop significantly in the days before her period. She now takes steps to prevent that by taking an iron supplement at that time. As for what you can do, given the timing of your cycle and the marathon, my first advice would be to do a very good taper and eat healthy. Include some red meat in your diet if you are not a vegetarian.

If you are a vegetarian, look into a supplement that is a complex that includes folic acid, vitamin C, and iron.

"Then relax. Give yourself some positive talk about the fact that you have trained well and will perform well. Worrying about your cycle could actually be like a self-fulfilling prophecy since our bodies are so responsive to what's going on in our minds. You may consider having a blood test for an anemia profile: not just measuring your hemoglobin but your TIBC, ferritin, and other factors related to having healthy red blood."

Amenorrhea

Q: I am a 16-year-old female who is very involved in sports. While participating in sports, I do not have my period. But when the season is over, and I have not worked out for a while, my period begins. Is this normal? How would not having my period affect me? I began menstruating when I was 13, so this has been going on for about three years.

A: Sometimes women runners lose their periods if they train excessively, which drops their percentage of body fat below what may be considered a healthy level. There is no exact number because people differ so much, but when women get much below 12 percent body fat, a series of problems may develop. One such problem is amenorrhea, which is a cessation of the menstrual cycle.

You need to consider the following questions: What is your level of body fat? Do you follow a good nutritional routine or do you just pick at your food? Have you bought the low-fat approach to diet so much that you're not getting enough nutrients? It is possible that the cessation of your period may be caused by a number of factors other than exercise.

Young female runners who attempt to lose weight in a misguided attempt to improve performance are more prone than men to eating disorders, and one of the problems is the amenorrhea you describe. Here are some of the problems you need to be concerned about.

- Almost three times higher incidence of stress fractures
- Premature osteoporosis that can affect your bone health

- Possibly a higher risk of heart disease
- An inability to conceive easily (just because your periods have ceased doesn't mean that you can't get pregnant)

I don't mean to alarm you; I'm glad you were intelligent and concerned enough to ask the question. Unfortunately, some young women might look on cessation of their menstrual cycles as an advantage, removing discomfort. But the long-range health problems involved with amenorrhea are not worth ignoring.

Chafing Heart Monitor

Q: I have begun to train with a heart monitor, but unfortunately, it chafes at the point where it contacts my sports bra, particularly on long runs. Is there any way to overcome this problem?

A: I posed your question to Kate Kinney, an experienced middle- and long-distance runner who coaches in the Denver area. Here is what she had to say.

"Unfortunately, many women regularly experience this discomfort, so you are not alone. I have had difficulty using a heart rate monitor with a sports bra. My first suggestion is to see if wearing some type of soft, nonchafing shirt under the bra and heart rate monitor helps. You will have to wet the area of the shirt under the heart rate monitor. If the weather permits, a lightweight vest over everything may make you feel less self-conscious.

"My other suggestions include taping padding to the edges of the monitor and straps, or using moleskin or some of the burn and blister pads available at drugstores under the problem areas. Even though it is tough to get off, sports tape applied directly on the skin will help with chafing. Also, consider seeking a sports bra with a wide band, since that will limit movement. Not all sports bras are equal, and you may need to experiment to find the one that works best for you, regardless of fashion."

Kinney also recommends learning how to use perceived effort and breathing rates as cues for training in addition to the heart monitor. "This will give any sore areas time to heal in between heart rate monitor workouts," she suggests.

Safety

Q: I love to run, but none of my friends will run with me, and my mom insists that I not run by myself. Her main concern is my safety. What are some safeguards that I can follow to put her at ease?

A: Admittedly, we live in a dangerous society, but hundreds of thousands of runners in America go running out the door and return safely each day without being molested or getting hit by a car. Considering statistics related to traffic accidents, you're probably safer outside a car than inside it. The more runners who seize the roads (*carpe viam*, being the motto of the Dead Runners Society, a message group on the Internet), the safer it will be for all of us, as there is strength in numbers.

You should sit down with your mother and see if the two of you can come up with some safe times and places where you can run. The track at school is one such place. Public parks frequented by other runners, at times when those runners are using those parks, is another place. Low-speed-limit roads usually are safe, but be sure to run facing traffic. Anywhere in daylight when and where there are others walking, hiking, or biking is a safe place to run. Or consider joining a team or a running club. I hope that your mom can be made to understand that running can be a very safe and healthy activity if done at the right time and in the right place. I hope that you will also realize that she has a legitimate reason to be concerned about your safety and not protest too much if she says, "Absolutely not. You can't run there!"

Running after Pregnancy

Q: My wife was a runner in college. We've been married for two years, and she hasn't run for nearly that length of time. She is now eight months pregnant and is already planning her "comeback" into running once the baby is born. What are your suggestions about starting back slowly and when it is safe to begin again?

A: I'm hoping that her body will tell her when it's safe to start back. Tell your wife to forget that she once ran in college and think like a beginner. Even though hospitals routinely kick women out the door 24 to 48 hours after delivery, it does take time for the body to heal. Walking might provide a better start-up exercise than running.

As important as what she does is what you do. There is a tremendous amount of stress associated with a young infant, and it is important for you to help your wife. The more help you can provide, the more it will make it easier for her to run. Maybe it's only offering a half-hour of babysitting a day while she goes for a walk around the block, or takes a nap. Whatever it is, just do it.

The fact that your wife didn't run during pregnancy isn't a problem but could slow down her return to running. Maybe you should consider buying her a baby jogger. When the child gets older, she may enjoy having him or her along for the run.

When You Gotta Go

Q: I am a beginning-level female runner. I have read a lot about hydration and have one difficulty with drinking lots of water. I try to drink water throughout the day. Not long after I start to run, I feel the urge to urinate. Do you have any suggestions to keep this from happening? What do racers, particularly women, do during training and marathons to prevent this?

A: You accepted too freely the idea that everybody needs to drink lots of water. We do, but the body only can absorb so much before it starts getting rid of it. What you need to do is manage your balance better. You want to be fully hydrated, but not so much that it sends you screaming into the nearest gas station.

Experiment with how much you drink and when you drink it. Usually, I advise marathon runners to stop drinking two hours before they race, otherwise they will be eliminating some of that fluid through their kidneys after they start rather than as sweat. I also advise them to resume drinking 5 minutes before the race begins and to continue throughout the race, since usually that fluid will go right into their air-conditioning systems, emerging as sweat.

But not always. I've run several marathons where I was running at a pace slower than normal yet drinking at the same level, and I overflowed. Since I didn't care about my time, ducking into the bushes wasn't a worry. It will take some time before you discover how to manage your fluid intake and elimination.

Fertility

Q: Until a month or so ago, I was running a maximum of 28 miles a week. I have since stopped because I am trying to get pregnant and felt that this was interfering with my ovulation cycles. Also, I recently had a miscarriage and blamed it on excessive exercising and overheating my body. I asked my doctor, but she did not give it much attention. I would appreciate any advice you could give.

A: Twenty-eight miles a week does not seem like an excessive amount of running. That's only slightly more than the average mileage for the readers of *Runner's World* magazine, according to surveys. But you didn't tell me where you were coming from. For someone who had started to run just a month or two ago, a jump to 28 miles a week would be a lot. For a more competitive runner who was used to 50- and even 100-mile weeks, it could be relaxation time. The body usually accommodates well to loads placed on it, as long as those loads are not excessive.

It also depends on whether or not running is the only "excess" in your life. You didn't give me any information as to what else you might be doing in the way of exercise, such as cycling or lifting weights or attending aerobics classes. Diet also can have a major influence, particularly among those trying to lose or maintain weight. For example, if you were following a very restrictive diet in an attempt to maintain an artificially low weight for your body type, that could have a negative impact on your health and cause cessation of menstruation. Other activities, involving family and work, also may be placing extra stress on your body. Only you can tell.

Certainly, women fail to get pregnant for all sorts of reasons that are unrelated to exercise. And women get pregnant even while running high-mileage routines. Everybody is different. The miscarriage may have been from the running, but as your gynecologist would tell you, there could be multiple other reasons for your present inability to conceive.

I did discuss your case with several physicians and exercise scientists to see what they thought, and their comments mirrored my thoughts. One clue is in the menstrual cycle. Are your periods normal? A frequent exerciser who had only four or five periods a year would fall outside normal. But someone whose periods came regularly every four weeks, but varied in length, might also be said to have abnormal cycles. As you can see, there's a lot we don't know about the miracle of birth, so ceasing to run may or may not do the trick for you.

Stress Fracture

Q: I am 46, not menopausal, and have recently had a pelvic stress fracture. Now I have been diagnosed with a "pre-osteoporosis" condition. I've been running again for about five months (with my doctor's okay), and I love it, but I am terrified of getting hurt again and having to stop. I run 3 miles a day, about five days a week, and so far, no problems. I'll be doing my first 5-K in a couple of weeks. Am I pushing too hard?

A: I don't think so, but what does your body tell you? Our bodies are good at sending us pain signals when they are being abused. The fact that your doctor cleared you to run again is a good sign. As for that 5-K, no problem. You're already running 3 miles regularly. I suspect with the thrill of the race, you'll be able to cover the extra 140 yards or so without too much extra stress. Just start near the back row and run your usual training pace.

If you have a pre-osteoporosis condition, hopefully that will motivate you to do a few other things to improve your bone density. Running isn't enough. Hopefully, your doctor already gave you this advice, but maybe I can underline it. A lot of stress fractures are caused by poor nutrition. You need to not merely add calcium to your diet (skim milk, for example) but also you need to get the rest of your nutritional house in order.

Were there any biomechanical problems that contributed to the fracture? Perhaps you and your doctor discussed this, but a lot of upper-leg injuries begin where the foot hits the ground. Just to be safe, you might consider making an appointment with a podiatrist—and take your running shoes so he can examine them for any unusual wear. Sometimes something as simple as better shoe selection can prevent problems from developing.

You also need to do some strength training to build your bones, and I hope your doctor offered some advice as to which exercises might be most helpful for you, particularly in the "core" section of the body. At least until you become used to strength training, machine weights are safer than free weights. Calisthenics in which you use your own body for resistance are good as well. There are also some excellent exercise machines that combine upper- and lower-body movements. I recommend doing strength training at least two days a week, either in addition to your running or in place of it on those two days.

If you combine aerobic training with strength training and good nutrition, and get your biomechanical act in order, you will look back 40 years from now and consider your recent stress fracture as a warning signal that caused you to make lifestyle changes that resulted in lifelong good health.

Woman's Best Friend

Q: I'm a female, and I would feel safer if I were running with a dog. Do you know what breeds of dogs would be good for running? I have a German Shepherd, and I currently run 4 miles a day, five times a week.

A: German Shepherds make great running companions. So do Labradors and Golden Retrievers. Large, long-legged dogs tend to perform better than short-legged dogs, to nobody's surprise.

But you can't suddenly pull a dog away from his cozy spot in front of the fireplace and expect him to run 4 miles with you on the first day. Dogs need to be trained to run long distances, just like humans do. Once that dog has been trained to run 4 miles, he will be able to outrun you. He also will start to get nervous and anxious when he knows it's time to go for his daily run.

Davia Anne Gallup, author of *How to Run with Man's Best Friend*, offers some additional tips on how you can help your pet become a good training partner.

1. Keep your dog on a leash when you run, so you can control the animal's gait effectively.
2. When forced to run on streets, run facing traffic with your dog in the heel position on your left side; the dog is less likely to interfere with cars.
3. Be consistent with your commands and use lots of praise.
4. When crossing busy intersections, stop, tell your dog to sit, then proceed when clear.
5. Because of traffic considerations, early morning or evening is naturally a better time to run.
6. Wear light-colored clothing and/or reflective gear in the dark, including a reflective collar for your dog.
7. Before starting, let your dog relieve itself. Be discreet and respect other people's property.

8. Traffic-free roads or soft paths make the best running surfaces for dogs. Concrete and blacktop should be avoided, especially during summer months when these surfaces can get very hot.

9. Many running tracks and other areas, such as beaches, do not allow dogs. Respect the rules.

10. Never enter a race with your dog without getting the approval of the race director. Doing so would be inconsiderate to runners who fear dogs or might trip over one.

12

Aging Runners
Master Longevity

- **Slowing Down**
- **Life Changes**
- **Maximizing Performance**
- **Maximum Heart Rate**
- **Back to Running**
- **Turning 40**

- **Recovery Strategies**
- **Look Far Ahead**
- **Three-Day Schedule**
- **Lifting Weights**
- **Comparing Oneself to Others**
- **When to Quit**

During the summer of 1957, I ran the mile in the Central American Athletic Union track and field championships on the cinder track at the University of Chicago's Stagg Field. Only six entered, but it was a tough field. Ted Wheeler and Phil Coleman had represented the United States in the Olympic Games the year before. Jim Bowers, then a freshman at the University of Illinois, had set a national high school mile record the previous year. Dick Pond, another collegian, would place high in the NCAA Championships in a year or two. The sixth runner had never broken 5:00 for the mile before and was basically mismatched.

So was I—although I didn't want to admit it. I hung on to Ted and Phil's pace for three of the four laps. When they kicked, I was left in the dust, although I did finish third in a personal record of 4:13.6, which sounded faster then than it does now.

That was my high-water mark in the mile, an event I didn't run that often, at least in top competition. I was 26 years old and just beginning to learn how to train. Three years later, I placed fifth at the 1960 Olympic Trials in the 3000-meter steeplechase and four years after that, fifth (first American) in the 1964 Boston Marathon in 2:21:55. By then I was 33 years old, and although I would continue to compete as a masters athlete, all my personal records came between the ages of 26 and 33. The only other runner from that Stagg Field mile to continue as a masters was Jim Bowers, who after two decades of relative inactivity, set a number of American track and road masters records.

Aging is part of the normal human experience. So is running progressively slower as you age. Not all athletes handle this situation well. They don't want to admit that they are not as fast in their forties as they were in their thirties and twenties. Others of us recognize that each birthday offers an opportunity to set personal records in new single-age categories. While preparing this book, I ran a 1500-meter race at the World Veterans' Athletics Championships in Durban, South Africa, more for fun than because I thought that I might win a medal. I felt as fast as at Stagg Field four decades before. I just didn't look at my watch after I finished.

Slowing Down

Q: I have done several marathons and many half-marathons, and I cannot improve my times anymore. I did some interval training during my most recent race buildup, which helped me to keep an 8:00-mile pace for the first 8 miles, then I really slowed down. What's the secret? At 47, though very healthy, will I ever be able to run, say, a 1:35 half-marathon?

A: Probably not. Slowing down is a fact of life. Somewhere in our thirties, most people reach a peak of strength and endurance and then begin to slow down. That's why the Boston Athletic Association makes allowances for people over 35 qualifying for its marathon. I've known a few individuals who started running in their thirties or forties who continued to set personal records into their fifties and even sixties. But that's because they gradually increased their training or learned to train more efficiently.

For a quarter-century, I have participated in an ongoing study on the effects of aging, supervised by Michael L. Pollock, Ph.D., director of the Center for Exercise Science at the University of Florida in Gainesville. Dr. Pollock began studying a group of two dozen athletes, most of whom he first tested at the National Masters Championships in 1971. That was my first year as a master, so I am the youngest of the group. Almost all of us are still alive a quarter-century later, and half of us are still competing.

At 5- and 10-year intervals, Dr. Pollock invited us back to his laboratories for extensive tests, sometimes lasting two to three days. During the first decade, some of us seemed to defy Father Time. Aggressive training allowed us to maintain our high maximum oxygen capacity scores. Though our fitness level remained much higher than the general public's, we all eventually showed a decline, which Dr. Pollock identified as 5 percent through our forties, 5 to 10 percent through our fifties, and 10 to 15 percent through our sixties. Declines become even more steep after that, though this fit group continues to maintain its level above that of the general public.

My fastest marathon at age 65 was more than an hour slower than my all-time best. I understand that I'll never be able to run in the 2:20s again, maybe not in the 3:20s either. It's partly a matter of the body aging, partly a matter of motivation.

That doesn't mean that you can't be the best *you* for this particular time of your life. Taking your focus off time will actually allow you to beat Father Time.

Life Changes

Q: I am 41 years old and have been running for 13 of the last 15 years. I was a serious road racer until I retired from competitive running when my son reached Little League age. While coaching his team, I ran only for fitness. Eventually, I had to give that up because coaching took too much of my time. Four years ago, I quit coaching and resumed running about 25 to 30 miles a week. I am much slower now, and my last marathon was 10 years ago.

Sometimes I miss competition and the training, especially things like the afterglow of a good 22-mile training run. I get depressed when I review old log books and see how good I used to be. I just can't turn my legs over like I used to. Still, there is a lot to be said for pure running: fewer injuries and less tension about setting personal records. I feel a certain level of enjoyment when I take the short drive out of the city to run my favorite courses without worrying about a Saturday race. While I am out there, I think about my fellow runners at the track grinding out quarters. Will I ever be content at this stage? Have you been through it?

A: You sound pretty content right now. I feel the same about Sunday runs in the Indiana Dunes State Park with fellow members of the Dunes Running Club. Don't get me wrong: I still race on the track and on the road and do hill repeats and interval 400s. But if I had to choose between those Sunday runs and setting more world, American, and personal records, it would be an easy choice. There is a certain purity to each day's run that transcends superficial race results.

I'm not certain I ever reached your philosophical depths in comparing now with yesterday, but the point is that you aren't trying to relive your past. I commend you for taking time out from your running to spend more time with your son, and for returning to your first love, running. I suggest that you focus on the now rather than the once-was. Sit down and make a list of all the things about running you like and things you still enjoy doing—or want to do. Part of that list is already in your question above. Pick up one of the many books about running by George Sheehan, M.D. He was *Runner's World* magazine's philosopher and tackled the same doubts you are having. Maybe it will help whenever memories of those old training logs threaten to fog your view of the present.

Maximizing Performance

Q: I have been an avid runner since I was 28, but I've been on a steady decline since I peaked at 38. It seems that my recovery time is the key. I can't train as hard since I can't recover as quickly. Do you have any training tips that would allow me to maximize my performance at age 46?

A: What is happening to you happens to all of us. Somewhere toward the end of our thirties, the curve turns downward on performance. I ran some of my faster races in my forties (notice that I didn't say "fastest"), but that was only because I knew more about training, and my body's reactions to training, than I did in my twenties and thirties. Here are three things to incorporate into your weekly training.

1. Program more rest days. One day of rest between hard workouts may not be enough. You may need to program two or

three easy days so that you can run at a high peak of intensity when you do run hard. Intensity is the secret to performance at all age levels.

2. Cross-train more. On those in-between days, use other sports to maintain and build your aerobic efficiency. Swimming and cycling are good alternate activities. Don't overlook the value of a good walk.

3. Do more strength training. As we age, we lose muscle mass and gain fat, even when our weight remains the same. One way to combat this is to do strength training using both machines and free weights.

Maximum Heart Rate

Q: I have read that maximum heart rate is basically a hereditary trait and can't be increased, but that it decreases with age. To what extent does my maximum heart rate affect my ability as a runner? Is it going to prevent me from improving speed and/or endurance? Also, how fast will it decrease? Should I expect declines in speed and endurance now that I am 46 years old? I am just starting to use a heart rate monitor.

A: Increasing your maximum heart rate is not the trick; you need to improve your ability to train at a level close to that maximum heart rate for longer periods of time. "Performance cannot entirely be linked to heart rates," suggests David L. Costill, Ph.D., director of the Human Performance Laboratory at Ball State University in Muncie, Indiana. "Some of the most successful distance runners have had relatively low maximum heart rates." When people begin to exercise, their resting heart rates often decline as their hearts become more efficient in pumping oxygen to the muscles. I'm not sure that their maximum heart rates increase as much as does their ability to achieve their potential. For many unfit individuals, attempting to attain a maximum heart rate is to risk sudden death.

My maximum heart rate for most of my running career was near 160. (My resting pulse rate was as low as 30.) Exercise scientists, however, will tell you that you cannot entirely predict performance by measuring heart rates. Cardiovascular capacity is only one factor that determines a good long-distance athlete. Everyone varies, and everyone varies in their reactions to training. Yes, your maximum heart rate will decrease gradually as you age. My current maximum heart rate (as measured at the Cooper Clinic in the spring of 1997) is 150. That's a decline of only 10 beats per minute over a period of four decades, much less than most formulas would predict and barely significant in the realm of exercise science. I'm running much more slowly now, but not entirely because of my maximum heart rate.

Back to Running

Q: Do you have training suggestions for a 50-year-old ex-runner, who, after a year's layoff, wants to get into some kind of training routine again? Do I start again as I have in the past, or should I treat my older body differently?

A: A little bit of both. You have to forget at least some of what you learned in your previous life as a runner and think like a beginner again—at least until you get back to near your previous level.

The rule of thumb that many exercise scientists go by is for every day you detrain, it takes two days to retrain. In other words, it may take you two years to build back up to near the point where you were before you took that year off. Hopefully, that won't discourage you from coming back. Just be cautious doing it.

Also, it makes sense to schedule regular physical examinations. You may want to do so now, and make sure that the exam includes an exercise stress test. I say that not to scare you, but as a reminder that regular exams every two to three years can prevent bad things from happening.

Turning 40

Q: I've competed at the national level for many years, but my career has been up and down with no consistency. The problem has been sciatica. First my right leg, then left. I've taken time off, gone to a chiropractor on a regular basis, and gotten massages—all to no avail. Now all of a sudden, I have developed pain in the groin area on both sides of my legs. I thought maybe my lower stomach muscles were weak, but I do stomach crunches on a regular basis and don't believe this to be the problem. Since I turn 40 in October, I have a very good chance to compete on the national level as a masters runner if I'm not relegated to the rocking chair. Any thoughts?

A: What you describe are typical overuse injuries. All that running at the national level can take a toll on the body. The miles do add up. Sciatica can be a nagging problem, and sometimes there is no cure. I could suggest some exercises, but what you probably need to do is reevaluate the training that has led to your successes—and failures. If you kept diaries, what were you doing before the injuries? What were you doing before your very best performances? Don't look only in the weeks before those injuries and performances; look months before. What patterns can you discover about how you trained for success?

That doesn't mean that you can't continue to train the same way, but you may need to make modifications based on what you learned over the past several decades as a runner. You may surprise yourself by what you may be able to accomplish as a master. I was able to train at a high level into my late forties, and even ran my second-fastest marathon (after a series of 100-mile weeks) at age 49. But I can't do that training anymore. Sit down and rethink your training. Maybe you need to program in more rest or substitute cross-training for some of your running. If you want to continue to compete on the national masters level, some modifications will be needed, otherwise the injuries will continue to hold you back.

Recovery Strategies

Q: Despite a regular program of stretching and cross-training, it seems that I can't avoid hamstring injuries. I am in my mid-forties and currently am hobbled by that problem. I run 40 to 65 miles per week. Unfortunately, my training is limited to a stationary bike right now. Any suggestions for avoiding the problem?

A: You've already figured out the obvious cures: stretching and cross-training. What's left is cutting mileage. My feeling is that 40 to 65 miles per week is a lot of miles, particularly if you're cross-training as well. If you also are doing speedwork on the track, that would provide more stress. And you didn't tell me about your racing schedule.

I would cut the stationary-bike mileage way back for two to three weeks to see if you can solve the immediate hamstring problem. Continuing to pursue alternate training methods while being injured can sometimes delay recovery.

Once you clear up the immediate problem, however, you need to consider the chronic problem. How can you keep this from happening again? That's probably going to require some downward modification, which could be temporary or permanent, in your training schedule, either in quantity of miles or intensity of those miles. You've already figured out some of the answers, so it's a matter of trying to figure out the rest.

Look Far Ahead

Q: I am a 38-year-old woman who has been running for 15 years. I recently had some back pain and was diagnosed with a deteriorating disc in my lower back, along with a bone spur a few vertebrae up. I was told that after I go through physical therapy, I can go back to running, but only every other day. Will this cause more problems down the road? Should I start walking and swimming as an alternative and quit running?

A: There was no suggestion from your question that your doctors told you to quit running; they told you to moderate your running. What you should do is ask yourself where you want to be 10, 20, 30, and even 40 years from now. If you quit running now, will you miss it? Assuming the deterioration continues, will you mind giving up running 10 to 20 years from now?

Every-other-day training works well for a lot of runners. Why not accept that as your current routine? If you like exercising daily, simply pick another sport to do on alternate days. Continue to monitor your body on a regular basis and obtain regular physicals. I believe that some form of strength training would be appropriate for the muscles surrounding your problem area, but definitely check with a sports doctor or physical therapist before you start pumping iron.

Not everybody takes the time to think, at age 38, what they'll be doing in sports in the future. Now is your chance. Planning can help prevent a lot of problems.

Three-Day Schedule

Q: I'm a recreational runner, age 55, who travels frequently and has difficulty maintaining a solid schedule. I've never trained seriously, but I've been active in sports my whole life. Can you recommend a good three-days-a-week program? I am not fast, but I want to maintain some physical conditioning for good health and keep the pounds from piling up after eating all those dinners I encounter on the road.

A: Most schedules designed for younger runners can be modified to accommodate older people. You simply need to plug in more rest days. Where other schedules suggest 3 miles of easy running on a "rest" day, you should take the entire day off. In schedules that are designed to allow 3 or 4 "hard" days during a week, simply stretch the time period to 10 days or two weeks, with the same number of "hard" days.

Since you plan to run only three days a week, you already have the right idea in mind. For those three days, I suggest the following three workouts.

1. Long run. I don't care how far you run this workout, but run it slowly. I suggest between 60 to 90 minutes. Train at an "easy" pace, 65 to 75 percent of your maximum heart rate, gentle enough so you can carry on a conversation without getting out of breath.

2. Tempo run. Do a run between 30 to 45 minutes, but pick up the pace in the middle of the workout, accelerating to a peak about two-thirds into the run. Hold that fast pace for a few minutes—as long as you can comfortably maintain your speed—then back right down.

You should start and finish this run at the "easy" pace described above. In the middle, run at a pace that I would describe as "crisp," meaning 80 to 85 percent of your maximum heart rate.

3. Strides. Warm up with a mile or so, then stretch and do some 100-meter strides at a "crisp" pace. (Strides are basically easy sprints.) Do anywhere from four to eight. You can end the workout there and finish by jogging another mile.

Or you can do a speed workout, including some repeats of 400 or 800 meters (depending on your goal) at paces that could be anywhere from "medium" (75 to 80 percent) to "hard" (85 to 90 percent) depending on the distances that you run. Make sure that you cool down afterward by jogging another half-mile or so.

If strides or speedwork seem too ambitious for you, simply go for a run of 30 to 60 minutes at your own pace. You'll be able to maintain a surprisingly high level of fitness on a schedule such as this.

Lifting Weights

Q: I've run nine marathons with a personal record of 3:18. I'm 48 years old, and the only weight training I do is 25 pushups a day. Will more weight training help my marathon times? I do a lot of hill running.

A: More weight training may improve your marathon times, but not by much. That's not the reason you want to weight train. As you get older, you lose muscle mass. It's good to resist that trend just to maintain a high level of fitness. But in the long run, running is more important than weight training when it comes to running faster. I weight train for reasons other than making myself a faster runner. Mainly, I'm interested in maintaining my lean body mass; strength is as important as aerobic fitness as we grow older.

Pushups offer a good beginning for any strength-training program. Roll over on your back while you're on the ground and do some crunches (shortened situps) as well. Then, if you can find a bar, add pullups to your routine.

Here's another routine, suggested by Vern Gambetta, former director of conditioning for the Chicago White Sox and Chicago Bulls and now president of his own consulting firm, Gambetta Sports Training Systems, in Sarasota, Florida. Stand poised on one foot, legs flexed, well-balanced. Do half-squats. You can do these in three variations: leg behind you, leg to the side, or leg moving back to front.

Single-leg squats will help you improve your balance as well as strengthen your legs. They're better than double-leg squats because you double the resistance (your own body weight) by using just one leg instead of two. Also, by doing them one leg at a time, you train both legs equally. When you lift with both legs, one leg sometimes will take more weight than the other.

For additional strength training, consider joining a health club or purchasing a multipurpose machine for your home. The hills you run also will help you maintain strength (particularly in your quads) more than running the flats.

Comparing Oneself to Others

Q: I just ran my first 5-K in 24:07, and was it ever great. I know that I am racing against myself and not necessarily others, but I am competitive and would like to know how I did compared to the average racer.

A: Based on the time I ran recently in a race, you would have finished 12 seconds in front of me. But there was snow on the course plus a couple of hills. And that's the rub. We're not only running against the pack; we're running against others in our age and sex groups. And conditions differ from race to race.

My first reaction is to tell you not to worry about where you finished relative to the pack. Simply enjoy the experience. Or get a copy of the results of the race you ran and compare yourself to others in that one specific event. *National Masters News* does publish a booklet, *Age-Graded Tables*, that may interest you. The subtitle is *Quickly and Easily Compare Your Performances at Different Ages and in Different Events*. The charts are somewhat complicated, so I can't easily tell you how well you did. The booklet costs $6 and is available from *National Masters News*, P.O. Box 50098, Eugene, OR 97401.

When to Quit

Q: I have run three times a week, 2 to 3 miles a workout, for 16 years. I am now 52 years old. During this time, I didn't pay much attention to what other runners were doing or saying. I just ran. Three months ago, I was in a 5-K race for the first time in 10 years, and I was surprised to see the number of people older than me in the race. Recently, I had begun thinking that perhaps 52 is too old to keep running and I should slow down. Now I am not sure. When is old? What are the signs that you should begin to slow down? Do you just keep running as long as you feel good?

A: You don't have to worry about when to slow down. It will happen whether you want it to or not. Of course, you could increase your training level and probably improve your 5-K times for another 5 to 10 years, but I sense that is not your goal.

After the 1985 World Veterans' Athletics Championships in Rome, I rode the bus to the airport with Paul Spangler, then in his eighties and a multiple gold-medal winner in those championships. Paul and I chatted all the way. We passed a field of sunflowers in full bloom, and Paul was taken by their beauty. He told me that his goal was to be the first masters athlete to compete at the World Vets at the age of 100.

It didn't happen. Paul was out for a run a week or so before his 95th birthday and suffered a fatal heart attack. Paul Spangler served as a great example for masters runners. I'm not sure if I'll still be around and running in championship events at age 100, but it's a goal we all should have.

13

Young Runners

First Exposures to the Joys of Running

- **Right Amount of Mileage**
- **Worried about Injuries**
- **Running with Mom**
- **Coach to Youngsters**
- **A Fun Activity**
- **Too Much Training**
- **Young Marathoner**
- **Genetics**
- **Tough Program**
- **Between Seasons: Winter**
- **Between Seasons: Summer**
- **Scholarships**

I never participated in running as a sport when I was a youngster growing up on the south side of Chicago. No age-group programs were available. I biked a lot and often swam long distances in the lake but never thought of this as sport. I ran only two years of track in high school and didn't discover cross-country until I attended Carleton College in Northfield, Minnesota.

Although my full-time job is writing, I coached track and cross-country at the high school level on two occasions. The first was during the 1960s at Chicago's Mount Carmel High School, my alma mater. One of my runners won city championships in the mile and cross-country. I stopped coaching, even though I enjoyed it, because it took time away from my own running.

A quarter-century later, I returned briefly to coach at Elston High School in Michigan City, Indiana. One of my runners on the boys' track team qualified twice for the State Championships in the 800. My girls' team placed fifth at State, the first time an Elston team had qualified for State in eight years. The same girls won the state meet the next two years, although under another coach.

My children and grandchildren had more opportunities to participate in running races while younger than I did. Of our three children, all did some running while young, but only the oldest competed seriously. He still is ranked in the top 10 in several events at Indiana University. Our second son ran the high hurdles and pole-vaulted in high school but found his niche playing tennis at Kalamazoo College in Michigan. He has a position with *Tennis* magazine similar to my position as a senior writer with *Runner's World* magazine. My daughter is more a recreational runner, although she has completed two marathons.

It's too early to tell whether our seven grandchildren will become runners, although two of the boys are leaning in that direction. During the 1996 presidential election campaign, Bill Clinton made Michigan City his last stop en route to the convention in Chicago. Maybe 40,000 people crammed into the local park. To avoid traffic, we walked from my oldest son's house to the park, and afterward, the two boys decided that they would run home with their father. My grandchildren may or may not fulfill my dream of running in the Olympics, but it was nice to see the torch being passed to another generation.

Right Amount of Mileage

Q: My son is almost eight years old, and we run 2 miles a day. How much is too much at his age?

A: Two miles is a reasonable distance for a boy that age. Make sure that he's doing it because he wants to run, not because you want him to run. If he decides that running is less important than baseball or football or some other activity, let him move on so you're not forcing him to follow your behavior patterns. Or make a bargain with him: "How about a weekly run, the two of us?" That might make it something special that he'll remember 20 years from now.

Your best strategy is to offer a good example, not only with your running but with your other health habits. And keep your approach to physical activity loose and relaxed. Even the 2 miles a day of running that your son does at this age will provide him with a base of physical fitness that will help him in sports and other activities and provide him with a lifetime of good health.

How much is too much? I hate to offer a number because every child is different. A generation ago, when the running boom got moving in the 1970s, some parents pushed their children to set age-group records and run marathons at the same age as your son. This meant that some very young children were running 40 to 50 miles a week or more. I'm not sure much physical or psychological damage was inflicted on these children, but I often wonder how many of them are still running today.

Let your son determine how much running is good for him, with your guidance, of course. If he enjoys running, there's no reason he can't continue to run 2 miles or more a day.

Worried about Injuries

Q: My 8-year-old daughter has always loved running. She currently is involved in a community track program for children 7 to 12 years old. She runs three days a week for at least 2.5 miles, with additional timed sprinting (100, 200, and 400 meters) and runs up stadium stairs. She is in good health but becomes sore after some of her workouts. Should I be concerned about any risks? A pediatrician cautioned me about stress fractures.

A: Assuming that your daughter has no major biomechanical impediments, she should be able to avoid injuries as long as she trains properly. Of course, that's not always easy, is it? As children become ambitious in their running, as they go for prizes and trophies, as they become members of school teams with ambitious goals, the level of stress rises, and with that the increase of risk of injuries.

But three days a week sounds about right for a community training program. As long as your daughter runs at the fun level, I wouldn't worry. Running up stadium steps might be considered by some as excessive, but there are a lot worse things that she could be doing. Don't try to push your daughter, but let her find her own way. Encourage her in her running ambitions. By the time she enters high school, if she wants to continue running, she can increase intensity. The training she will have done in her youth program will work to her advantage as long as she doesn't overtrain. Stress fractures can happen to anyone, but they shouldn't scare people away from our sport.

Running with Mom

Q: I have run seriously for 20 years, and now my 9-year-old daughter has started running with me in the mornings. We run 4-plus miles, three times a week. Should I be aware of any special needs or concerns for such a young runner? Any training tips? We have had trouble finding her good running shoes.

A: No training tips. Just let her run. The program you have her on sounds fine. Every now and then seek a scenic spot for a run. Also, make her aware of traffic and, without frightening her, tell her that she needs to be alert at all times and careful about where she runs.

Concerning shoes, the many children who run occasionally can use whatever soft shoes they happen to use for all other sports. With your daughter running that frequently, though, you need to buy her a good pair of running shoes. Go to a specialty running store if the general sports stores don't have enough models and sizes to fit her properly. Providing young runners with good footwear can be expensive because they may outgrow the shoes before they wear out.

There's an old saying in running about avoiding injuries that I know you as a 20-year veteran have heard many times: Listen to your body. I might modify that to say: Listen to your child. Listen to her wants and needs. Communicate. The temptation will exist for you to use running to bond more with your daughter and open her eyes to the wonders of the sport. Some of that is good, but try not to overdo it. Just make sure that you are opening a door for her and not pushing her through it.

Coach to Youngsters

Q: I recently agreed to coach my son's seventh- and eighth-grade cross-country team and would appreciate some general direction about its summer training. I bought a book about training young distance runners, which is helping me understand the biomechanics and physiological aspects of running. It fails, however, to offer any schedules for summer conditioning. The team consists of approximately 40 kids: beginners and experienced runners, boys and girls. I'd like to provide two separate schedules, based on experience and motivation. The program will be mainly self-directed. We may get together once a week as a team during the summer months. I know how to include some speedwork, some hills, and some easy jogging, but not much more. Any suggestions regarding how many runs a week, how far, and how easy?

A: Three or four runs a week should suffice at that age level. How far? You should concentrate on time, not distance. A half-hour most days, with one workout a week fairly structured, with you providing close supervision and control, would be good. How easy? Let the kids pick their own paces. Try to make the experience as much fun as possible.

You're likely to have a few motivated individuals (not necessarily always the fastest) who will want to do more. Simply have them fill in the days between on their own, with whatever distance they want at whatever pace they want. Caution them about the need to take periodic rest days so they don't overtrain. I'm inclined not to overorganize young runners, preferring to dampen their competitive fires until they get into high school.

On the one day a week that you do get together, try doing what I call grass drills. Go to a track or a golf course. Begin by jogging 800 to 1600 meters. Stretch. Do some strides (for instance, 4×100 meters at a good pace, with walking between). Stretch. Do some bounding drills (skipping is one such drill that kids find fun). Stretch. Maybe some more strides. Jog another 800 meters to cool down. The workout shouldn't take much more than 30 to 40 minutes, and it's a busy workout that the kids will enjoy.

A Fun Activity

Q: I have a 10-year-old daughter who just loves to run. She got hooked on the sport after running in Steve Scott's 1-Mile Fun Run in Carlsbad, California. She has now run 7:12 for the mile and runs three days a week. After soccer season, she wants to train so she can run under 7:00 in the next Fun Run. What would be a good training routine for her in order to stay in shape and still have fun? And can you direct me to any running clubs in the Southern California area for her to be a part of? Also, she has expressed an interest in running a 5-K. I'm sure that she can do it, however, I want to make sure that she doesn't train so hard as to injure her young body. I would like running to remain fun.

A: Breaking 7:00 in the mile should be no problem. Simply aging one year should provide more than 12 seconds improvement for a runner her age. Playing soccer, she will get plenty of running and so needs to do little extra than that dictated by the coach. Once soccer season is over, have her run three to six days a week. It almost doesn't matter what she does as long as she has fun. Pick some pleasant place to run, and plan a trip to some new area once a week or so. And keep the pressure off.

The Amateur Athletic Union sponsors age-group races and would know of clubs for children in your area. Their national headquarters is in Orlando, Florida. Another good source is USA Track & Field, located in Indianapolis. For more information on locating a running club, see page 19.

If she is interested in running a 5-K, let her do it. She could probably run that distance, at least to finish, based on her soccer background alone. Normally, I would recommend that children wait until they join a high school cross-country team before moving up in distance so they don't become obsessed with running too early and, in effect, lose their childhood. But everybody moves at a different pace. Let the child's own desires be your guide.

Too Much Training

Q: My 12-year-old son has been running for one year, training 6 to 10 miles a week. Recently, he made the high school junior varsity cross-country team and is now running 25 miles a week. When the season starts, he will be racing twice weekly. His 5-K time has dropped to 18:45, but I'm worried that he is training too hard for someone his age. What do you think?

A: He may be pushing the edge for his age, but you can't argue with success. When I was coaching high school cross-country, I was happy if a runner ran that fast by the time he was 18 years old. Obviously, your son has some talent.

Despite whether you or I think that he is running too much, the point is that he is part of a team. If he wants to be part of that team, he needs to train with the team and follow the coach's direction. That coach has the responsibility for designing a program to benefit runners at different levels of ability and at different degrees of development. That's no easy task.

I'm usually inclined to go easy with young runners, not wanting them to do too much too soon and risk being burned out by the time they normally would be reaching physical maturity. But it depends more on what they want and how much they enjoy what they're doing. At least for the time being, relax and enjoy his success.

Young Marathoner

Q: I'm a 16-year-old female who ran a half-marathon this summer. My time was 1:43:00, and I felt so good throughout the whole race. It seems like the farther the distance, the better I do. Now I would like to try a marathon. Since I am still growing, will it be too hard on my body?

A: Don't be in a hurry to jump to the marathon too soon. My main objection to runners your age participating in even shorter road races is that it detracts from the normal school programs. If you don't run cross-country and/or track at this time, you should. This is a unique time of life to be part of a team and to develop your speed by racing and training over shorter distances. If you move too quickly to long distances, you may lose the benefits of short-distance training. And in the long run, you may run slower at long distances.

When my son Kevin was in high school, I wouldn't let him run a marathon until after graduation. Then, as a graduation present, I allowed him to run one that summer, but only if he promised to run the first half no faster than 7:00 pace. He ran the first half slower than 1:30, then sped up and finished in 2:48. He eventually went on to run a 2:18 by the end of college.

Genetics

Q: I run every day, and it seems like I don't improve. Other runners slack off in practice and then burn me in the meets. I train hard, but it seems that I get nothing out of it. The coaches don't tell me how or what to do differently. Do you have any suggestions?

A: Yes, relax and be patient. You may have bumped up against a glass ceiling in athletics and become a victim of what I call the unfairness syndrome. This refers to the fact that some people are more athletically talented than others. That is, they possess some genetic factor that allows them to succeed in certain activities.

It's not entirely a strong work ethic that allows Pete Sampras to succeed in tennis or Tiger Woods to succeed in golf. Sampras trains very hard, but you don't win Wimbledon entirely on hard work. Genetics is a major factor. As David L. Costill, Ph.D., director of the Human Performance Laboratory at Ball State University in Muncie, Indiana, once said: "If you want to be a successful athlete, carefully select your parents."

Regardless of what hand you have been dealt in the game of life, you have to work with what you have. If your specific mix of talents doesn't allow you to achieve success in your chosen sport, you may need to take a more realistic look at your goals or—I hate to say this—find another sport. Beating your teammates isn't necessarily a measurement of how good a runner you are. Continue to work hard and be the best you can, but remember that life isn't always fair. I hope that you can learn to enjoy running whether you beat your teammates or not.

Tough Program

Q: My 16-year-old daughter has been running varsity cross-country for five years. She and her teammates run 12 months a year with no time off. In preparation for the cross-country season, they turn up the intensity in the fall. My daughter runs really hard workouts every other day with easy ones in between. Her race times have been excellent and her performance has been improving during the last four weeks. But with this improvement, she has started having moderate pain in her right hip. It hurts the most at the beginning of her runs, but then eases up as her runs progress. Her hip is very sensitive to the touch at all times. We would welcome any insight you might have as to what is happening.

A: Your daughter is probably overtraining because of the intense program at the school. This is not a criticism of the coach, because if you want success at the upper levels, you need to train at a high level. But doing so increases the risk of injuries. Also, your daughter is at an age where her body is changing, which may be part of the problem with the hip. The fact that it feels better at the end of a run rather than at the beginning suggests a moderate rather than a severe injury, but she probably has some soft tissue damage that needs time to heal.

You don't want the moderate pain to develop into intense pain, and neither would her coach. Have your daughter talk to that coach, explain the problem, and see if the coach can modify some of her training (fewer miles, less intensity) to allow the injury to heal naturally. This is a former high school coach speaking, but believe me: runners do not always communicate well when it comes to problems that might affect their training. It takes a very alert coach to monitor several dozen runners simultaneously and know what's going on with their minds and bodies. The fact that the coach has your daughter on a hard/easy program suggests to me that the coach knows what he or she is doing.

Once the season is over, your daughter may benefit from some downtime to allow her body to fully heal before starting to get ready for track. Again, have her communicate this need and desire with the coach. She is having success, so I don't want her to completely back off, but there comes a point in every runner's life where discretion is more important than valor.

Between Seasons: Winter

Q: I am going to run the 800 and 400 meters in track this spring. I ran cross-country in the fall and want to make the switch in my training. Any advice for getting started?

A: Instead of being a matter of getting started, it's one of maintaining your training. Most successful runners build on their fall training to achieve higher levels of achievement in the spring.

If you were seriously involved in racing two or three times a week and participated in qualifying events leading to the state championships, you probably are a bit burned out from the effort and need some downtime: psychological as much as physical. You should take a week or two off to catch up on your studies, see your nonrunning friends, and participate in school activities. If you used cross-country mainly for conditioning (with an eye toward shorter events in the spring such as the 400 and 800), you should increase your training commitment, rather than back off.

Regardless, the next several months are usually a good time for base training: running long but easy. Put in some extra miles to build an aerobic base, but don't train at too intense a level. Depending on whether you can train on a track that isn't 2 feet deep in snow, you may want to do at least some easy speedwork but probably not more than once or twice a week. Early in the new year is the time for more intense speed training, even if it means using the school hallways as your indoor track. Don't overlook work in the weight room, particularly if you backed off on your strength training toward the end of the season. Once in a team situation, look to your coach for guidance. In the meantime, you can catch a head start on your competition by running consistently regardless of speed or distance.

Between Seasons: Summer

Q: Track season has ended, and I want to keep running over the summer. What is your advice for summer training for a distance runner? What type of schedule should I follow?

A: To achieve success in distance running, you need to give the sport your attention 12 months out of the year. Here are my thoughts on bridging the gap between spring track and fall cross-country.

Schedule. The best schedule is the one provided by your coach. Someone who sees you every day in practice can provide the best guidance. Times and distances and schedules and programs mean less than the personal touch that your coach brings to your training.

Kick back. With track over, you probably need some downtime. Don't rush right into high-mileage training, thinking that you'll get out of shape if you don't run every day. After you have raced frequently, not only does your body need a rest but also your mind needs refreshing. Take anywhere from one to four weeks off before getting back to full-time training. That doesn't mean that you can't run during this period, but don't run hard and don't run more than three or four days a week.

Reflect. During this downtime, reflect on the activities outside running that impact on your success. Are you eating as well as you should? Are you organizing your day so that you have time both for studies and social activities? Look back on your previous training and racing: Can you pinpoint reasons why you have or have not run successfully? Can you eliminate the negative reasons? Keeping a training diary will help in this regard.

Volume. In looking forward to the coming season, more is not always better. More miles and more workouts may only make you more tired. Again, follow your coach's training schedule, and don't add extra workouts away from the team under the mistaken belief that this will give you an edge on your teammates and competitors. Overtraining can result in injury and sickness. The best gains are earned from steady and consistent training.

What works. The best training programs involve a mixture of easy running over relatively long distances, fast running over short distances, and rest in between. Different coaches use different combinations in getting their teams ready for the seasons. Most high school coaches use the summer for base training, a lot of miles to develop the aerobic conditioning of their runners.

Scholarships

Q: I am a high school runner and think that I have a lot of potential but not enough confidence. I've broken school records and received All-Conference honors both years that I've been in high school. I'd like some information on scholarships. I've received numerous letters already, but I am not a senior so I haven't paid much attention to them yet.

A: College coaches spend a lot of time and effort sending recruiting letters to talented young athletes with the hint of scholarships in the offing, but the truth of the matter is that pickings are slim these days for track-and-field athletes and distance runners.

Because both the NCAA and various conferences place limits on the number of scholarships available to athletes, particularly in track and field, coaches have few to offer. As a result, unless you are a so-called blue-chipper capable of winning at the conference and/or scoring points at the national level, you are more likely to get a fraction of a scholarship. Coaches do this so they can spread the available aid around to more athletes on the team.

I wouldn't take those letters you receive too seriously. And if you're invited to visit a campus, don't become overly impressed if you get to eat lunch with a famous alumnus who was on an Olympic team. Look first at what that university can offer you as a student. Is it the type of college you want? Does it have courses in your area of major interest? Is the location to your liking? Is it the size school that you want? What do you think of everything at that university other than athletics? Be honest, and don't be overwhelmed because there are trophies from the Penn Relays in their trophy case.

Sooner or later, you probably want to consider what the school has to offer you as an athlete. You didn't get a chance to pick your high school coach, but you certainly do have a chance to select your college coach. You probably need to make at least one campus visit to help you with this decision. NCAA rules, of course, prohibit the coach from talking too often to you either by phone or in person. Do you like that coach who is sending you letters? What kind of training program does he offer? Ask to see training schedules, or ask members of the team what they do. What about those who will be your teammates for the next three to four years? A lot of thought should go into your decision because you are going to have to live with it for four years, and, indeed, for the rest of your life, both as an athlete and an individual.

14

Weather
Running Hot and Cold

- **Summer Struggles**
- **Too Much Sweat**
- **Overheating**
- **Headaches from the Heat**
- **Winter Training**

- **Cold-Weather Wear**
- **The Wind**
- **Morning Exercise**
- **Lunchtime Runs**
- **Saunas and Hot Tubs**

Standing on a grassy knoll on Chicago's lakefront and talking to my marathon training class one Saturday morning, I warned everybody that the weatherman had predicted hot and humid weather. "Drink plenty of fluids," I said, adding, "You might also want to pick a pace slower than usual."

And, even as the words tumbled parrotlike out of my mouth, I felt stupid saying that.

As I later told Bill Fitzgerald, the class co-director, "It didn't feel that hot." The temperature just before we began our workout at 7:30 a.m. was in the low 70s. A hefty breeze was blowing out of the southwest. "It felt pretty cool before we started," I told Bill.

Ten miles into the run, I didn't feel that way. I was soaked with sweat, but in the high humidity, it wasn't evaporating fast enough to cool my body. The water bottle on my belt from which I had been drinking was empty. I had just run through a stretch from Navy Pier to the North Avenue beach where there were no trees. The course being along the lake meant that we were exposed not only to the sun overhead but also to the sun reflected off the water.

I shut down the engine before being forced to shut down. I walked. I paused longer at drinking fountains. Even at that, I finished the run nauseated and groggy, not good signs. I had planned to meet Bill afterward, but after gulping several cups of Gatorade and water, I jumped in my car, cranked the air conditioner up to max, and headed for a cold shower. It would be nearly 6 hours before I began feeling good again. All of this came about after only a 12-miler at a slow pace.

I survived to run another day, but even when seemingly cool breezes fool me in the future, I will not take predictions of hot and humid weather lightly. Heat and humidity aren't the only problems runners have with weather. At another time of the year, cold and windy weather can plague us even more.

Summer Struggles

Q: I live in New Orleans and have been running for about three years. I cover 10 to 20 miles a week and also walk on my lunch hours. Since the early summer, my muscles have become very tight. If I do 5 miles on Monday, I can hardly do 2 on Tuesday. It is very hot and humid here. Does the heat have anything to do with it?

A: The heat has everything to do with it. Summer is a difficult time of year to run in the deep South, when runners get paid back for those pleasant runs they had in January. You're likley to feel excessive fatigue if your training regimen causes you to dehydrate and you don't compensate by drinking enough fluids before and after your runs. The best rule for hydration and rehydration is this: Drink more than you possibly think that you can get down. It's still probably not enough.

Heat and humidity also can cause a general feeling of lethargy that is both physical and psychological. It's difficult to run when you have to work too hard. Your fatigue, however, could also be from any number of related reasons, among them diet. Unless you eat a healthy diet rich in carbohydrates and with ample calories to balance your energy expenditure, you could be running on empty.

It is also possible that your fatigue is related to some yet unrecognized medical problem, not even related to running. So if all else fails, you may want to see your physician for a general physical exam.

Actually, the fact that you run 5 miles one day and 2 the next is not necessarily a bad idea. Most elite athletes follow a training regimen that alternates hard and easy days. The easy days allow them to recuperate from their last hard workout so that they can run strong in their next. So maybe you need to simply accept the fact that you can't run the same workout day after day without making some adjustments either in pace or distance, particularly in midsummer.

Try varying your workout routine. Check your diet and fluid management. I like the idea that you walk during your lunch hour, so you might want to do more walking than running during really hot periods, then reverse that ratio at times of the year when the weather turns cool.

Too Much Sweat

Q: I perspire to excess. I live in Florida and am training for the Marine Corps Marathon. I train in the early morning, but on my last long run of 16 miles, I suffered from heat exhaustion (losing 11 pounds on this run). I run with a water bottle and refill every 3 to 4 miles and sometimes store fluids along my running route. I'm thinking of doing that for the marathon as well. Is there any way to decrease the amount of perspiration?

A: No, unfortunately, there isn't. Alberto Salazar had the same problem. He used to sweat excessively, and it affected his ability to perform in hot weather. At a period during his career when he was in peak form, he placed well back in the 1984 Olympic Marathon, which was run in warm weather in Los Angeles. Salazar knew what his problem was and sought expert advice in the period leading up to the games from environmental scientists, including Lawrence E. Armstrong, Ph.D., of the University of Connecticut. He drank a quart of water 20 minutes before the start of the marathon and another quart 5 minutes before but still couldn't overcome the fact that he perspired to excess. He lost 12 pounds during the race, approximately 8 percent of his body weight. So you have company.

Your fitness level dictates how much you sweat only to the extent that being in very good shape allows you to cruise at a relatively faster pace with less stress than someone not quite so fit. But this didn't help Salazar.

It's not easy training for a fall marathon in Florida, because most of the long runs in the traditional marathon buildup must be done at the hottest time of year. Training for the Disney World Marathon, which is in January, is much easier because the longer runs come in the fall. Yes, stashing fluids along the course may help, although there are ample water stations in the Marine Corps Marathon so you shouldn't need to do so. Fluid replacement in the marathon itself may be less a problem than in workouts, since the weather will be cooler in November. But if you sweat as much as you say, it will still be physically impossible for you to drink enough fluids during long workouts to compensate for 11 pounds lost in sweat. You can drink, but at normal stomach emptying rates, the fluid won't get absorbed into your system quickly enough to help your air-conditioning system.

You need to rethink your training program and consider eliminating long runs over 10 miles during the hottest part of the year. Sure, I know that all of the schedules (including mine) suggest that 20-milers are necessary for those preparing for marathons, but they weren't designed for people training through Florida heat. One strategy would be to break your long runs in half: run a 10-miler in the morning, rehydrate thoroughly, then do a second 10-miler in the evening. Another strategy, which requires long-range planning, would be to do your mileage buildup during the cooler spring, then coast through the summer with shorter workouts, returning to the long training for a brief period before the race. If this doesn't work, you may need to go to Marine Corps with diminished goals, selecting a time that is slower than you might otherwise achieve if better trained. Then use the great weather you have during the winter to plan for a fast time in a spring marathon.

Overheating

Q: I have been running 3 miles a day for five or more years. My trouble is that I get so red in the face that it is quite embarrassing. I don't sweat much and was told that I radiate my heat rather than sweat it out. I can't increase my distance because I become really hot and red. (My temperature remains elevated for about 2 hours.) I want to race, except I get so red that people constantly ask me if I am okay. I look like I am about to explode. I drink a lot of water before running, but it seems to do no good. I know my sweat glands work because I sweat when I am nervous (cold sweat). I am about 20 pounds over-weight, but I can't increase my aerobic activity because of the redness. What is wrong with me?

A: Different glands are involved with nervous sweating and sweating from exercise. Have you consulted a physician about your inability to sweat? I'm not sure a physician could help much, but this would at least confirm that you are one of a limited number of people whose sweat glands don't function properly. This could be caused by a variety of factors, mostly linked to heredity, but the bottom line is that you need to be very cautious when running in warm weather.

There was a woman in one of my beginning running classes a decade or so ago who didn't sweat and couldn't run past 3 miles. She knew that that was her limit, so she trained accordingly. Drinking extra water won't help if the water isn't released in perspiration. Dousing the skin with water to simulate the body's natural sweat production is only partially successful. Losing that 20 pounds might permit you to run more easily but would not necessarily help with your sweating problem.

You may consider limiting your competitive efforts to cold-weather races, those where weather conditions (45 degrees or colder) will provide an air-conditioning effect. Even in cold weather, however, you will need to be cautious about heat and not overdress. Stick with the shorter-distance races and workouts, unless you can find some medical solution to your problem.

Headaches from the Heat

Q: In hot weather, I get headaches around the eye sockets after I run. These can last up to 6 hours before disappearing and can be quite debilitating. I never get them during the winter.

A: Here are a number of suggestions. Pick the ones that you think relate to you.

Cover up. When running in the summer, always wear a cap to keep the sun off your head. Similarly, wear sunglasses. The headaches may be from exposure to the sun. (This is good advice even if you don't get headaches.)

Cool down. Run at times of the day when heat is less likely to be a problem: early in the morning or in the evening. Running on trails in the woods instead of on hot concrete can protect you from the heat.

Cut your distance. If the headaches come after long runs, modify your summer training. I always felt that summer was a good time to run short and fast rather than long and slow.

Relax. Reserve time immediately after the workout to lie down and relax. Maybe you can nip the headaches before they occur. If aspirin or other medications help limit headache symptoms, you may want to take the aspirin immediately after finishing the run so it will quickly reach your system. I'm not sure that I would medicate during the run.

Drink up. One cause of your headaches may be dehydration. Make sure that you are well-hydrated before and after, but particularly during, your runs. A lot of people overlook the "during," particularly in workouts.

Gatorade recently did some research suggesting that carbohydrate intake during workouts can speed recovery and prevent some of the negative effects of excessive workouts, such as immunity suppression. Nothing in the Gatorade study suggests that taking carbo-drinks might help you avoid headaches, but give it a try. Investment in a water belt will make it easier for you to stay hydrated.

Those are a few suggestions, but from talking to people troubled by chronic headaches, I know that solutions are varied and difficult. In the long run (for the long run), you also should consult a doctor.

Winter Training

Q: What would you suggest as a winter training program for middle-distance running? What about sprinters?

A: It depends on where you live. If you live in the upper Midwest like me, winter's cold can make training difficult if you don't have access to indoor facilities. I use the cold months for base building, going out and covering some easy, slow miles, all bundled up, not worrying about time or distance. I also snowshoe and cross-country ski.

Winter is a good time of the year to work on strength as well as aerobic base. Usually, I spend more time on the weight machines this time of year than other times when I am more anxious to head out the door. Developing strength is essential for middle-distance running.

If you have access to a pool, you might try swimming and aquarunning for your aerobic base. If you can use a treadmill, don't do all of your running on it at a steady pace. Try some interval sprints. Go easy to warm up, then crank the speed up to near 800-meters race pace for 30 to 60 seconds, then back down to easy, then back up again.

Sprinters could use a similar routine. Even though people who run 100 meters need strength and speed, they also need aerobic power. The fastest sprinters are not those quickest out of the blocks but those who slow down the least as they near the finish line. I don't know that much about Michael Johnson's training, but I'm going to bet that he does some easy and long running in the off-season.

If you live in San Diego, you may think that the above advice doesn't apply to you, but it does. You need a time of year when you back off your regular training to concentrate on strength and aerobic base, too. I've always felt that living in a cold climate was an advantage for distance runners (if not for sprinters and middle-distance runners) because it forced us to change our training to survive, which is a good thing. How many marathoners on our Olympic teams can you name who came from California or other warm climes? Keith Brantly lives in Florida, but consider the number of Minnesotans who have run fast marathons: Barney and Janis Klecker, Bob Kempainen, Garry Bjorklund, Ron Daws, Buddy Edelen, and Dick Beardsley, to name a few. They come from the Land of Sky-Blue Waters, but I don't think that it's the water. Winter may be good for runners because it forces us to change our training.

Cold-Weather Wear

Q: I would like to know the proper attire for winter running so that I will not overdress or underdress. I only run 2 miles, four days a week, and would like to continue this routine through the winter months. When is it too cold to run outside?

A: As far as I'm concerned, it's never too cold to run outside. One of the coldest workouts I can remember was a run at the Maplelag, a cross-country ski resort in northern Minnesota, where the temperature had dropped to -18°F. A couple of local runners heard that I was staying there and came by to run with me. We all wore several layers of clothes. Actually, the sun was shining, there was relatively little wind, and it was a pleasant workout.

If you only plan to run 2 miles, you probably don't need to worry too much about overdressing. If you overheat and get soaked with sweat, you'll be back indoors before getting chilled. The farther you run outdoors, the more care you have to give to dressing properly. Here are some tips.

Layer your body. The key to running in cold weather is layering. Multiple layers of thin fabrics will keep you warmer than a single thick layer. By layering, you trap air, which is the best type of insulation. Thin layers are also lighter, so you'll be able to run faster. A nylon jacket that you can remove and tie around your waist is convenient if you get warm toward the end of the run.

Wick away sweat. Choose fabrics that are very breathable, allowing moisture to move outward and away from your body, evaporating in the atmosphere. Cotton usually is a poor undergarment since it traps water close to your skin, which can be cold. There are so many miracle fabrics these days boasting "wickability" that it's difficult to keep track of them. Read labels and ask the salespeople when buying.

Stay dry. The outer shell you expose to the snow and wind is important because, while you want moisture going out, you don't want it coming in. A tightly knit outer fabric may be necessary to keep you dry. The worst days for running outdoors are when it's raining and just above 32° F. That's much less pleasant than a few degrees colder when the rain turns to snow.

Concentrate on extremities. If your hands or feet get cold, you'll feel miserable no matter how much you've wrapped the rest of your body. A single pair of socks is usually enough for me, but some runners use multiple pairs. Mittens work better than finger gloves since allowing your fingers to remain close together keeps them warmer. Again, the secret is multiple layers. On very cold days, I wear wool mittens covered by leather shells.

Don't forget your head. Heat escapes from the head, so a wool cap is essential. On very cold days, I also wear a balaclava, which is like a sock that fits around the head with a small opening for the eyes, nose, and mouth. You may want to cover your mouth with a scarf on cold days, although I never do. I wear sunglasses not only as protection against sun reflected off white snow but also to keep the wind out of my eyes.

Seal the edges. Pay attention to where one clothing part overlaps another so that cold air can't reach unexposed skin. You can be warm over most of your body and still suffer frostbite to exposed parts. The key points are the ankles, wrists, and neck. The balaclava mentioned above can help seal the area around your neck, which is essential for trapping warm air within.

Take fluids. You don't think that you'll overheat in winter? Dehydration can be almost as much of a problem in cold weather as in warm, particularly because we're less inclined to drink. Knowing this, pay more attention to drinking fluids before and after your runs.

Avoid too much clothing. Overdressing can be more trouble than too little clothing. If you overdress and overheat, you may become soaked with sweat, making for an uncomfortable second half of the run, particularly if you are forced to run home into the wind. Concerning choice of direction relative to the wind, that's a mistake that you'll only make once if you're paying attention. It's better to run into the wind at the start of your workout than at the end, when your energy level is lower. That's good advice any time of year, but it's particularly important in the winter.

The Wind

Q: I'm running a marathon in a few days and the weather forecast calls for strong winds. My goal pace is 8:00 per mile. How should I adjust my pace for running against, and with, a strong wind?

A: It's not easy, and it depends on how much the wind is blowing and even at what point in the course it is blowing. Running against the wind probably will slow you down more in the final 6 miles than in the first 6 simply because of accumulated fatigue. Running with the wind at your back isn't always an advantage either. In one marathon I won many years ago in South Dakota, I turned the corner at 18 miles happy to have the wind behind me. But it was a hot day and I overheated. I actually ran the last miles slower than I had into the wind. Fortunately, everybody else behind me was having similar problems.

Normally, you'll lose some time going into the wind but not gain all of it back with the wind behind you. I'd suggest going out conservatively, say 8:15 to 8:30 pace in the early miles, to save energy you may need later. You probably also need to avoid looking at your watch, which may cause you to worry that you are going either too fast or too slow. Listen to your body for signals on how fast to run. If you're running to establish a set time, weather conditions can thwart you. If your goal is only to run a time equal to your ability on the given day, victory may prove easier to attain.

Finally, if the weather conditions are truly awful, you might consider backing way off your pace or bailing out of the race early, figuring to save your legs for another effort several weeks or months down the road. Bill Fitzgerald, who works with me in coaching marathon runners in Chicago, found himself running poorly in a race several years ago. But Fitzgerald had a backup plan. He ran easily and stopped at 18 miles, using the marathon as a workout. Two weeks later, he ran another marathon and qualified for Boston. All marathoners need to formulate backup plans for those days when the weather turns nasty.

Morning Exercise

Q: I am 42 years old and have begun to enjoy running more and more. I would like to run at least three times a week for about 5 miles each time. In the past, I have run in the evenings after work, but now that it is winter, it gets dark and colder much earlier. I have decided to bite the bullet and switch my runs to the morning. Is there any special regimen for early-morning runs? Should I have breakfast first?

A: Everybody determines the early-morning routine that works best for them by trial and error. I suggest that you simply drink a glass of orange juice before heading out the door, waiting until later for a fuller breakfast. Your body will be stiff after getting out of bed, so consider walking the first quarter-mile before breaking into a run. Layer your clothing to stay warm. You'll eventually learn what is too much and too little. Experience is a great teacher.

Lay out your clothing the night before a morning workout, so you don't have to think too hard when you get up. Your wife will be happier if you aren't stumbling around the bedroom pulling clothes out of drawers and asking her where you left your mittens.

I have a thermometer mounted under my deck so I know how cold it is and what to wear, but I sometimes step outside to check to see which way the wind is blowing before deciding how much to wear. Since you'll be running in the dark, you definitely should wear some reflective gear so drivers (who also will be only half-awake in the morning) can see you. There are some excellent reflective jackets on the market now.

Lunchtime Runs

Q: I live in Ottawa, Canada, so winter training has to take place on my lunch break since I find it too dark and cold to run after work. I plan to start running long on the weekends in preparation for a May marathon. My problem is that I've just changed jobs and can't afford to run 40 to 60 minutes at lunch like I used to. How can I get a worthwhile lunchtime workout in 25 to 30 minutes of running time?

A: You can get all the running you need during the lunch hour. Simply accept the fact that you have less time. Run the same pace most days, although once or twice a week you might consider picking the pace up slightly during the middle of your runs. (Make sure that the footing is good when you do this.)

Adjust your training schedule so that you do most of your mileage on the weekends, when you will have time to train in daylight. Run for an hour at marathon pace on Saturdays and 2 to 3 hours at a pace slower than that on Sundays.

Use Mondays and Fridays as your rest days to recover from and for the weekend training. That leaves Tuesdays, Wednesdays, and Thursdays for runs of 25 to 30 minutes. Some people juggle their work schedules, coming in early or leaving late to allow themselves a window of opportunity to train a bit longer on other days of the week, but this may not be an option for you. Once spring arrives, the days will become warmer and longer, allowing you to shift some of your training.

Saunas and Hot Tubs

Q: Do you recommend the use of a sauna, steam room, or hot tub as part of any exercise program? If yes, what are the conditions?

A: My introduction to the sauna came while touring Finland with an American track team back in the Middle Ages. I ran the 3000-meter steeplechase in Turku on a September evening so cold that I thought I saw ice floating in the water pit. I was quite happy to retreat from the track to a sauna. The Finns believe that their saunas contain *sisu*, the legendary spirit that makes them stronger and faster.

The heat in a sauna is dry; the heat in a steam room is wet. Many American health clubs dating at least back into the last century had steam rooms so that members could relax in them after a hard game of squash or handball. I would think that postworkout relaxation might be the best use of both saunas and steam rooms. I've never particularly enjoyed using either. Perhaps I am too impatient.

When I remodeled my basement several years ago, however, I did install a whirlpool. It comes in very handy after midwinter running, skiing, or snowshoeing. It's a good way to get warm again. I use the whirlpool for more than that or relaxation. I also do my stretching in the whirlpool and find that the hot water helps loosen me up. (Some exercise physiologists disagree with this approach, but it works for me.)

Can this make you a faster runner? I've never seen any research to favor either saunas, steam rooms, hot tubs, or whirlpools. But if you enjoy sitting and soaking, that should be excuse enough. I certainly know that I probably would do less stretching without a whirlpool in which to do it.

Nutrition

Eat for Power and Performance

- Eating before a Cross-Country Meet
- Meals before a Road Race
- Energy Loss
- Gels
- Morning Runs
- Carbo-Loading
- Caffeine
- Vitamins
- Junk Science
- Creatine
- Vegetarianism
- Nausea
- Ammonia Breath
- Fat-Burning

Most questions that I receive related to nutrition can be divided into two categories: eating for performance and eating for good health. Answering questions on performance is fairly simple. Answering questions about good health—the nutrition in our daily lives—can get more complex, which explains why there are so many books in the stores about subjects ranging from cooking to weight loss.

I have a very simple principle that I apply to my eating for both performance and good health. I learned what I know about nutrition from Joanne Milkereit, R.D., a dietitian connected with the Medical University of South Carolina in Charleston. We co-authored a book titled *Runner's Cookbook*. Joanne told me that every runner should put the following words on the refrigerator: "Eat a wide variety of lightly processed foods."

Those eight words make more sense and contain more wisdom than anything on nutrition I've heard before or since. Keep them in mind as you read my answers to runners with nutrition questions.

Eating before a Cross-Country Meet

Q: What is good to eat before a cross-country race 5000 meters long? Our team usually runs meets at about 4:00 or 4:30 in the afternoon.

A: With 4 to 5 hours between lunch and your race, there is ample time for whatever you ate at noon to digest, assuming that you didn't overdose on pizza. Unlike marathoners, you don't need to worry about carbo-loading. Your regular diet (assuming you eat well) should supply you with ample energy to run 5000 meters, a race too short to dip deeply into your reserves of muscle glycogen. Thus, you want to eat enough in your prerace meal to maintain energy without disturbing your stomach. You'll find that bland foods that are high in carbohydrates work best. If the food in the cafeteria displeases you, pack a lunch so you can gain better control over your prerace meal.

Also, eat a good breakfast. A hearty breakfast that contains a mix of grains and fruits can fill your energy tank for the day. Some nutritionists even recommend that breakfast be the biggest meal of the day, although Americans aren't always culturally ready to accept such advice.

One caution: Don't eat or drink much in the last hour before you go to the starting line, holding the mistaken belief that you need a sudden energy boost. The opposite may occur. Experiment with different eating strategies. When you find one that works, stick with it.

Meals before a Road Race

Q: I recently read that you should eat the morning of a race. I am worried, however, that this will cause me stomach distress, or worse, a prolonged trip to the bushes. Is there any way to have my carbs and an empty stomach, too? Is a sports drink an acceptable substitute for breakfast?

A: Yes, prerace eating can cause you stomach distress if you are not used to it. I tell people in our class for the Chicago Marathon never to do anything in a marathon that you haven't already done in practice.

The same applies for shorter races, although you can use shorter races (5-Ks and 10-Ks) to practice eating tactics.

I find that by eating 2 to 3 hours before a morning race, I have ample time to clear my digestive tract. How much I eat depends partly on the length (and importance) of the race. I give more attention to premarathon meals than I do to eating before a local 10-K run that is mainly for recreation. For that local 10-K, I might not bother to eat at all. If the race is important to me, and in the morning, I'll rise early enough so that I can eat something before I drive to the race. Sometimes that something is only fluids, which will clear the stomach fast.

Stop drinking at least 2 hours before the starting time of the race, otherwise you may find yourself ducking into the bushes after the gun goes off. Normally, it takes that long for fluids to move through the system and into the kidneys, ready for elimination. Several minutes before the start, you can start drinking again because those fluids will be absorbed by the body and eliminated as perspiration.

If I have time (2 to 3 hours), I'll eat a light breakfast: orange juice, toast or a bagel, and coffee. Sports drinks are okay for shorter races, but if you plan to be on the course for more than 3 to 4 hours, such as in a marathon or ultramarathon, solid food is better. David L. Costill, Ph.D., director of the Human Performance Laboratory at Ball State University in Muncie, Indiana, refers to this as topping off the fuel tank. Even though you have a pasta dinner the night before the marathon, your body will have burned some muscle glycogen just in the normal process of moving around.

The bottom line is, experiment. Determine at practice races how your body reacts to different fueling and refueling strategies. You can make a mistake in a 5-K and not suffer serious consequences, but in a marathon, you need all systems at go.

Energy Loss

Q: I am training for a marathon, but I have been feeling bad on my long runs of 12 to 13 miles. I run out of energy, and when I finish, I feel like throwing up and passing out. I have not been eating anything on my runs and have not been drinking much either. Also, I don't have a good appetite since increasing my mileage. I am a 5-foot-2, 115-pound female who's 28 years old. How many calories should I eat a day to maintain an energy level adequate to cover the necessary mileage? Can I drink some of them, as the running seems to really dull my appetite?

A: Let's not talk calories. You probably need a minimum of several thousand calories a day to keep moving, but your needs are more basic than counting calories.

First, you need to experiment with fueling yourself before, during, and after your runs. Try eating a snack 1 to 2 hours before your runs: some carbohydrate, such as a sports drink or bagel. Then get to a sports store and buy a water belt to carry with you while you run, or find a route that will take you past drinking fountains. In purchasing your water belt, make sure that it has some pockets into which you can stuff some of the new carbohydrate-based gels or energy bars. And grab some more carbs after you finish. Research by John L. Ivy, Ph.D., at the University of Texas at Austin, suggests that you can replenish your muscles best if you refuel immediately after depleting them. Fruits and sports drinks are good at doing this if they don't upset your stomach.

To better educate yourself about a healthy diet, I recommend that you consult a registered dietitian. Ask him to analyze your diet and make recommendations related to calorie intake. Lastly, you might want to check with a general practitioner to determine whether some underlying medical problem is causing your energy to drop during runs. It could be something as simple as low iron stores, in which case adding 3 ounces of lean red meat to your diet once a week could help.

Gels

Q: I'm training for a marathon and have tried gels during my long runs. I've noticed an improvement in my strength and speed at the end of my 20-milers. How do you carry gels comfortably with running shorts and a singlet?

A: I've experimented with various gels on training runs and have run several marathons using them. I feel that they are a very useful product. Depending on the brand, they provide 80 to 120 calories per packet, theoretically enough energy to get you another mile down the road.

Gels come in plastic packets similar to ketchup and mustard packets that you find in fast-food restaurants. They look like, and have the consistency of, petroleum jelly. Most of the gels on the market are flavored, everything from banana to chocolate. Each packet provides a spoonful or two of the product, and they're easy to squeeze into your mouth. Wash them down with a cup of water for best results. Gels are best used during long-distance races, not before when there are easier and cheaper ways to boost your energy. For short-distance races such as a 5-K or 10-K, gels are probably superfluous.

If you plan to use gels during a marathon, take them at regular intervals with slightly more emphasis on the end of the race. For instance, in a marathon, I might open a gel packet at 9, 15, 20, and 23 miles. On several occasions, I've noticed an energy surge right after taking them, although I suspect that may be more psychological (the placebo effect) than physical. Don't overlook that psychological advantage, however. I would find myself at 8 miles looking forward to mile 9 when I knew that I could open a packet, just like Christmas. I wish that gels had been available earlier in my career when I was experimenting with ways to boost my energy to carry me past the wall at 20 miles in a marathon.

They're very easy to carry attached to your singlet. Simply take a single safety pin and pin the plastic packet toward the bottom of the singlet, positioned so you can tuck the bottom into your shorts. That way, the packet doesn't bounce around. You may look a bit silly running with five to six packets dangling from your shirt, but you'd look a lot sillier sitting on the curb at the 20-mile mark.

If you decide to use gels while racing, it is very important to experiment with them while training. In one marathon, I tried a different product that I picked up at the prerace expo and discovered that I liked neither the taste nor the convenience of the package.

Morning Runs

Q: I am a morning runner who usually hits the road around 6:00 A.M. My routine is to roll out of bed, grab a cup of coffee, then start my run. I do not eat anything prior to the run, so my last meal before I run is about 10 hours before. Should I have something small, such as fruit or an energy bar, in order to increase my strength during my run?

A: People differ in their energy needs and their abilities to run with food in their stomachs, so you may or may not feel stronger if you eat before your run. I usually grab a glass of orange juice and go. On mornings when I have more time (an hour or two) between awakening and running, I may have something more to eat: toast, applesauce, or even my usual breakfast of cereal with raisins, bananas, and whatever fruit happens to be in season. Before morning races, I'm usually fussier, but most morning workouts are not done at full speed. Undigested food in the stomach is less of a problem.

Sooner or later, however, it comes down to what is the comfortable prerun nutrition plan for you. Fruit before going out the door makes sense, but it also may upset your stomach and send you into the bushes. An energy bar might work since you could consume it on the run, if the workout lasts long enough. Test various routines to see what disturbs your stomach and what does not.

Carbo-Loading

Q: I am puzzled as to what runners mean when they talk about carbohydrate-loading, done before a marathon. An old article in *Runner's World* magazine talked about doing a depletion run, then loading for best results. But others say that the most recent data indicates that one should not deplete, just increase the intake of carbohydrates three to four days before the race. What are your thoughts on carbo-loading?

A: Carbo-loading today has a different meaning than it did 20 years ago when runners first became aware of the need to increase their intakes of carbohydrates before a marathon. When someone mentions the term "carbo-loading" today, I often feel obligated to explain that it doesn't work the way science once thought that it did and that they're better off carbo-loading by adding carbohydrates the last three to four days before the race.

Scandinavian scientists originally developed carbohydrate-loading back in the 1970s for use by Nordic skiers. The routine seemed to work, so it was copied and modified by long-distance runners.

The most efficient fuel for endurance athletes is carbohydrates, which is stored in the muscles as glycogen, a form of sugar. The muscles burn glycogen similar to the way your car burns gasoline. As for fats, the body stores it first as fat, which later can be broken down into glycerol and carbon residues, making its way back into the carbohydrate pathway. With proteins, the body can convert them more directly into glycogen, but this and fat transfer are less efficient processes that might be compared to your car running on low-octane gasoline that causes the engine to knock.

The body can store enough glycogen in the muscles to run for 2 hours, close to 20 miles of running for a well-trained athlete. At around

20 miles, if and when you run out of glycogen, you hit the wall. Your pace drops, and running becomes more difficult.

It's actually a bit more complicated than that since the body will burn some fats in combination with carbohydrates right from the start. The ratio of fats versus carbohydrates burned depends partly on how fast you run and how well you have trained your muscles to burn both carbohydrates and fats. If you run fast, you will burn primarily carbohydrates (actually muscle glycogen). If you run slower, you will burn a somewhat higher percentage of fats with those carbohydrates. This will allow you to preserve some of your glycogen for the end of the race, and thus you will be able to run past the wall with energy still remaining in your tank.

This is why I recommend that runners do their long training runs at a slow pace. By running at this pace, they teach their bodies to convert fats more efficiently. If you can preserve glycogen stores for the closing miles, you'll finish the race faster. The bottom-line message is that the more glycogen you can cram into your muscles, the better. Here's where carbo-loading comes in.

The early research was based on the premise that you could cram (or load) more glycogen into your muscles if you depleted them first. Thus, back in the 1970s, the better marathoners would go for a "depletion" run of 20 miles the weekend before their races, which drained their muscles of glycogen.

For the next three days, marathoners followed a low-carbohydrate diet. This maintained the glycogen level of their muscles at an artificially low level. Then, in the final three days before the marathon, they switched to a high-carbohydrate diet, which supposedly caused an overdose reaction, forcing the muscles to absorb a higher percentage of glycogen than otherwise might be the case. The example used was that if you squeezed all the water out of a sponge, it would absorb more than if it had never been squeezed.

The carbo-loading diet worked, sometimes. A number of marathoners (including myself) had very good performances after carbo-loading. But sometimes we crashed. There were a number of problems with this regimen.

1. Hindsight suggests that a hard 20-miler one week before a marathon was too destructive on the muscles, even for elite athletes used to high mileage.

2. Life without pasta is no fun, and runners tended to become depressed during the low-carb depletion phase the first three days of the week. This was not good for their attitudes leading into the race.

3. Some runners required more than three days of high-carbs to replenish the glycogen that was depleted during all of the above.

Research by Dr. Costill and others eventually suggested that you can get all the benefits of carbo-loading by concentrating on the high-carbohydrate phase during the final three days while forgetting the depletion phase. As a result, all of us are now much happier. Today, when runners talk about carbo-loading before a marathon, they're referring to a big plate of spaghetti with bread on the side washed down with a high-energy drink the night before the race.

Caffeine

Q: How does caffeine affect the body's ability to burn fat? Can I lose weight by drinking several extra cups of coffee a day?

A: That's been a point of controversy among exercise scientists for years. Some scientists wondered whether coffee might help people lose fat by speeding up their metabolisms. Caffeine has been shown to increase the blood fat levels. Theoretically, by supplying more fat in this form to the active muscles, those muscles should burn more fat and less carbohydrate during exercise, especially prolonged exercise. But Tim Noakes, M.D., of the University of Cape Town Medical School in South Africa and author of *Lore of Running*, found that if you follow the high-carbohydrate diet that is recommended for endurance athletes, you may negate this metabolic effect. In other words, a cup of coffee with that plate of pasta offers you no extra edge.

Dr. Noakes states: "Caffeine is one of the most powerful ergogenic (performance) aids, legal or otherwise. How it acts is still not entirely clear. I suspect that it has stimulatory effects on both the brain and on the muscles and that these effects are more important than the metabolic effects that may or may not increase fat metabolism during prolonged exercise."

The bottom line, suggests Dr. Noakes, is that you should not count on losing weight if you drink a few extra cups of coffee. The most effective means for weight loss remains combining exercise with a sound dietary routine in which you can burn more calories than you consume.

Vitamins

Q: A number of runners that I run with take vitamin supplements. They say that vitamins help them run faster. I've always thought that as long as I ate a reasonably well-balanced diet, I wouldn't need to take vitamins. Am I kidding myself, and should I be following their lead?

A: While there may be specific reasons why individual runners might have a vitamin deficiency and thus, might need some form of supplementation, I'm a nonbeliever when it comes to looking for nutrition at the drugstore. I'd rather send you to the grocery store, specifically to the aisles where you find fresh fruits and vegetables.

A number of runners use the excuse that they have poor diets as a reason for taking vitamin supplements, but they're kidding themselves. If you're starving yourself through a mistaken belief that you can improve performance by losing weight, or if you come from a Third World country and are actually starving, vitamin supplementation may help, but you'll still be missing other important nutrients in food that are necessary for good health. Even if you're only achieving two-thirds of the Recommended Dietary Allowance for vitamins and minerals, you probably don't need supplements, states Ellen Coleman, a sports nutritionist with The Sport Clinic in Riverside, California, and author of *Eating for Endurance*.

"There is no vitamin supplement that will improve running performance," says Coleman. "What's more, if you eat a balanced diet that provides enough calories, you probably don't even need the supplement. Despite what a lot of people think, runners don't have greater vitamin needs than sedentary people. Besides, the more food you eat, the greater your vitamin intake will be. And since runners generally eat more than sedentary people, they get more vitamins and minerals relative to their needs."

Junk Science

Q: I frequently see advertisements in running magazines and other publications promising performance improvements from certain supplements. Should I take these ads seriously?

A: No. A recent issue of the American Running and Fitness Association's *Running & Fit News* had something interesting to say about what ARFA advisor Mary Jo Feeney called junk science.

"There are many products that make persuasive claims to revolutionize your health and fitness," Feeney says, "but the true path is eating a balanced, low-fat diet, together with enjoying plenty of physical activities. Remember that dietary supplements, including vitamins, minerals, herbals, amino acids, and others, don't have to have a Nutrition Facts label like the one required on foods. And they don't have to undergo testing for effectiveness and safety, which are required for drugs."

Feeney listed the 10 red flags of junk science, quoting the Food and Nutrition Science Alliance.

- Tips that promise a quick fix
- Dire warnings of dangers from a single product or regimen
- Claims that sound too good to be true
- Simplistic conclusions drawn from a complex study
- Tips based on a single study
- Dramatic statements that are refuted by reputable scientific organizations
- Lists of "good" and "bad" foods
- Tips made to help sell a product
- Recommendations based on studies in publications that are not formally reviewed by others knowledgeable in the same field
- Tips from studies that ignore differences among individuals or populations

Feeney summarizes: "If you see any of these in the claims for a product, walk away and don't spend your money." I couldn't have said it better myself.

Creatine

Q: What can you tell me about an energy supplement called creatine? Can it improve performance?

A: I'm not a fan of performance-enhancing drugs, both for ethical and health reasons. My recommendation is not to take creatine.

The reason? It's expensive, at up to $30 for a week's supply, and it's questionable whether or not it actually helps performance. For distance runners, it may actually inhibit performance. Why do I make that statement? I contacted Melvin H. Williams, Ph.D., professor emeritus in the department of exercise science at Old Dominion University in Norfolk, Virginia, and the author of *The Ergogenics Edge: Pushing the Limits of Sports Performance*, and here is what he had to say.

Dr. Williams said that the sports world first became aware of creatine as a muscle-building supplement after Linford Christie of Great Britain won the 100 meters at the 1992 Olympic Games. Allegedly, Christie used creatine. Some research suggests that if you do strength training, the creatine will facilitate the regeneration of ATP (adenosine triphosphate), which provides immediate energy for muscle contraction. Several studies, including some on Swedish cyclists and Australian rowers, suggested that this provided a performance edge in sprint events, particularly about 4 to 6 seconds into the event. You can understand why a sprinter like Christie might be interested, particularly since supplementation with creatine, which occurs naturally in the body, is not on the International Olympic Committee's list of banned drugs.

But many other studies, including one conducted by Dr. Williams himself, showed no performance gains. He looked at sprinters at 60 meters and saw no difference between those taking creatine and the control subjects. "I couldn't duplicate the earlier results," admitted Dr. Williams. A study with Australian swimmers showed no effect at 25 and 50 meters.

Despite mixed opinions within the athletic and scientific communities, Dr. Williams concedes that there may be some advantage for bodybuilders and sprinters. "Power sports may benefit," he says. "But taking creatine could be a disadvantage for distance runners." One study of baseball players by Dr. Williams showed that they gained 5 pounds in one week. Distance runners might not appreciate such weight gain. The Swedish study that showed an advantage for events lasting 6 seconds also showed a disadvantage for a 3.6-kilometer terrain run. Participants ran slower because creatine increased their body mass.

What about side effects? One possibility is cramps, caused by creatine getting into the muscle and diluting electrolytes. Another possibility is decreased muscle flexibility and an increased risk of muscle pulls, which happened with a group of decathletes. A dietitian for a major-league baseball team that takes creatine discovered a significant increase in creatine kinase, an enzyme that is a marker for muscle damage. Nobody yet can predict what long-range health problems may be caused by overdosing on creatine.

Vegetarianism

Q: I am a female vegetarian who is very active in sports, but I get run-down a lot because of poor nutrition. I have started to make an effort toward healthier eating. I need some advice about protein-filled foods without a lot of fat, because I am trying to turn the fat I have into muscle.

A: Practicing vegetarianism can be a very healthy way to live. For instance, vegetarians have a lower incident of cardiovascular problems than us carnivores, but (and this is an important "but") you have to understand how to eat properly, otherwise you wind up with insufficient energy for training, or even normal living. You seem to already have discovered that fact.

A number of people who decide to become vegetarians simply cut red meat out of their diets, but that's not enough. What are you going to put *into* that same diet to ensure that you replace the vitamins and nutrients lost? Even 3 ounces of red meat a week will help keep your iron stores high. Runners should take care not to become iron-deficient, since it will compromise the ability of their red corpuscles to deliver oxygen to the muscles. Menstruating women have to pay special attention to maintaining high iron stores.

Because he is a vegetarian, I asked *Runner's World* magazine's executive editor Amby Burfoot to comment. "Protein usually isn't a problem unless someone is restricting calories, which this woman very likely is. Strict vegetarians should take B_{12} tablets, and of course, a female runner vegetarian may have to be careful about iron intake. Tell her to make spaghetti sauce like Italians: in a cast-iron skillet."

Vegetarians should also select cereals and breads that have been iron-enriched. Prune juice is rich in iron. So are refried beans, if you happen to eat in a Mexican restaurant. Also, spinach, tofu, peas, and broccoli are good ideas. If iron deficiency is going to be a lifetime problem for you, I suggest that you make a serious study of good nutrition.

Avoiding foods with fat to turn fat into muscle is not the way it works in the human body. When you eat fat, it gets broken down into sugar compounds, the same as carbohydrates or proteins. And all three can get deposited as fat. You can't turn stored fat into muscle. You can lose fat and gain muscle, but there's no easy and direct transfer of fat to muscle despite what the people promoting so-called fat-burning supplements would like you to believe. Losing weight is a matter of balancing calories in (eating) with calories out (normal activities, including exercise). Strike a negative balance, and you'll lose weight. Physiologically, it's simple; psychologically, it's much harder.

Nausea

Q: A problem that I have with longer, harder workouts, or longer races such as the marathon or triathlon, is extreme stomach upset. I try not to drink or eat too much, but I never hit the balance. Are there any tricks or medications that might help?

A: I sympathize with you. Normally, I don't participate in ultramarathons, but on one occasion, I competed in a snowshoe race that I knew would take me 6 hours to complete. I tried to refuel with a combination of soft drinks and candy bars, but it didn't work. My stomach became so upset that I eventually dropped out two-thirds through the race.

I've had better success, however, in lengthy cross-country ski races, grabbing whatever has been thrust at me along the trail—everything from blueberry soup (favored by Scandinavians) to chocolate chip cookies. In both long triathlons and bicycle races, I've had success packing fruits and candy bars under the seat of my bike. My favorites: peaches and Three Musketeer bars. There's less jarring in both ski and bike races. You're right, though. It is a fine balance.

That's what long workouts are for: to experiment with various replacement foods and fluids and energy bars. Perhaps you've already heard about the new gels that come in small plastic pouches (see "Gels" on page 182). But in events lasting for more than 4 hours, most endurance athletes find that they need solid food instead of, or in addition to, fluids and gels.

Postrace nausea in long-distance races is often caused by dehydration. If you fail to drink enough during a marathon and your body weight falls by more than 2 percent because of fluid loss, you may become sick because of the stress on your body. Ironically, this may lessen your desire to drink, which is one reason why I encourage runners to drink early and often during long races and in workouts.

I also get a number of questions from high school runners who become nauseated and throw up at the end of cross-country races, which are seldom over 5000 meters. In this case, it's less a matter of dehydration and more a matter of stress: running at a pace that takes them to 95 percent of maximum and above. A poor choice of prerace foods can complicate this problem.

Some athletes become so nervous that they vomit before competition. Bill Russell, the great center for the Boston Celtics, experienced this problem, although it didn't seem to affect his ability to perform. Ellen Coleman, a sports nutritionist with The Sport Clinic in Riverside, California, and author of *Eating for Endurance*, used to work as a nutritional consultant for the California Angels and describes one player who threw up before games. She eventually cured his problem by prescribing a liquid pregame diet rather than high-fat foods that take longer to digest.

So it's back to the drawing board. You simply need to test a number of replacement strategies both in training and in races of less importance to discover what works for you, and I stress "for you" because everybody is different.

Ammonia Breath

Q: I am a 31-year-old male who is in fair shape, and I can run a 10-K or ride a bike 30-plus miles anytime. One thing happens to me fairly often when I push myself past a certain point: A strange ammonia smell comes to me. It actually seems to be coming from inside my head. What is going on?

A: I checked with David L. Costill, Ph.D., director of the Human Performance Laboratory at Ball State University in Muncie, Indiana, and here is what he had to say.

"What usually happens is that people begin to burn fuels inefficiently, and the by-product for people who train hard, or who push to the edge in races, is that they start to metabolize proteins and produce ammonia. This usually only occurs with people who don't have much in the way of carbohydrate reserves. They've shifted over to burning fats and proteins. In a long run, it's a reflection that you're running out of fuel. Your body is forced to tap into other sources of energy, which are not efficient."

Dr. Costill continues: "Diabetics have this problem, or someone who has been starved, including people on no-carbohydrate diets. Their breath can smell like ammonia, although the smell more likely is acetone, one of the ketone bodies produced as a result of the inefficient burning of lots of fats. It's like having poor combustion in your car, which creates more waste products. Most runners are not used to burning alternate fuels, so they don't handle them well."

People who run marathons run out of carbohydrate-based glycogen several hours into the race and are forced to burn fats. This is one reason that they hit the wall. Normally, I wouldn't expect someone running only 10-K or biking 30 miles to have this problem. You should check your diet and focus on getting 55 percent of your calories from carbohydrates. By doing that, you not only should be able to get rid of that ammonia smell but also your improved diet will allow you to perform better.

Fat-Burning

Q: I'm a 19-year-old collegiate softball player, majoring in nutrition. I want to shed some extra fat in order to improve my speed and quickness. I must admit that I eat a lot, but it is always healthy food, mostly carbohydrates. At most, I run about 2 miles, three times a week, not including practice, weights, and extra sprint workouts. In one of my classes, I was told that in order for one's body to burn fat, one must work out aerobically beyond 20 minutes. I would run for that long, but I get extremely bored. To be honest, I feel that I am only gaining fat. What should I do to improve my overall condition?

A: I disagree with what you were told in class, and so does Nancy Clark, R.D., of Sports Medicine Brookline in Massachusetts and author of *Nancy Clark's Sports Nutrition Guidebook*. We both agreed that if you run 2 miles, you should burn approximately 200 calories. It's like a meter in a taxicab. It's going to start clicking away the minute you get in the backseat. And you'll burn calories as soon as you start running. Burn calories, and you can burn fat. If you don't eat excessively, you eventually will decrease the fat in your body. You may have misinterpreted something that you heard in class, because if you run 2 miles in 20 minutes, or run for 10 minutes on two occasions, you'll burn 200 calories, which if combined with other aerobic workouts of shorter or longer duration will result in fat loss.

Clark says that the secret to losing fat is to run a calorie deficit. If you eat 3,000 calories a day and burn 3,200 calories that day, you'll begin to lose weight. If you burn only 2,800 calories a day, you'll begin to gain it. The way to lose weight is not necessarily to go out and run for more than 20 minutes but rather to bring your eating and exercise habits into balance.

Weight Loss
Shed Pounds Sensibly

- Scale Shock
- Calorie Burn
- Plateau
- Losing Weight Gradually
- Fat-Loss Strategy

- Fear of Injury
- Body-Fat Measurement
- Shedding 100 Pounds
- Anorexia Nervosa
- Fad Diets

If weight loss has become a fixation for Americans, it is because so many of us are overweight. According to Joanne Milkereit, R.D., a dietitian connected with the Medical University of South Carolina in Charleston, 30 percent of us are overweight. "More disturbing," says Milkereit, "is that the numbers are growing. And the numbers are growing faster among children than they are among adults."

Ironically, and more the subject of this chapter, many others perceive themselves as being overweight even though they would not be considered so by any reasonable standard. These body-conscious individuals often want to lose weight to look better, feel better, or, for those engaged in sports, to perform better. According to the National Institutes of Health, an estimated one million Americans suffer from eating disorders and 50,000 will die from those eating disorders.

While researching this book, I attended the Gatorade Scientific Conference in La Quinta, California. Among the speakers was Linda Houtkooper, Ph.D., a nutrition specialist at the University of Arizona in Tucson. Dr. Houtkooper said, "The pressure for athletes to perform has never been greater. Many athletes are taught that enhanced performance will result from low body weight and, specifically, low body fat."

Attendees were invited to offer comments after each lecture. I suggested that if we only talked about young athletes, we were merely seeing the tip of the iceberg. I suspect that increasing numbers of adult athletes also have problems controlling their weight. I receive numerous inquiries from individuals seeking to lose weight, many of them with unrealistic goals, such as one woman who wanted to lose 20 pounds within three weeks.

Many manufacturers produce pills to cause weight loss. I notice increasing numbers of supplements that promise to trigger fat-burning. It became obvious from listening to the presenters at the Gatorade Scientific Conference that most of these products simply do not work.

The best way to lose weight is to combine a nutritional diet with exercise and create a calorie deficit. Do that and you can lose weight and (maybe) perform better. I stress that in my responses to the many readers who question me about the subject of weight loss, but I often wonder if they get the message.

Scale Shock

Q: I recently started long-distance running: 40 minutes, three times a week. The only problem is that I've started to gain weight, and it's worrying me. I am 5 feet 4 inches and now weigh 134 pounds. Obviously, this extra weight is not making it easy for me. What's happening and what should I do?

A: Relax, and don't worry about what could be a temporary weight gain, or perhaps more likely, a readjustment in the fat/muscle balance of your body. I spoke with Judy Tillapaugh, R.D., a dietitian who coaches women's track and cross-country at Indiana University–Purdue University at Fort Wayne. Her reaction was the same as mine. "Too many of us look only at the bathroom scale and not the whole person."

It's not uncommon for a sedentary person to gain weight rather than lose it when starting to exercise. The reason is that they replace fat with muscle. Muscle is more dense, thus it weighs more. The more sedentary the individual, the higher the ratio of fat to muscle and the more likely it is that he will shrink in size before the numbers on the bathroom scale start descending. In fact, one way that very thin people can gain weight is to begin to exercise.

Tillapaugh suggests that you should focus on girth and feelings rather than the bathroom scale. Are you more trim now that you've started exercising? Do you feel better? Are you more confident in your ability to accomplish tasks? There are other reasons for running beyond losing weight, although weight loss often is what gets people started.

Your weight gain should be temporary. In fact, some of it may be fluid, if thirst causes you to drink a lot after you run. (If those fluids, such as soft drinks or juices, contain calories rather than being water, that could be part of the problem.) Think less of a specific goal weight and more of a healthy weight range so you don't get trapped worrying about every little pound gained or lost from day to day and week to week. Once you adopt a regular running routine, you may begin to see a reversal of the trend. Tillapaugh and I both encourage you to continue running while considering the whole person.

Calorie Burn

Q: I am 20 years old. I want to start running and go on a diet to lose 40 pounds. How many minutes do I have to run to lose weight?

A: It's not so much a matter of minutes; it's miles.

A person who weighs about 150 pounds burns 100 calories for every mile covered running. Someone who weighs more (or less) will burn more (or fewer) calories, but 100 is a handy number to work with in explaining calorie burn.

One pound equals 3,500 calories. Eat 3,500 calories worth of food, and you'll gain 1 pound. Burn 3,500 calories exercising, and you'll lose 1 pound. Given that figure, you need to run 35 miles to lose 1 pound, 350 miles to lose 10 pounds, and 1,400 miles to lose 40 pounds. Averaging 27 miles a week, it would take you one year to lose 40 pounds. That much mileage may sound intimidating to a beginner, but it's about what the average reader of *Runner's World* magazine runs weekly.

You don't necessarily need to run nearly 4 miles a day to lose weight. You can combine diet with exercise. You can eat less. In fact, running often has the effect of at least temporarily suppressing your hunger. You also can't snack on chocolate chip cookies while running. Some people snack out of boredom, and running has the capability of filling boring times of the day. If running motivates you to cut even 250 calories from your daily diet (those chocolate chip cookies), that would be the equivalent of 2.5 miles running.

You want to create a calorie deficit. The combination of 250 calories dieting and 250 calories running would create a calorie deficit of 500 calories daily, or 3,500 calories a week. Voilà, you've just lost 1 pound.

That's theory, of course, and weight loss is not always as easy to achieve in practice, nor is it easy to maintain that weight loss. Maintaining weight loss will require a permanent lifestyle change. I can't promise that you will lose 40 pounds because of your new running routine, but you certainly will be choosing the correct strategy if you can combine diet and exercise.

You're probably going to find that the first 10 to 20 pounds will roll off relatively easy, assuming that you definitely are overweight. Once you have achieved your early weight loss, it will get progressively tougher as the body fights to preserve a certain percentage of fat for good health. Another conundrum is that the lighter you get, the fewer calories you will burn running, because you will have less weight to impede you.

Plateau

Q: I have been running up to 8 miles or working out on treadmills and stair machines five times a week for five years. I have become stagnant. I can't seem to run any faster or farther. Plus, I have gained about 7 pounds recently. Do you have any ideas how I could put more intensity into my workout and lose some of the weight?

A: There are three ways to lose weight: run more miles, eat less food, or combine both of them. More intense workouts are not necessarily going to work for you unless you can cover more miles in the same period of time.

But even that offers a problem. You don't necessarily double your calorie burn by doubling your mileage, at least if you consider calories burned over a 24-hour period. Chris Melby, Dr.P.H., a professor of nutrition at Colorado State University in Fort Collins, suggests that if you overtrain, you also may become overfatigued. That may cause you to eliminate "background" activities during other parts of the day that previously burned some calories. "You might be less likely to walk the dog if you're tired from too much exercise," comments Dr. Melby. Fatigue might also cause you to sleep more. So in considering your plateau, you might want to analyze what else you're doing during the 24 hours to burn calories. And consider also whether or not that extra 7 pounds you've added is muscle, thus not necessarily a negative factor.

What you need is a goal. Select some challenge or something to motivate you to a higher level of effort. This is one reason why seemingly sane people decide after running without racing for 20 years that they want to do a marathon.

It doesn't need to be a marathon, or anything even connected with a running race, but maybe there is some goal that might allow you to move from that plateau on which you now find yourself.

Losing Weight Gradually

Q: I've been jogging 2.5 miles a day, at least five days a week, for about four months. I'm 27 years old and weigh 215 pounds. I've been eating less also, but I've only lost 4 pounds. I had hoped that I would be losing more weight than that. Shouldn't the pounds just be dropping off?

A: Weight loss doesn't always come easily. A person who weighs about 150 pounds burns 100 calories for every mile covered running. Even though someone weighing 215 pounds would burn more calories than the 100-per-mile figure, it's best to stick with that number for convenience. Figuring 3,500 calories per pound, you would need to have burned 14,000 calories to have caused your 4-pound weight loss.

You run 2.5 miles a day, five days a week, which is a total of 12.5 miles a week. If you round that off to 10 miles, you can calculate that you burn 1,000 calories a week through your exercise routine. If you've been running for four months, I'm going to credit you with 16 weeks of running, so that comes to 16,000 calories. Exercise scientists would look at the difference between 14,000 and 16,000 and say that the difference is not "statistically significant." In fact, someone your size could easily have a day-to-day weight variation of several pounds without doing anything differently.

Four pounds of weight loss doesn't seem like much reward for four months of work. But if you keep your exercise routine up for another four months, you will have lost 4 more pounds, and at the end of the year, you should have shed 12 to 15 pounds.

If you were, indeed, eating less, you probably should have dropped a few more, but all in all, you're not doing that bad. There have been documented cases of people losing more than 100 pounds in a year, but usually these individuals are seriously obese. And sometimes, despite early successes, they gain that weight back. In all honesty, you probably are much better off losing pounds gradually than rapidly. The secret is to keep it up, or rather keep it off.

Fat-Loss Strategy

Q: For fat loss, is it better to run longer and slower or shorter and faster? What running program do you recommend for optimum weight loss?

A: It's better to run longer at a slow pace because in running, you burn calories related to how much ground you cover. Scientists describe this calorie burn in foot pounds. They measure the number of pounds you push over a given distance. In this respect, walking and running differ very little in their abilities to burn calories. Walk a mile and you burn approximately 100 calories; run that same mile and you also burn about 100 calories. It's how much ground you cover, not how fast you cover it. That doesn't seem fair, but it's true.

Still not convinced? If you walk 3 mph, you'll burn 300 calories. If you run 10 mph (but go only 3 miles), you also will burn 300 calories. If you extend that run at 10 mph for an hour and cover 10 miles, you will burn 1,000 calories. That doesn't make that workout "better." It depends upon your goals.

Of course, the number of calories burned varies depending on your weight, and it also can vary depending on your economy, the efficiency with which you walk or run. An inefficient runner with very bad form who rumbles along the ground thrashing his arms to counterbalance his pounding stride burns more calories than a smooth-striding elite runner who seems to float across the pavement. That's at least one advantage back-of-the-pack runners have over those who win the prizes; they probably burn more calories per mile.

Inevitably, the best program for weight loss is one that allows you to run more miles. If that means slowing down to preserve energy so you can cover more miles in a workout, do it. Or, if you have limited time for your training, such as a half-hour at lunchtime, you may want to speed up so you can cover the maximum amount of distance.

My advice would be to combine slow running and fast running with rest, in an organized training program that allows you to maximize your talents, whether your are a rumbler or a floater.

Fear of Injury

Q: I want to get back to running, but I am worried because I am 40 pounds heavier than before. Will the extra pounding cause me back or knee pain? If I keep running, regardless of the pain, will that cause any permanent damage? I have put off starting a running regimen because of the weight. Should I run now, or diet until I lose those 40 pounds, then start running?

A: If worrying about possible back or knee problems is what is holding you back, you may never get started. That also may be true if you wait until you lose those 40 pounds before beginning to run.

Don't worry about back or knee problems until they happen. But you shouldn't have to experience any pain if you return to running at a moderate pace. Think like a beginner. Start by walking. Simply by exercising at a moderate intensity, you should begin to shed some of that extra weight. When that happens, add jogging to your routine. You can combine walking and jogging in a single workout, or alternate between those workouts.

At the same time, you should also be getting your nutritional act together. The best way to lose weight is to combine diet and exercise. So limit some of your food intake. Don't go on a crash diet, but even removing 200 to 300 calories a day from your daily eating routine will allow you to reduce more weight. Remember, however, how long it took you to gain those 40 pounds. Don't be in too much of a hurry to lose them; if you overtrain or diet too much, you might suffer some injuries that could delay reaching your goal. Follow my advice and, within 6 to 12 months, you should see a new you in the mirror.

Body-Fat Measurement

Q: What is an appropriate body-fat percentage for a 44-year-old recreational runner? Got the calipers; got the formula; need the goal.

A: Elite male runners have body-fat percentages close to 8 percent, elite females 12 percent. That's unrealistic for many of us. A more sensible goal would be somewhere between 12 and 16 percent for men and between 16 and 20 percent for women. You could post somewhat higher numbers and still be considered fit.

Formulas aside, I've often found tremendous variation in percentages depending on the type of measurements done: calipers, deep water, electronic impedance, and others. My own body-fat percentages (using different forms of measurement) sometimes have varied as much as 5 to 6 percentage points, when my weight and fitness level was the same. One problem in attaining accurate body-fat measurement is the amount of subcutaneous fat stored deep beneath the skin, where the calipers can't reach.

In the laboratory, very precise measurements can be made using electronic machines that scan the body, but these machines often cost many hundreds of thousands of dollars, resulting in very high fees any time you use them. And in all honesty, I'm not convinced that they provide a body-fat number more meaningful than the number you can get with the calipers in your hand or the number on your bathroom scale.

What will work for you is to look at only your body-fat percentages and not the body-fat percentages of others, whether elite or healthy runners. You'll be able to see, as you train, whether or not your body fat is coming down. One of the best devices for determining body fat is the bathroom mirror.

Shedding 100 Pounds

Q: I am 48 years old and, until 10 years ago, used to run 50 miles a week. I want to resume running, with a weekly goal of half my previous mileage. In the past two years, I have gained a lot of weight, maybe 100 pounds, but my doctor says that it is okay to exercise. I have not taken good care of myself recently, but I want to feel better and become more active.

A: I don't mean to discourage you, but forget about a return to running until you shed at least some of those 100 pounds. Also, forget about the type of training you did a decade ago. Trying to repeat some of your old workouts is a sure recipe for an injury that will slow your comeback attempt.

Begin by walking. This will help you shed some of the extra weight. Assuming that you also watch your diet, the pounds should come off easily at first. Eventually, though, it will get tougher as you begin to approach your previous weight. Achieving that exact weight may be very difficult because your body has changed and you have aged in the last 10 years. A reasonable goal would be to get your weight down to within 25 pounds of your previous running weight. Once you achieve that goal, you then need to evaluate your efforts to that point and consider how much farther you can go with your weight loss. I don't mean to set up artificial barriers, but I don't want you to get discouraged. Combining diet and exercise is the best way to lose weight, so take a very close look at your diet. And don't look merely at the number of calories for different foods but also look at the nutrient value of those calories.

Walk for a week, or two weeks, whatever it takes to get used to exercising again. When you feel comfortable with this routine, you can begin to alternate some jogging and walking. After a while, you may be able to do continuous runs. But I would be very cautious until you get rid of some of that fat. Think of how hard it would have been when you were doing those 50-mile weeks to have been forced to carry a 100-pound pack on your back. That's what you're stuck with now. But if you can maintain your motivation, you can reach your goals.

Anorexia Nervosa

Q: I started running to lose weight about two years ago when I was 16. Soon enough, however, I began to eat improperly, and I went from being a 120-pound, 5-foot-4 girl to a 93-pound weakling. I'm better now and my running has improved, but food overwhelms me at times. I find myself lost in hard workouts to burn off calories, even when I have little energy. I'm now 102 pounds. I love to run, but I don't know if my tough workouts make it harder for me to start eating better and feel normal again.

A: Your case is frightening to me. It's one of the reasons why I bark at other (mostly female) runners who pepper me with questions related to what I consider excessive weight-loss desires. You're far from normal now. You're still showing all the symptoms of anorexia nervosa and certainly need counseling from a registered dietitian and/or someone such as a psychiatrist who can dig down to the roots of why you are doing this to your body. Your tough workouts, probably combined with insufficient nutrition, are part of those symptoms.

In fact, excessive training for which the goal is burning more calories and losing more weight is also part of your problem and even has a name: *anorexia athletica*. Run more miles and burn more calories, many obsessed runners believe. In actuality, individuals who do this hit a point of diminishing returns because excessive exercise makes them excessively fatigued. This forces them to sleep more and move more slowly as their bodies fight to preserve energy. One friend of mine who ran more than 100 miles a week while in high school recalls being so tired that he could hardly walk up stairs between classes. On one occasion when his coach called off a Saturday morning practice session, he went back to bed and slept until Sunday morning.

Following is the American Psychiatric Association's description of the symptoms of anorexia nervosa.

- An intense fear of gaining weight or becoming fat, even though you're underweight
- A negative change in the way you experience your body (for example, claiming to feel fat even when you are in fact emaciated), with an undue influence of body weight or shape on self-perception
- Weight loss to less than 85 percent of your normal body weight or, if during a period of growth, failure to make 85 percent of the expected weight gain
- Refusal to maintain body weight over a minimal normal weight for your age and height
- Denials of the seriousness of the current weight loss
- Absence of at least three consecutive menstrual cycles

While young women are more likely to become anorexic than men, I can cite at least one male cross-country runner, overweight when younger, who stopped eating out of fear of becoming fat again. He ended the season in a hospital. People have died from anorexia nervosa, the most publicized example being that of singer Karen Carpenter.

Nutritionist Nancy Clark, R.D., of Sports Medicine Brookline in Massachusetts and author of *Nancy Clark's Sports Nutrition Guidebook*, summarizes the problem: "The majority of people with eating disorders exercise compulsively. The athlete with anorexic tendencies exercises as a means to create a calorie deficit and be thinner; the athlete with bulimic tendencies exercises to burn off the calories consumed during a binge." (Bulimia is a disease that is marked by self-induced vomiting or the use of medications, including enemas and diuretics, to prevent weight gain.) Clark continues: "Extreme eating disorders usually reflect an inability to cope with life's day-to-day stresses."

Excessive exercising, dieting to the point of starvation, and the binge/purge syndrome of bulimia are all part of a downward health spiral guaranteed to inhibit performance rather than improve it. It is impossible to perform well as a runner without eating properly. Starvation as a way of maintaining an artificially low weight is extremely dangerous. Runners who recognize themselves in any of the behavior problems mentioned above should seek help immediately.

Fad Diets

Q: I have recently learned from many sources that a diet high in protein and fat and low in carbohydrates (while supplementing with vitamins) is a good way to lose fat and hold onto muscle. I am currently on this diet and have to say that it has worked! The only drawback that I've noticed is a sluggish feeling all day. Am I headed for a health problem here? I like the weight loss because my runs appear to be easier since I've lost 10 pounds.

A: Your source provided you with a fad diet that works in the short run but has little promise for the long run. You're sluggish because the body has to work hard to convert fat and protein into glycogen. Carbohydrates are much more efficient as a fuel for exercise.

One of the reasons why you lose weight on low-carbohydrate diets is that you lose fluids and become artificially dehydrated, a bad idea for exercisers. With insufficient carbohydrates, you also store insufficient glycogen in your muscles. (Glycogen bonds with water, one reason why you have more fluid in your system while following a diet rich in carbohydrates.) The problem is that without carbohydrates/glycogen, you don't have enough energy to exercise at a level to keep weight off efficiently.

Fluid loss, of course, is only temporary. Even if you do drain 5 to 10 pounds of fluid out of your system by becoming dehydrated, and thus lose weight, you eventually will reach a plateau where you will have no more fluid to lose. Most of these kooky diets work, even though their promoters don't admit it, by getting people to cut calories and starve themselves. But a better weight-maintenance routine would have you eat a balanced diet and create a calorie balance by using exercise to burn as many calories as you eat.

Go back to a diet that has a better blend of carbohydrate sources such as whole grains, fruits, and vegetables. Some fats and proteins are necessary, but they should not dominate your diet. Use a well-balanced diet that includes lightly processed foods, and you can get rid of those vitamin pills as well. It has been proven that the only successful way to maintain weight loss over a long period is by combining exercise with a healthy diet.

17

Health and Fitness
The Greatest Motivators of All

- **Enough to Stay in Shape**
- **Asthma**
- **Arthritis**
- **Allergic Reaction**
- **Bursitis**
- **Diabetic Marathoner**

- **Headaches**
- **Numb Feet**
- **The Flu**
- **Wrinkles**
- **An End to Smoking**

One reader asking for advice on a medical problem began his question by stating, "I did not see an M.D., D.P.M., or D.O. by your name, but hopefully, you know someone who can help me with my problem."

My response was to say that, no, I was not a doctor, and I try not to pose as one, but Ann Landers is not a psychiatrist and she has spent half a century dispensing a fair amount of psychiatric advice to her readers. Like Ann Landers, when a question arrives in my mailbox requiring a level of scientific or medical expertise that I don't possess, I contact an advisor who can provide that expertise.

In many instances, however, I can provide what might be called anecdotal advice based on my experience as a runner and the knowledge that I have gleaned while writing articles and books about health and physical fitness for the past 40 years.

Many questions that I receive relate to health; many relate to fitness. In fact, recent surveys of **Runner's World** magazine readers suggest that obtaining information on how to improve their health and fitness is a major reason why people continue to subscribe to our magazine.

Enough to Stay in Shape

Q: Is a 3-mile walk three times a week enough to keep a 48-year-old woman in shape, or is more needed?

A: Yes and no. It depends partly on your definition of being in shape. That much exercise would come close to meeting the American College of Sports Medicine (ACSM) standard for achieving health benefits. The ACSM recommends that we all exercise 20 to 60 minutes, three to five times a week. You fit right in.

But Michael L. Pollock, Ph.D., director of the Center for Exercise Science at the University of Florida in Gainesville, and one of the individuals who helped formulate the ACSM standards, suggests that you also consider some strength training. "You need to train all the muscle groups," says Dr. Pollock, "and that includes the hips, abdomen, and upper body. Walking won't do that."

Pumping iron might seem a strange activity for a 48-year-old woman, except when you consider that you are only a dozen years from the age when women begin to fall victim to osteoporosis, which is the progressive weakening of the bones from mineral loss. Fortunately, there are many exercise machines that you can use in the privacy of your home. You don't have to go to a gym and work out next to the bodybuilders.

Walking (or jogging) more often (or farther) would produce additional health benefits, specifically in the areas of improved cardiovascular response and weight control. Kenneth H. Cooper, M.D., author of *Aerobics*, points to 15 miles a week of walking or jogging as enough to achieve a good level of physical fitness. He says that when you go beyond 15 miles, you're doing it for reasons other than fitness. And I agree.

The average reader of *Runner's World* magazine does just that. Our readers average about 25 miles a week and participate at least occasionally in a 5-K or 10-K race. Those who compete in marathons run 40 to 60 miles a week. But now we're approaching the upper reaches of staying in shape. Inevitably, you are the one who decides how far you want to go and how much you want to do.

Asthma

Q: I have a problem with exercise-induced asthma. Can you give me some hints to help relieve the symptoms? Would changing my diet or taking vitamins help?

A: Exercise-induced asthma seems to be a growing and common problem these days among runners and among the general population as well. One study suggests that the incidence of asthma has doubled in the past two decades. One reported cause is that younger people now suffer fewer childhood infections, such as whooping cough and tuberculosis. Apparently, such infections once trained the immune system not to react to irritants such as dust and pollen. Without such infections, you're more likely to suffer problems from asthma and other allergic reactions. The study suggested that we might be able to limit asthma attacks by using a tuberculosis vaccine, but scientists are not yet ready to endorse that approach.

Asthma should not be taken lightly. Reportedly, 5,000 Americans died from asthma attacks in 1995, a 44 percent increase in only a dozen years. According to the National Institutes of Health, asthma cases shot up 34 percent during the same period. It's particularly a problem with children in larger cities. Twelve million Americans now have asthma.

Why do we get asthma? Genetics is a factor. If your parents have asthma, that increases your chance of getting it, too. Other factors that might trigger an asthma attack: cigarette smoke, auto exhaust, pollen, household dust, animal dander (dandruff), and insects. Other causes include infections (a cold or the flu), stress, allergies, and exercise. By inhaling irritants, you may inflame your airways, or bronchi. This will cause mucus to build up. The muscles surrounding the bronchi tighten or spasm, and the airways narrow. Suddenly, you have trouble breathing.

Symptoms include wheezing, chest tightness, and coughing. Muscle-relaxing spray drugs (bronchodilators) can relieve symptoms for runners with mild asthma. For those who have more severe symptoms, steroid-based drugs can help.

There's no evidence that taking vitamins can reduce your symptoms. Changing your dict would help only if some food allergy is causing your problem.

I coached a high school runner named Megan Leahy, who had several attacks of exercise-induced asthma in races her freshman year. She'd be running with the leaders, then all of a sudden, boom! Megan would fall to the back of the pack. It was like she had collided with a wall. Her mother worked closely with a physician to adjust her daughter's medication. According to one pulmonary function test, Megan's lung capacity was only 30 percent of normal. Eventually, Megan began to manage and control her asthma. As a senior, she placed second at the state cross-country championships, helping her team win its second straight state title.

Now a scholarship athlete at a Big Ten university, Megan still has problems, particularly in the spring because of certain pollens in the air. She finds that she experiences more difficulties when she goes out too fast, so she prefers running a steady pace (not always easy to achieve in competition).

If you have exercise-induced asthma, you can't go it alone or depend on self-medication. There are many prescription drugs available, some of which will help, some of which will not. You very definitely need to consult with a physician who understands the problem and who knows how to treat it. Keep in mind also that individual runners differ greatly as to why they have exercise-induced asthma and in the ways they overcome it.

Arthritis

Q: I have been diagnosed as having arthritis in my right ankle, probably as a result of multiple ankle sprains in my misspent youth. I have continued to run but not as long or hard as I used to. Am I going to make my arthritis worse or cause myself more problems if I continue running?

A: From all I can gather after talking to numerous physicians, running does not cause arthritis. They say that arthritis is more a congenital problem. In other words, you are what your parents are. That doesn't mean that some injury (your misspent youth) or running might not complicate the problems of arthritis. Some experts feel that increased bloodflow caused by running can lessen the problems of arthritis, but the ankle is an area without a lot of bloodflow to begin with.

Doctors often find that they need to approach each case differently. If running troubles your arthritic ankle, you might need to find some other activity that puts less strain on it. Cycling, swimming, or even walking might serve as a more satisfactory lifetime exercise. Or, you might need to try some supplementary exercises or stretches to strengthen the muscles around the ankle. Try ankle raises: standing barefoot and rising up on your toes. If that doesn't help, check some books on stretching and weight lifting for other possibilities. In the meantime, I would continue to run as long as your ankles let you without fear that you are causing further damage.

Allergic Reaction

Q: I just started jogging a week ago to lose a few extra pounds. I'm 5 foot 2 inches, 120 pounds, and 23 years old. Tonight, I pushed myself more than ever on my jog uphill. After about 25 minutes, my hands and lips began to swell. My tongue got so big that I couldn't even swallow. My heart was racing, the skin on my face felt tight, and I was huffing and puffing. I stopped running and walked until I finally found a drinking fountain, then gulped a lot of water down and rested for a minute. I was about a quarter-mile away from home, so I got up and walked slowly, but my symptoms became even worse. I could feel my lips swelling even bigger, and then I began to lose my vision. Everything was turning to spots, until my vision was almost gone. I felt like I was going to faint, but luckily, I could see just enough to make out my house. My entire body was shaking as I approached the door, and I collapsed to the floor the minute I got inside. My lips are still swollen, but finally, 3 hours later, I'm functioning fine again. What happened to me tonight? Should I swear off jogging forever?

A: You should have dialed 911 while you still had strength. Seriously, you could have died, particularly if the swelling in your throat had reached a point where it began to cut off your air supply.

I suspect that you pushed too hard after having only been running a week and triggered some sort of allergic reaction. It might not happen again, but please tread more gently into the night as you pursue your running goals.

You're not alone in your experience. A similar thing happened to me, and fortunately, someone was around to take me to an emergency room. It was about 15 years ago, and I was teaching a jogging/walking class at a tennis club in town. Meanwhile, members of our running club were working out at another part of town, and I planned to join them for dinner afterward. After the class, I began to run the 6 miles between the club and the restaurant.

Several miles from the restaurant, the call of nature forced me to duck into the bushes. Emerging, I continued running and began to feel a tingling sensation similar to what you described. Things deteriorated from there. I was having trouble breathing by the time I reached the restaurant and went straight to the restroom, figuring that splashing some water on my face would help. I looked in the mirror and saw that my face was swollen like a pumpkin.

One of the club members drove me to the emergency room, where a doctor gave me an injection for what appeared to be an allergic reaction. After about a half-hour, the symptoms declined. I never found out what caused the problem. A bee sting? Poison ivy? At one point in my run, I had passed a farmer who was spraying his crops. Had I breathed in some insecticide?

With your problem, I don't think that it was a vitamin deficiency. Dehydration might have contributed to your problem. Try to think of what else was happening around you as you ran. If an incident like this happens again, seek treatment immediately and see an allergist.

Bursitis

Q: I was diagnosed with bursitis of the hip about a year ago, and it hasn't improved much despite RICE (rest, ice, compression, and elevation), two cortisone shots, and too much ibuprofen. I run 3 to 5 miles, three times a week. The hip doesn't hurt while I'm running, and it didn't improve when I took two months off. My doctor says little about whether I should continue to run. What's your advice? And can I ever train for a marathon under these circumstances, or must I wait until the bursitis vanishes completely, if it ever does?

A: Bursitis is a tough problem to cure. It's more a condition than an injury, so it doesn't always respond to treatment, as you already have discovered. You've tried all the traditional remedies that I might have suggested.

Bursitis is an inflammation of the bursae, which serve as cushions between bones and tendons, between tendons, and between bones and the skin. They are tiny pouches in different areas of the body, and friction and stress occur there frequently.

Lyle J. Micheli, M.D., writes in the *Healthy Runner's Handbook*, "An overuse bursa injury, known as bursitis, occurs when irritation of the bursa causes fluid to flow into the sac and become inflamed. In a bursa that lies between two tendons or between a tendon and a bone, irritation is usually caused by repetitive movement of the tendon over the bursa."

Among the preventive measures that Dr. Micheli suggests are improving strength and flexibility and proper warmup and cooldown. Treatment includes protecting the bursae from further impact, RICE, anti-inflammatories, and at the far end, surgical removal. In addition, I might suggest therapeutic massage as one way of relieving the pain, but that's more a guess than a medical opinion.

Concerning your question, I would continue to train as long as you can run without too much pain. (You may need to program more rest days.) As for a marathon, your body probably will tell you whether or not that is possible. You didn't say what type of physician you're seeing, but if he is not able to offer more help, you may want to seek advice from a different specialist more familiar with sports injuries.

Diabetic Marathoner

Q: I was diagnosed with insulin-dependent diabetes almost five years ago. I keep my sugars under good control, and I am well within my ideal body weight. I want to train for, and subsequently run, a marathon. Is this an attainable goal?

A: My father-in-law had diabetes. It eventually caused him to go blind, so I do have a strong understanding of the problems faced by people with diabetes. None of our three sons or seven grandchildren have been diagnosed with the disease, but the genetic sword is over their heads.

Yet many people with diabetes live healthier lives than so-called normal people, particularly if they are diagnosed early and educate themselves on how to manage their disease. They learn to eat right and exercise, something that too many members of the American public have not yet learned to do.

"There's no reason that you can't run a marathon, as long as you take proper precautions," says Robert Cantu, M.D., of Concord, Massachusetts, a past president of the American College of Sports Medicine. "One of the most important precautions is to *not* keep your diabetic condition a secret from those around you. Warn your training partners and race partners about your condition so that if you start getting blurry-eyed and begin to weave because of an insulin reaction, those around you won't mistake it for heatstroke. At least on the long runs, you probably don't want to run alone."

Exercise allows many diabetics to reduce the levels of insulin that they must take to control their diabetic conditions. I'm sure that you've already discovered that and learned that it's a good idea to carry some sugar candies to counter a low blood sugar as a result of vigorous exercise. I would think that the new quick-calorie gel products would be particularly useful for people with diabetes.

Running a marathon is difficult for anybody because of the stress, and this is more true for you. But I'm hopeful that with proper precautions, you can achieve your goal of a marathon finish.

Headaches

Q: I get a headache and become short of breath when I run. What should I do?

A: Becoming short of breath is natural when you run, at least to a point. Your body systems, including those feeding the brain, need fuel, just like your automobile needs fuel. The fuel used by the muscles is glycogen, but it takes oxygen to break it down. Your heart beats faster, pumping oxygen to the muscles. You begin to breathe harder to bring more oxygen from the lungs.

If you're not in good shape and don't have a good aerobic base, you get out of breath faster because you have an inefficient oxygen-delivery system. This is natural.

Having headaches is not natural, although they may be linked to an inefficient cardiovascular system, which fails to deliver enough oxygen to the brain. The brain isn't getting enough fuel for its needs, so it sends out a signal in the form of a headache. Presumably, if you slow down, the headache should disappear.

Headaches can be caused for numerous reasons, however, and some people have headaches that are severe enough to be classified as migraine headaches. I called Seymour Diamond, M.D., of the Diamond Headache Clinic in Chicago, who is an international expert on headaches. Dr. Diamond cited numerous reports of runners' headaches in the literature.

"Exertional headaches can occur in some individuals," he said. "Although most of these headaches are from benign causes, the patient should be thoroughly evaluated to rule out a more serious origin of the headaches. Therapy is available, such as the use of a nonsteroidal anti-inflammatory agent prior to the activity."

At the risk of alarming you, the headache could also be a signal being sent by your body to announce a more serious medical condition. Have you had a physical exam lately? You sound like a beginning runner, and I always recommend that beginners (particularly those 35 or older) get stress tests before starting too vigorous an exercise regimen.

Play it safe. Visit your doctor. Request a physical exam with a stress test. Once cleared, you can return to running without worry, and hopefully, without those headaches.

Numb Feet

Q: I am an 18-year-old runner training for a marathon and have begun to do long runs of 12 miles or more. Last weekend was my first time at this distance, and after about 6 miles, my feet began to tingle like they were asleep. Why is this happening, and how can I prevent it from happening again?

A: I posed your question to Paul D. Thompson, M.D., director of preventive cardiology at Hartford Hospital in Connecticut.

Dr. Thompson suggests that it may be because your feet swell as you run. This means that your shoes become tighter toward the end of a long run than at the beginning. The tight shoes cause the numbness. One solution would be to lace your shoes less tightly and make sure that the shoes you use for your long runs are not too tight to begin with.

Another possibility is that your problem may be related to compartment syndrome, where the leg muscles enclosed in sheaths expand to the point where they begin to bring pressure on the nerves within those sheaths. This may cause tingling of the feet and the legs. Dr. Thompson says that this condition usually improves as people get in better shape, but not always. One other solution that he suggests is to wear thicker socks, which provide more cushioning. When the feet swell, they will be less likely to cramp, because the socks will compress them.

The Flu

Q: While training for marathons, I reach the point of doing 20-mile long runs and then get the flu shortly thereafter. As a result, I lose critical training time and don't run the marathon. This has happened three times. I take plenty of vitamins. Why is this happening?

A: Vitamins are not the answer, at least not those you buy in a drugstore. The best vitamins are those that come packaged in fresh foods. Despite all the hype about vitamin C, there's little proof that it can help to boost your immunity against the flu and typical winter colds.

David C. Nieman, Dr.P.H., of Appalachian State University in Boone, North Carolina, once surveyed 2,311 finishers of the Los Angeles Marathon and found that 13 percent suffered an upper respiratory infection the week following the race, compared to 2 percent among a control group, which was comprised of marathon runners who did not run the 1987 Los Angeles Marathon but had trained for it similarly and were equally experienced. When we get our mileage up high, it often causes our immune systems to crash. Dr. Nieman discovered that those who trained over 60 miles a week were twice as likely to get sick.

Here are some tips on how to avoid colds and the flu.

Avoid people with colds. Cold viruses are spread both by personal contact (shaking hands, for example) and by breathing the air near people.

Wash your hands frequently. Also, avoid touching your mouth, nose, or eyes after being in contact with someone who is ill.

Get a flu shot. If it doesn't prevent you from catching the flu, it may help reduce the symptoms.

Drink sports beverages before and after hard runs. Maintaining high glucose levels seems to improve immunity.

Avoid mental stress. Work or home stress combined with hard training can be a bad combination.

Take a cautious approach to weight loss. Dieting can depress the immune system, especially if you lose weight too quickly.

Maintain a balanced diet. Poor nutrition, particularly a diet deficient in vitamins and minerals, can depress immune system function.

Get plenty of sleep, and at the right times. With insufficient sleep, your immune system can crash. Jet lag can be a factor.

Try not to overtrain. Marathon training, almost by definition, involves overtraining. Too many miles, however, can make you ill.

While Dr. Nieman's research showed increased problems for those training more than 60 miles, it's my feeling that it's not so much how much you run but how you get there. Thus, an individual who increases his weekly mileage from 20 to 40 may be at more risk than a runner who runs 80 miles weekly but is comfortable at that level. There's no question in my mind, however, that overtraining is one of the main reasons why runners catch upper respiratory infections while preparing for marathons.

Wrinkles

Q: In a book by a prestigious New York cosmetic surgeon, the author advises against running, especially long-distance running. He claims that it causes facial wrinkling and a haggard look. Do you have any recommendations or advice?

A: Did the author really say that? That's a little bit like suggesting that you give up sex because it causes pregnancy. What about the fact that running and various other forms of physical fitness have the potential to extend life?

Go to the starting line of any 5-K or marathon race and examine the faces of the runners entered. Do their faces look wrinkled or haggard? How do they look compared to the rest of the nonexercising population? You're more likely to get wrinkles from smoking or sitting in the sun than by running.

That doesn't mean that runners don't need to cover up. Knowing what I now know about skin cancer, I wish that I had run more frequently with a cap to shade my face while younger. Suntan lotion also will protect against the sun. Pick a high sun-protection factor and slather it on well before you run so it has time to dry before you start to sweat. Double-layer, if necessary. Runners need to be particularly cautious when running midday in summer. But stop running? No way.

An End to Smoking

Q: I am a smoker and would like to begin a running program to help me quit. How many times a week should I walk or run? Is it safe to run every day?

A: It's safe for most people to run every day, but you don't want to do too much too soon. This is particularly true since you may have compromised your health, depending on how long you smoked. Nicotine not only affects the lungs and raises the risk of cancer but it also affects your cardiovascular system. Start out very slowly and watch for any warning signs that might signal undiagnosed heart disease, such as tightness in your chest. It's also a good idea to get a medical checkup before you start, just to be safe. The longer you smoked and the older you are, the more important it is to have a stress test before starting vigorous exercise.

Now that I've thoroughly scared you, I hasten to add that running and walking on a regular basis is an excellent way to kick the smoking habit. That's because fitness activities allow you to set goals. Your goal becomes to walk a mile, or walk for 20 minutes, a day. For some people, the next goal will be to run that mile without stopping. A lot of us who have run for many years have forgotten how heady an experience it can be for someone not used to exercise to run a full mile nonstop. After that, your goal might become running 2 miles or 3 or entering a 5-K race just to finish and win a T-shirt. At some point in your life, you might even consider running a marathon, although I don't advise that right now. Regardless, your focus becomes doing something positive (getting in shape) rather than doing something negative (quitting smoking).

You may want to settle for an every-other-day routine, at least until you become comfortable with running. Start with a half-hour workout routine. Begin by walking for 5 minutes, then alternate jogging and walking, letting your body tell you when to stop and start. Don't be intimidated by faster runners around you. We all were beginners at one time or another, and I think that you'll find the running community very supportive of your efforts. Finish the last part of the half-hour by walking for 5 minutes.

If you want to train every day, which might be a good idea since you're trying to do something else daily other than smoke, go for a pleasant half-hour walk on the off days. Try to pick a scenic or interesting location so the walk is something that you look forward to. Once you're comfortable with running three or four days a week, 2 to 3 miles a day, you may decide to remain at that level. That routine is plenty for good health, although you should add two days a week of strength training for total fitness. Once you get in shape, you'll discover that you will want to avoid cigarettes for fear of compromising your training. But be sympathetic to other smokers around you. They may want to quit smoking, too, but don't have the courage you have already displayed.

Index

Beginner runners
    adding distance and, 2-3
    breathing while running
        and, 4
    fatigue and, 7-8
    fitness and, 5-6
    frequency of running vs. distance
        and, 9
    injuries and, first, 6-7
    progress of, 10
    similarities and differences among,
        1-2
    slow vs. fast running and, 8-9
    walking-to-running switch for,
        3-4
    weight lifting and, 5
Bicycling, 60, 65
Binge/purge syndrome, 204
Biomechanics. *See* Technique for
    running
Black toes, 121
Bladder problems, women runners
    and, 139
Blisters, 120-21
Body fat
    amenorrhea and, 136-37
    anorexia athletica and,
        203
    anorexia nervosa and,
        202-4
    bulimia and, 204
    eating disorders and,
        202-4
    losing, 199-201
    measurement, 201
    muscle vs., 195-96
Boston Marathon, 85, 95
Bounding drills, 37-38
Breast cancer, women runners
    and, 133-34
Breathing while running
    altitude and, 51-52
    beginner runners and, 4
    stomach cramps and, 105
Bulimia, 204
Bunions, 123-24
Burnout, overcoming, 25-26
Bursitis, 211-12

C

Caffeine, 186
Calf injury, 109-10
Calorie burn
    exercise and, 193, 199
    nutrition and, 193
    slow vs. fast running and, 8, 199
    weight loss and, 190-91, 196-97
Camps, running, 28
Cancer
    breast, 133-34
    skin, 216
Carbohydrates, 184-86
Carbo-loading, 184-86
Carriage, running technique and,
    31
Chafing, 99, 137
    heart rate monitor and, 137
    of legs, 99
Children. *See* Young runners
Chondromalacia patella, 112-14
Cigarette smoking, quitting, 216-17
Circadian rhythms, 23, 44
Clothes. *See also* Shoes
    breathable, 174-75
    caps and hats, 175
    chafing and, 99
    for cold-weather running,
        174-75
    layering, 12-13, 174
    mittens, 175
    overdressing and, 175
    socks, 124, 175
    water-resistant, 175
Clubs, running, 19, 147
Clydesdale runners
    shoes for, 130
    training for, 48-49
Coaching young runners, 159-60
Cold, common, 102, 215
Cold-weather running, 173-74
    clothes for, 174-75
    hydration and, 175
    time of day for, 176-78
    wind and, 176

Compartment syndrome, 111-12
Conversion rates, cross-training, 61, 63-64
Crashing after marathon, avoiding, 82-83
Creatine, 188-89
Cross-country meet, nutrition and, 180, 191
Cross-country skiing, cross-training and, 62-63
Cross-training, 57-58
    conversion rates and, 61, 63-64
    cycling, 60, 65
    duathlon, 66-67
    marathon, 68-69
    motivation for, 69-70
    power lifting, 59
    shoes, 127
    skiing, 62-63
    snowshoes, 66
    Spinning, 65
    swimming, 61-62
    in training routine, 60-61
    triathlon, 67-68
    weight lifting, 58-59
Cycling, 60, 65

D

Deep lunge exercise, 35
Dehydration, 211
    cold-weather running and, 175
    hot-weather running and, 173
Detraining, 50-51
    aging runners and, 149
    injuries and, 97-98
Diabetes, 212-13
Diet. See Nutrition
Dietary fats, 184-85
Dieting, 204-5. See also Weight loss

Distance
    beginner runners and, 2-3
    frequency of running vs., 9
    increasing, 41-42, 74
    of tracks, 53-54
    training for, 41-42
    young runners and, 157-60
Dogs
    as partners for women runners, 142-43
    as threats to runners, 55-56
Downhill running, 38-39. See also Hill training
Drinking technique in racing, 92-94. See also Hydration
Duathlon, 66-67

E

Easy/hard approach to motivation, 25
Eating disorders, 202-4
Elliptical trainer, 14
Endorphins, 2
Energy, nutrition for, 181-84
Energy bars, 184
Equipment. See also Clothes; specific types
    baby joggers, 16-17
    brand names and, 11-12
    heart rate monitor, 16
        chafing and, 137
        for training, 49-50
    inside vs. outside workouts and, 15
    layering clothes and, 12-13, 174
    tights, 12
    total-body workout, 13-14
    treadmills, 14-15, 46-47
Estrogen, women runners and, 132-33

H

Half-marathon, 88–89
Half-taper program, 89–90
Hamstring(s)
   injury, 114–15
   strength training, 58–59
Hats, 175
Headaches, 172–73, 213–14
Head position, running technique
      and, 31
Health problems. *See also* Injuries
   advice on, 206–7
   allergy, 210–11
   arthritis, 209–10
   asthma, 208–9
   bursitis, 211–12
   cold, common, 215
   cold-weather-related
      clothes and, 174–75
      dehydration, 175
      time of day for running and,
         176–78
      training and, 173–74
      wind and, 176
   diabetes, 212–13
   eating disorders, 202–4
   flu, 214–15
   headaches, 172–73, 213–14
   hot-weather-related
      dehydration, 173
      fatigue, 169–70
      headaches, 172–73
      overheating, 171–72
      perspiration, 170–71
   nausea, 191–92
   numb feet, 214
   smoking-related, 216
   wrinkles, 216
Healthrider, 14
Heart rate, 49–50, 148–49
Heart rate monitor, 16
   chafing and, 137
   training and, 49–50
Heat and humidity, 169. *See also* Hot-
      weather running

Heatstroke, 13
Heat treatments, 102
Heel drops exercise, 107, 109
Heel hold exercise, 35
Hill training
   marathons and, 81–82
   numb toes and, 34–35
   running technique and,
      38–39
   treadmills and, 46–47
Hip pain, 116
Honolulu Marathon, 13
Hot tubs, 178
Hot-weather running
   fatigue and, 169–70
   headaches and, 172–73
   heatstroke, 13
   hydration and, 173
   overheating and, 171–72
   perspiration and, 170–71
Hurdle exercise, 35
Hurdler's reach exercise, 114
Hydration
   cold-weather running and, 175
   hot-weather running and, 173
   prerace, 181
   while racing, 92–94
   urination problems and, for
      women runners, 139

I

Iliotibial band injury, 115
Immune system, training and,
      133–34
Infection, upper respiratory, 133
Influenza, 214–15
Injuries. *See also* Foot problems
   Achilles tendinitis, 106–7
   ankle sprain, 107–8
   beginner runners and, 6–7

Injuries *(continued)*
  calf, 109–10
  chafing, 99
  cold treatments for, 102
  compartment syndrome,
    111–12
  detraining and, 97–98
  hamstring, 114–15
  heat treatments for, 102
  hip pain, 116
  iliotibial band, 115
  knee, 100, 112–14
  overuse, 149–50
  overweight runners and, 200
  plantar fasciitis, 104–5
  progressive pain, 116–17
  rest and, 97
  runner's knee, 112–14
  running after, 100
  running through pain and, 103
  shinsplints, 97, 110–11
  shoes and, 119
  soreness vs., 101–2
  stomach cramps, 105–6
  stress fracture, 141–42
  stretching and, 98, 107, 115,
    117
  technique for running and, 97,
    141–42
  training and, 98–99, 117–18
  unstable surface for running and,
    108
  of young runners, 158
Interest in running, lack of, 20–21
Interval training, 44–45
Iron, 135

J

Jitters, racing, 91–92, 171–72, 192
Junk science on nutrition, 187–88

K

Kneecap pain, 112–14
Knee grab exercise, 114
Knee injuries, 100, 112–14

L

Lactic acid, muscle soreness and,
  101
LaSalle Banks Chicago Marathon, The,
  131
Layering running clothes, 12–13,
  174
Lifting weights. *See* Weight lifting
Love of running, passing on, 156–57
Lunchtime runs, 177–78

M

Marathon(s)
  aging runners and, 75
  ammonia breath and, 192–93
  attraction of, 71–72
  avoiding crashing after, 82–83
  Boston, 85, 95
  breaking three-hour barrier in,
    77–78
  cross-training for, 68–69
  diabetes and, 212–13
  first, 72–73
  flat running and, 81–82

goal setting, 75
hill training and, 81–82
increasing distance and, 73
Marine Corps, 170
motivation and, 20
postrace syndrome and, 84–85
speed and, 73
training
  errors, 76–77
  final run, 83–84
  minimum, 75–76
  overtraining, 78–79
  weight lifting, 79–80
as "training" run, 80–81
weight lifting and, 79–80
young runners and, 162
Marine Corps Marathon, 170
Meals. *See* Nutrition
Menstrual cycle, women runners and,
  135–36
Metabolism, 23
Migraine headaches, 213
Mileage. *See* Distance
Mittens, 175
Morning runs, 43–44, 176–77,
  183–84
Morton's toe, 122
Motivation, 19–20
  burnout and, 25–26
  for cross-training, 69–70
  difficulty of teaching, 18–19
  easy/hard approach to, 25
  goal setting and, 22–23
  lack of, 20–21
  marathon run for, 20
  partners and, 26–27
  personal, 28
  plateaus in exercise and, 19
  racing, 86–87
  runner's high and, 27–28
  stamina and, 20–21
  time of day for running and, 23
  time management and, 21–22
  workouts for, 25
  for young runners, 23–24
Muscle
  body fat vs., 195–96
  soreness, 101–2

N

Nausea, nutrition and, 191–92
Nervousness, racing and, 91–92,
  171–72, 192
Nicotine, 216–17
Nordic skiing, cross-training and,
  62–63
NordicTrack, 11, 13
Nutrition
  amenorrhea and, 136–37
  ammonia breath and, 192–93
  anorexia athletica and, 203
  anorexia nervosa and, 202–4
  bulimia and, 204
  caffeine and, 186
  calorie burn and, 193
  carbo-loading and, 184–86
  creatine and, 188–89
  cross-country meet and, 180,
    191
  eating disorders and, 202–4
  for energy, 181–84
  fad diets and, 204–5
  fitness and, 179
  gels and, 182–83, 191
  junk science on, 187–88
  for morning runs, 183–84
  nausea and, 191–92
  for performance, 179
  prerace, 90–91, 180–81, 191
  vegetarianism and, 190–91
  vitamins and, 187

O

Overdressing for running, 175
Overheating, hot-weather running
  and, 171–72

Overtraining
  amenorrhea and, 136–37
  anorexia athletica, 203
  avoiding, 52–53
  injuries, 149–50
  for marathon, 78–79
  young runners and, 163–64
Overuse injuries, 149–50. *See also*
      Overtraining
Overweight runners, injuries and,
      200. *See also* Clydesdale run-
      ners

P

Pace, 36–37
Pain
  hip, 116
  kneecap, 112–14
  progressive, 116–17
  running through, 103
Partners, running
  dogs as, 142–43
  for motivation, 26–27
Performance, maximizing aging
      runners', 147–48
Personal records (PRs), 88
Perspiration, 13, 170–71
Plantar fasciitis, 104–5
Plateaus
  exercise, 19
  weight loss, 197–98
Post-marathon syndrome (PMS), 84
Postrace nausea, 191
Postrace syndrome, 84–85
Power lifting, 59
Precor elliptical trainer, 14
Pregnancy, running after, 138–39
Progress, checking on, 10
Pronation, 122–23
PRs, 88

Q

Quadriceps strength training, 58
Quarter squats exercise, 113

R

Racing. *See also* Marathon(s); *specific*
      races
  age-group, 161
  drinking technique in, 92–94
  expo, 20
  first 5-K, 87–88
  half-marathon, 88–89
  hydration
    before, 181
    during, 92–94
  motivation for, 86–87
  nausea after, 191
  nervousness and, 91–92, 171–72,
      192
  nutrition before, 90–91, 180–81,
      191
  personal times and, 88, 144–46,
      154
    young runners and, 160–61
  recovery after, 94–95
  routine, 92
  running routine after, 94
  tapering program and, 89–90
Recovery strategies
  for aging runners, 150–51
  postrace, 94–95
Rest
  injuries and, 97, 108, 211
  after racing, 95–96
  between workouts, 46
Rest, ice, compression, elevation
      (RICE) treatment, 108, 211

Road race. *See* Marathon(s); Racing
Routine, racing, 92
Runner's high, 27–28
Runner's knee, 112–14
Running Wild, 17

S

Sabbaticals from intense running, 26
Safety concerns for women runners, 138
Saunas, 178
Scenic runs, 19
Scholarships, 166–67
Shinsplints, 97, 110–11
Shoes
    for Clydesdale runners, 130
    cross-trainer, 127
    ground shock and, 119
    increases in size of, 128
    injuries and, 119
    numb toes and, 34
    proper fitting, 126–27
    selecting good, 125–26
    soft, 125–26
    for young runners, 159
Side bend exercise, 35
Skiing, 62–63
Skin
    cancer, 216
    chafing, 99, 137
    dry, 124–25
    wrinkles, 216
Slow vs. fast running, 8–9, 199
Smoking
    cessation, 216–17
    related health problems, 216
Snowshoes, 66
Socks, 124, 175
Soreness, injuries vs. muscle, 101–2
Spandex running tights, 12

Speed
    fartlek, 48
    increasing, 37–38, 42, 73
    marathon and, 73
    technique for running and, 37–38
    training for, 42
Spinning, 65
Sports drinks, 173
Sprain, ankle, 107–8
Stair drop exercise, 35
Stamina, lack of, 20–21
Steve Scott's 1-Mile Fun Run, 168
Stomach cramps, 105–6
Straight-leg lifts exercise, 113–14
Strength training, 58–59, 113, 141–42
        See also Weight lifting
Stress fracture, 141–42
Stretching. *See also specific types*
    dangers of, 117
    exercises, 35, 107–9, 114
    injuries and, 98, 107, 115, 117
    routine, 34–35, 107
    in whirlpool, 178
Stride length, 30, 32–33
Sugars, 184
Sunglasses, 175
Sun protection, 216
Supination, 122–23
Supplements
    fat-burning, 190–91
    vitamin, 187
Surface for running, unstable, 108
Sweating, 13, 170–71
Swimming, 61–62

T

Tapering program, 89–90
Technique for running, 30–31
    arms and, 31, 36
    carriage and, 31

U

Unfairness syndrome, 162-63
Uphill running, 39. *See also* Hill
    training
Upper body strength training, 59
Upper respiratory infection, 133
Urination problems, women runners
    and, 139

V

Vegetarianism, 190-91
Vitamins, 187

W

Walking
    fitness and, 207
    switch to running from, 3-4
    through water stations in race,
        93
Wall leans exercise, 107, 109
Water intake. *See* Hydration
Weather conditions, 168-69
    cold
        clothes and, 174-75
        hydration and, 175
        time of day for running in,
            176-78
        training and, 173-74
        wind and, 176

hot
    fatigue and, 169-70
    headaches and, 172-73
    hydration and, 173
    overheating and, 171-72
    perspiration and, 170-71
    hot tubs and, 178
    saunas and, 178
Weight gain, 195-96
Weight lifting. *See also* Strength
        training
    aging runners and, 153
    beginner runners and, 5
    in cross-training, 58-59
    in marathon training, 79-80
    power lifting, 59
Weight loss
    amenorrhea and, 136-37
    anorexia athletica and, 203
    anorexia nervosa and, 202-4
    body fat loss and, 199-201
    body-fat measurements and,
        201
    body fat vs. muscle and, 195-96
    bulimia and, 204
    calorie burn and, 190-91,
        196-97
    eating disorders and, 202-4
    fad diets and, 204-5
    goal setting in, 198
    gradual, 198-99
    plateau in, 197-98
    preoccupation with, 194-95
    program for, 201-2
Whirlpools, 178
Wind, cold-weather running and,
        176
Women runners
    amenorrhea and, 136-37
    anorexia athletica, 203
    anorexia nervosa, 202-4
    bladder problems and, 139
    breast cancer and, 133-34
    bulimia and, 204
    chafing heart rate monitor and,
        137
    dogs as partners for, 142-43
    eating disorders and, 202-4

SOUTHEASTERN COMMUNITY COLLEGE LIBRARY

3 3255 00056 0046